QUARTERBACKING BART STARR

BART STARR

with MARK COX

QUARTERBACKING

PRENTICE-HALL, INC., Englewood Cliffs, New Jersey

QUARTERBACKING BART STARR
with MARK COX

Library of Congress Catalog Card Number: 67-25951
Printed in the United States of America

Current Printing (last digit):
10 9 8 7 6 5 4 3

PRENTICE-HALL INTERNATIONAL, INC., *London*
PRENTICE-HALL OF AUSTRALIA, PTY. LTD., *Sydney*
PRENTICE-HALL OF CANADA, LTD., *Toronto*
PRENTICE-HALL OF INDIA PRIVATE LTD., *New Delhi*
PRENTICE-HALL OF JAPAN, INC., *Tokyo*

Photo credits: page 4, Albert Kraus, Inc.; 31, Laughead Photographers; 61, 66; Malcolm W. Emmons; 113, Tony Tomsic; 160, 187, Daniel R. Rubin; 243, Lee Balterman for SPORTS ILLUSTRATED © Time, Inc.; jacket and end papers, 17, 33, 35, 36, 37, 38, 62, 77, 78, 79, 88, 91, 92, 94, 95, 100, 112, 116, 120, 121, 122, 126, 127, 136, 143, 150, 159, 165, 197, 205, 212, 213, 214, 215, 217, 221, 222, 246, 247, 266, 267, 269, 271, 291, 292, 293, 296, 301, 302, 303, 304, Vernon J. Biever; 41, 42, 43, 44, 45, 46, 47, 48, 49, 50, 51, 52, 53, 54, 56, 76, 77, 79, 83, 84, 85, 87, 89, 90, 91, 93, 94, 99, 100, 103, 104, 105, 109, 110, 111, 112, 115, 117, 118, 198, 199, 202, 203, 206, 207, 208, 209, 216, 223, 232, 233, 234, 235, 236, 237, 238, 239, 242, 250, 251, Ed Feeney.

Cover drawing by Robert Sweetland

To my wife Cherry,
without whose love and understanding,
I never could have attained
sufficient stature in football or in life
to be extended the privilege
of writing this book.

foreword

For all too many years, Bart Starr was referred to as the most under-rated quarterback in football. Today this is no longer true. By the time the 1966 football season finally had been completed with the historic Super Bowl, the young man christened Bryan Bartlett Starr had been voted the National Football League Player of the Year by the writers, the Jim Thorpe Trophy as the Most Valuable Player of the National Football League by the players, and unanimous choice for All-Pro Quarterback.

What is a lot more important to him, his contributions to the Green Bay Packers had figured mightily in leading his team to a record of 12 victories against two losses, his fifth Western Division title, his fourth NFL championship, and the first annual Super Bowl supremacy.

Yet Bart Starr typifies modesty. Following the Packers' championship triumph over Dallas, he brushed aside all personal compliments:

"You can't talk in terms of individuals. You have to talk in terms of team."

This is the real Bart Starr. His team philosophy is one of the many facets of his character that have contributed to his greatness as a quarterback, as a leader, and above all, as a solid citizen.

You will learn much about Bart Starr in the following pages—his problems, his pleasures, and generally what has motivated him into becoming the Number One quarterback in professional football. You will find him sharing this learning with his readers in a manner of frank, earnest candor without reference to his personal accomplishments.

In the Packer locker room there is a poster over the entrance to the training room. Printed in gold on a green background are the words "Anything is ours providing we are willing to pay the price." This is one of Coach Vince Lombardi's favorite sayings, and paying the price is exactly what Bart Starr has done to become the football player that he is today. He has paid the price for success through hard work, quiet determination, and firm belief in the coaching precepts of Vince Lombardi.

In the official National Football League record book, the category for Passing Efficiency, Lifetime lists Bart Starr as Number One. Trailing him are Sammy Baugh and Otto Graham. If any category was suitably headed for Bart Starr, it is Efficiency. Today, the hallmark of professionalism is the Green Bay Packers, and the perfect quarterback to marshall the meticulous Green Bay offense is Starr.

Bart's ascendance to the top ranking of pro quarterbacks was marked by the years of unheralded success in heading the Packers to their great success. He has quarterbacked his team to more championships than any other player in history. While the plaudits of the fans went to other more flamboyant players, Starr consistently kept the Packers winning. And, after all, that's what it's all about.

Bart Starr is one of the great quarterbacks, and it just might be that when he has finished playing, the experts will call him the greatest. Whether they do or not will never concern Bart. He is a team man first and foremost and stands for all of us, young and old, as a classic example of the "good guy" finishing first. His friend and teammate Zeke Bratkowski said it best: "Bart commands respect, from his teammates and the other players, because he knows the game and because he's all-pro off the field too."

Bart Starr deserves every accolade as a man and a player. It has been an honor for me to be associated with him in the publication of his book.

Mark Cox

acknowledgements

To Coach Vince Lombardi, Phil Bengtson, and the other members of what I feel is the finest coaching staff in football, for the counsel, guidance, and many contributions they made in the writing of this book.

To my teammates Bob Skoronski, Boyd Dowler, Doug Hart, and Larry Moore for their time and trouble in posing for the instructional photographs.

To photographers Ed Feeney of Chicago, who shot the sharp, graphic instructional photos; Vern Biever of Port Washington, Wisconsin, whose camera has so dramatically recorded Packer game action through the years, who combed his files to furnish us with many of the illustrations included, and who supplied photographs for the jacket and end papers; and Tony Tomsic of Cleveland, who surely must cheer for his hometown Browns on Sunday afternoons, but whose interest in contributing some of the game action art here is greatly appreciated.

To professional secretary Mrs. Elsye Davis, who not only typed, but often retyped, every word in this manuscript.

To the editorial team at Prentice-Hall that put all of this together—Bill Grose, Barbara Van Osten, and Joe DiDomenico.

And to Mark Cox of Chicago for his assistance in planning, writing, and editing this publication.

contents

OFFENSIVE TERMINOLOGY USED IN THIS BOOK

Onside — Side to which the play is called.

Offside — Side away from the play called.

Strong Side — Side to which the flanker is set.

Weak Side — Side away from the flanker.

Split End — Receiver on the weak side (whether split or closed).

Tight End — Receiver on the side of the flanker.

Wing or Flanker — The outside flanking receiver to the strong side.

Swing — Pass expression calling for a back to take part in the pattern.

Flood — Pass expression where both remaining backs take part in the pattern to the same side.

Even — Defensive line spacing with no lineman over the center.

Odd — Defensive line spacing with lineman over the center.

Fold — Maneuver where lineman steps behind the block of man next to him to block the linebacker on seal upfield.

Slam — Hard shoulder contact and release for another assignment.

Cutoff — Maneuver to slow up pursuit of defensive man.

Seal — Assuming position to pick up any offside pursuit.

Drive — Aggressive shoulder block.

Pinch or Double Team — Two offensive men blocking on one defensive player.

QB — Quarterback.

HB — Halfback.

FB — Fullback.

MLB (M) — Middle linebacker.

LB — Linebacker.

DEFENSIVE TERMINOLOGY

Stunt or "Game" — A maneuver among defensive linemen to confuse the offensive blocking.

Cornerman — Defensive halfback opposite a split end or flanker.

Strong Side Safety — Safety on the side to which the flanker is set (also the side where the tight end is located).

Weak Side Safety — Safety to the side of the split end or away from the flanker.

Red Dog — Defensive maneuver employing a linebacker to rush the passer in effort to create more pressure or to break up a play before it begins.

Blitz — Another term for red dogging, usually implying that more than one linebacker is involved.

Safety Blitz — A safety taking part in a blitz.

the Bart Starr story

1

My life story is football. I have lived it, loved it, played it, sweated with it, laughed at it, cried with it, and rejoiced in it for as long as I can remember. Although I am naturally biased toward it, I honestly feel football is the finest sport in the world today.

My Dad tells me that he gave me a football almost at the time I began to toddle around the house. Originally it was one of those tiny rubber ones. The size and quality of the footballs progressed right along with my growth through life—from the days of losing my baby teeth until I became big enough to play with the standard size ball.

It all started in our own back yard, where I was soon running, passing, kicking, and tackling with my folks. From there, my life of football moved into the corner vacant lot. To us, any open space was a potential playing field.

We didn't have an organized team or any type of organized play at that point in life. We didn't have a coach or even a nickname for our team. We would just gather a group together after school and on Saturdays, and play as long as we could move.

In fact, I can recall one of my early frustrations in life occurring when anyone would build a new house on one of our empty lots. All too often we would chop down the grass, nail up some wooden goal posts, with an occasional limed sideline or two, only to have the local real estate office sell us out of business.

Not many years past that stage, we made our first organized team—a group of youngsters sponsored by the Veterans of Foreign Wars in Montgomery, Alabama. To us, the biggest part of the whole deal was that everyone on the team had a uniform.

1

The first organized team on which I ever played was the VFW Post #96 of Montgomery, Alabama.

This was a real milestone in our lives. We couldn't have cared less that they fitted us like so many flour sacks, because every one of us imagined that we were equipped as well then as the Green Bay Packers are today. Even the ill-fitting uniforms didn't prevent us from seeing ourselves as a combination of spaceman, Batman, and Red Grange all tucked into the same peewee package.

From there our group progressed into an organized program of junior high school football. This was quite a jump because in those days there were no Pop Warner Leagues, Park Board teams, Tiger Leagues, or any other form of Little League organizations for football nuts like us. As a result, our first really well-organized team was our junior high school squad. I was a halfback and really loved the game. We learned a great deal—which wasn't too difficult because we had nothing but desire from which to start. We had a good coach, and as I look back on it, he did an excellent job of teaching us the game.

Naturally, the next stop was senior high. Our school in Montgomery consisted of three grades, the 10th, 11th, and 12th. Probably most of those enthusiasts who fill up the professional stadiums on Sunday afternoons feel that all of us were regulars from the day we first stepped on the football field. This certainly wasn't the case with me. In fact, it was a long haul before I ever made the varsity team right there at Sidney Lanier High School.

My problems came out early, for way back there in the 10th grade I made up my mind I was going to become a quarterback. Having played halfback, this was a pretty natural desire because most teams were running from the Notre Dame box at that time, and I had enjoyed being a halfback, handling the ball on most of the plays. However, when I reached the 10th grade, Sidney Lanier High School had gone to the "T" formation, and I realized immediately that I wanted to be a quarterback.

I feel sure the switchover from a "box tailback" to a "T" formation quarterback wasn't the only reason, but I did have a long way to go to make the club. I didn't even make the varsity my first year, although I was immediately convinced that I should have. My spirits sank lower and lower as the first few weeks went by and my activities were confined to the scrub team, where we would run the opponents' plays against the varsity during the week. Friday night games didn't hold much interest for me, as my week's activities were behind me at that point. We did have a few games of our own against some smaller schools' varsities, and one of the saddest experiences in my life occurred in one of those contests. I dropped a punt which enabled our traditional rivals to beat us, and I cried my heart out for an hour afterwards.

We won most of our games played against these smaller school varsities and a large school scrub team or two, but I still couldn't adjust to playing with the scrubs instead of the varsity. I honestly felt I was good enough to make the team, and one day, five or six weeks into the season, I went home and announced to my Dad that I was giving up football.

I can remember his exact words. He nonchalantly said to me, "Okay, son, it's all right if you do, but tomorrow afternoon I want you out back cutting down all the corn stalks in our garden. Then I want you to clean up the area and get it ready for winter. Cut down all the old growth and police up real well." My Dad was a master sergeant in the Air Force, and the term "police up" became familiar to me.

He knew that I hated this type of work, so, needless to say, I never got around to reporting to the garden. It was football for me from that day on. Obviously, it was an easy decision then, as it would be now—for I suspect that I have had a lot more fun playing football than I would have found in gardening.

It wasn't until my second year in high school that I got a chance to play. Even then the opportunity occurred only because of an accident suffered by our first team quarterback. In the first three games that year I must have played a total of about four or five plays. Then, in the fourth game, we were playing a fine team from Tuscaloosa, and our quarterback broke his leg. This gave me the opportunity I needed to move in to the starting quarterback spot, and you may be sure that I bore down as hard as I knew how to hold the position through the remaining year and a half of my high school days.

One of the great early thrills in my life occurred that junior year in the final game of the season when we were playing a team with the same name as our own—Sidney Lanier High School—from Macon, Georgia. This was an impressive high school football team that had enjoyed a great season. One of its favorite plays was a bootleg in which the quarterback literally hid the ball from the defense. He did this so adroitly that we really couldn't tell when he had the ball and when he had given it to the halfback.

We were so impressed by this maneuver that we decided to try it ourselves. We moved down near their goal line in the third quarter, and I decided this was the time to try it. Emulating the other quarterback, I tucked the ball down against my leg, rolled out to the right, and threw a pass into the end zone where one of our ends was all by himself. He caught the ball for the score, and we went on to win the game and close out an undefeated season.

The following year, when I was a senior, we lost only one game in a season that was highlighted by a trip to Louisville, Kentucky, where we played the football-celebrated Manual High School. Three of our four coaches had played for Bear Bryant at

Sidney Lanier High School team (1951)—my senior year. I'm (21).

At the High School All-American game in Memphis, Tennessee (August, 1952).

the University of Kentucky—Charlie Bradshaw, who now is head coach at Kentucky; Bill Moseley, our head coach (now in business); and Matt Lair, our line coach, who is now at Texas Tech. As a result, they were as happy as we were when we ended up winning by some 20 points. It was a big day for both the coaches and ourselves.

Some of the greatest coaching I have ever received came from this high school coaching staff—which, incidentally, was rounded out by Neal Posey, who is presently the athletic director and basketball coach at Huntingdon College in Montgomery. They served as a tremedous influence on all the boys on our team, and I learned many lessons from them which have proved meaningful to me down through the years. To this day, I remain grateful to them for what they have given me.

The thrills that come with football continued to mount for me. I was named to the All-American High School Team and was awarded a scholarship to the University of Alabama. Later that summer, between high school graduation and enrolling at Alabama, I was selected to play in the high school All American game in Memphis, Tennessee.

After the season started, my morale received another boost when I made the varsity as a freshman. That was in 1952, during the Korean War, and freshmen were eligible. I was thrilled to be a member of the varsity team, and during the course of the year I became the second-string quarterback. We used to lead cheers on the bench for the starting team to keep the score mounting, because we knew this was going to give us an opportunity to get in some action. I played enough to get my letter that freshman year.

My highlight of that year occurred in the final game when we were playing against Syracuse in the Orange Bowl. I threw the TD pass that broke the existing record for most points ever scored by a team in Orange Bowl play. You can imagine what a great moment this was in the life of a freshman who was just thankful for the opportunity to get in the game.

Incidentally, the center on that Syracuse team was Jim Ringo, a great competitor with whom I later teamed for eight years at Green Bay. Jim was All-Pro for five years with the Packers.

Alabama had a tremendous team that year, for those were the days of two-platoon football, and there were many outstanding players on the club, both offensively and defensively. There was so much talent on this squad that when the two platoons were eliminated by a rule change the following year, Alabama was probably hurt as much as any team in the country. Even though the depth in ability which our squad possessed was confined by this rule change, we did have a fine team in my sophomore year, winning the conference title again.

I finished second in the nation in punting that year, topped only by a fellow named Zeke Bratkowski, of Georgia. Of course, Zeke and I have become great buddies with the Packers, and our families today are the closest of friends. Alabama went on to play in the Cotton Bowl, but we lost to Rice Institute in a tough game that was highlighted by the famous tackle from the bench by Tommy Lewis on Dick Moegle. I'll never forget it.

This game became a real turning point in my career. From this point on, our team went downhill, and I skidded right along with it. Prior to the opening of the season, I was punting in practice one day and felt something snap in my back. Never having suffered any back troubles, I just assumed it was a little kink and kept right on working out. Since punting was a vital part of the game for me, I continued kicking to get myself in shape for the opening game.

As the practice days continued, my back grew progressively worse, to the point where I could hardly bend over and tie my

Jim Ringo, one of the all-time great centers, receiving instructions from the team photographer on picture day.

shoe laces. Even worse, I didn't have the slightest idea what to do about it. I missed the first three games of the year and spent two of the next three Saturdays in traction in a hospital. When I was finally released from the hospital, I managed to get into a few of the later games, but only in spots, and we finished the season with a record in the .500 vicinity. My skid in football had definitely begun.

In my senior year I was pretty well recovered from the back injury, but at this point Red Drew was replaced as coach by J. B. (Ears) Whitworth. Whitworth had come from Oklahoma A. & M.

and wanted to go with his younger players to start a rebuilding program for the future. The seniors were pretty much shunted aside, and our playing time was limited, to say the least.

The only time I can recall getting into a game early in the season occurred one day when things weren't going too well, and I guess he felt he had nothing to lose by inserting the old folks. You can imagine how I felt when on about the third play after I had gone into the game I suffered a sprained ankle and hobbled off the field. It was truly a miserable year. This was nothing short of a living hell for me, and I had never been so glad in my life to get a season behind me.

This was not a great chapter in the history of the fine football school of Alabama. As for Coach Drew, he has remained

This photo was taken just before I left home to join the Green Bay Packers in the summer of 1956. Whenever I had trouble finding someone to work out with, my Dad was always willing to help.

a friend through the years. I correspond with him frequently, and he is the first person I call when I visit Tuscaloosa now.

When the season was finally over, I was drafted in the 17th round by Green Bay. I am sure this selection came about only because our basketball coach, Johnny Dee, had recommended me to Jack Vainisi, the Packers' business manager. Johnny and Jack had been campus buddies at Notre Dame where, incidentally, Johnny returned as basketball coach. I was delighted to be picked even on the 17th round, and, of course, I have been grateful that it was the Packers who were willing to take a flyer on me. I wanted, more than anything, to make the Green Bay team and was dedicated to doing so.

Most of the summer was spent throwing footballs at a tire suspended in an "A" frame on my wife's folks' lawn. My wife would retrieve the throws for hours without ever a trace of impatience. I'm convinced this concentrated work enabled me to make the Packer team.

The first year at Green Bay pretty much paralleled my senior year in college. I sat on the bench while Tobin Rote quarterbacked the Packers, and I had a lot of time to look and learn. Tobin was one of the fiercest competitors I have ever known. He was a fantastic individual performer those days but didn't have the team in front of him to support his efforts. He deserves a lot of credit for being able to establish the records he did under the adverse conditions with which he was plagued at that time.

Tobin Rote, one of the greatest competitors I have ever known.

Tobin and his wife were also very considerate with us off the field. They invited me to join them frequently for dinner or other functions and went out of their way to make us feel welcome.

In my second year with the Packers, Tobin had been traded to Detroit for a couple of players and a draft choice, so I became the starting quarterback. Our record wasn't particularly complimentary, but I was able to log a full season's mileage and some very valuable experience that becomes necessary in the life of every professional quarterback.

Here, once again, the third year bugaboo hit me, and my career turned downward much the same as it had in my third year in college. It all started with a coaching change in the Packer organization. Ray (Scooter) McLean had replaced Lisle Blackbourn, and we suffered through a season in which we won only one game. The single victim was the Philadelphia Eagles, and we almost blew that one. They made a real charge at us in the last few seconds.

As I look back on that season, it's quite clear to me that my confidence sank to an all-time low. I was getting a first-hand lesson on how expensive the price of success can be. I knew that I had worked extremely hard and had literally expended blood, sweat, and tears in my preparation for the game throughout those early years. I knew I was totally dedicated to the game, and in my heart there burned an intense flame of desire to succeed.

Though this was a very unhappy part of my life, I can look back now and know that these years served a definite purpose in my preparation for the future in football. I continued to work very hard at practice, and I maintained every ounce of perseverance with which God had blessed me. However, I didn't realize during those first three hectic years with the Packers that my confidence had edged downward. This was an area in which I unconsciously had come up short.

Vince Lombardi arrived in Green Bay in 1959. With his astute analysis of individuals, it didn't take him long to realize that I had slipped into this shortcoming. It didn't take him much longer to set about changing my entire approach to the game of football and, I might add, even my basic approach to life. He changed my outlook completely and every part of my mental make-up along with it.

At that time, in 1959, I probably even had doubts about going out and becoming successful in any field other than football. Then the Lombardi system started to function. I learned that in proper motivation, preparation, dedication, and sound teaching and application in practice sessions lay the development of successful accomplishments. In developing accomplishments by these basic means, I learned that self-confidence came right along with the rest of his program, because self-confidence can only be developed through successful experiences.

Coach Lombardi was patient with me from the beginning. Yet he was very demanding, which caused me to concentrate on the objective. Powers of concentration began to develop in my thinking, and my performance reflected it.

He chewed me up when I committed a careless mistake, but in so doing, he proved to me quite conclusively that a person can't brood over one mistake, or waste time feeling sorry for himself, or take on any sort of persecution complex. This had been a vital shortcoming in my mental make-up in the past. I had continually fretted about my past errors, and misfortunes. I realized that I had fed negative thoughts into my mind for so long that I automatically performed accordingly—in a negative fashion. Today, after having worked under Coach Lombardi for the last seven years, I am completely changed, a totally different person. I honestly feel, if given an equal opportunity, I can become a success today in any field of venture in which I choose to concentrate.

My lack of mental toughness has become a thing of the past. Today I realize that once you have made a mistake, you must accept it for what it was, learn from it, profit by it, and then totally dismiss it from your mind. Profit by it, yes, by analyzing it, but do not let it linger, simmer, or smolder to the point of feeling negative. This had been my weakness for years. In the time that I have played for Coach Lombardi, this probably has been the most beneficial contribution he has made to my development as a quarterback and as a person.

When Coach Lombardi arrived in 1959, the three quarterbacks were Lamar McHan, Joe Francis, and myself. I didn't play much during the first few weeks of the season. Coach had decided to go with McHan, and we won our first three ball games. Then we lost five in a row!

The most disappointing day in 1959 for me came in New York when we played the Giants. I knew that Lamar McHan was hurt. I didn't really think Joe Francis could do the job, but Coach Lombardi went with Joe. I sat on the bench the entire game and didn't get a chance to play. We lost 20–3. I'm not a drinking man, though I enjoy beer occasionally, but that night after the ball game Ron Kramer, who hadn't played either, and

I went out and really saw New York and cried on each other's shoulder.

I later discovered that the loss to the Giants in New York was also Coach Lombardi's biggest disappointment of the season. This was his first year as a head coach in the NFL, he was returning to his home town, and his team was playing against a fine Giant team he had helped build. He wanted victory very badly, but we lost. Since that day the Packers have not lost to the Giants in exhibition games, in regular season games, or in championship games.

I began to play more after the Giants game, and in our game against Washington we broke the five-game losing streak, beating the 'Skins, 21–0. We finished the season with victories over the Rams, Lions, and 49er's, and I was the quarterback through those games.

Since we won our last four games of the year, I was given the starting assignment in 1960 to open the season. We lost to the Bears, 17–14, and that night after the ball game Lamar McHan happened to be at the same restaurant for dinner as Coach Lombardi. Lamar cornered Coach Lombardi and said that if he had been playing we wouldn't have lost.

I don't think that, at this point in my career, Coach Lombardi had the utmost confidence in me and, as a result, the following week he went back to McHan. We won our next few ball games and were doing pretty well in 1960 until a game against the Pittsburgh Steelers in Pittsburgh.

Lamar was having a tough time that day, and the Steeler's defensive line was helping to make it rough. A few passes were dropped on Lamar and he couldn't move the ball club.

Early in the second half, Coach put me in the game. As will happen many times when a new quarterback comes in, he'll momentarily spark the club. That's what happened in Pittsburgh, and we maintained the spark to come on and win the game, 19–13.

After the game, McHan made the comment to a few people that it was strange how they could catch my passes and drop his. I know Lamar didn't mean this but he was bitter at not playing and probably was frustrated at not having a good day. He is a real competitor and wanted to play so badly that he hated to be taken out of a game like that, and especially to have it end the way it did.

After the Steeler game Coach Lombardi called me into his office and told me I would have the job for the rest of the year. We won the Western Conference championship with an 8–4 record, but lost the NFL title game to the Eagles, 17–13.

After the 1960 season, Coach Lombardi traded Lamar to the Baltimore Colts; and in early 1961, while we were in training camp, he acquired John Roach, who was then with the Cleveland Browns. John and I became good friends, and in 1963 Zeke Bratkowski joined us. John left in 1964 to join the Cowboys and retired after that season. Of course, Zeke is still with us and all fans know the great job he has done for the Packers. I am very proud of the close relationship that Zeke and I enjoy. I think it is of the utmost importance that the two quarterbacks get along well, because, if they don't, many times loyalty is divided and team morale is hurt.

We had great seasons in 1961 and 1962 and won the championships both years, beating the Giants 37–0 in 1961 and 16–7 in 1962. Some experts say the 1961-62 Packers may have been the greatest team ever assembled. In 1963 I honestly felt we had as good a football team as we had in 1961 and 1962. In fact, I thought at times our team was even better in 1963 than in the two championship years. But we lost two games that year, both times to the Chicago Bears who eventually won the championship. For the Packers to lose to the Bears any time is bad enough, but twice in one year and costing the championship! The Bears lost only one time that year, though they had three ties. This cost us the championship, because we won 11, lost 2, and tied 1, while the Bears won 10, lost 1, and tied 3. In the NFL, ties don't count in the percentages so our percentage was lower than the Bears'. We had two games with them and lost them both, so the Bears deserved the title.

We had a great running game that year. I recall a game against the St. Louis Cardinals down in St. Louis when I think we probably had as good a day running the ball as I have ever seen. The Packers have been justly proud of our balanced attack, and our running game in 1963 was as good as I've ever seen it.

Many people thought we lost the championship that year because of the absence of Paul Hornung. Well, I disagree, though Paul is and was at the time a great football player. I don't think we missed him that much. Tom Moore had a great year for us in 1963, as did his backup men, Elijah Pitts and others, and so I don't really think that Paul's absence contributed to our downfall. It was a case of having lost both times to the same club, and this eventually beat us.

In that Cardinal game, I had the misfortune of breaking my hand—the only really serious injury that I have had—and that sidelined me for four games. This was when we got Zeke Bratkowski from the Rams, and so Zeke, John Roach, and I finished up the season. Although we didn't win the championship, we ended the year on a good healthy note by beating the Browns in the playoff game in Miami.

Paul Hornung was reinstated for the 1964 season, and I have never seen a man get ready for a season the way he did that year. He came to Green Bay in early May and began running outside and daily running the flights of stairs in the stadium until he had himself in the peak of condition. On opening day that year, Paul was probably in as fine shape as at any time I have had the pleasure of playing with him.

I point this up because, as we mentioned earlier, many felt the absence of Hornung had cost us the title in 1963. I don't know if this put pressure on Paul when he reported back but, while he had a good year playing, he had a miserable year kicking the ball. Of course, this is the difference between winning and losing any year, and we had the misfortune of losing a few games by just a few points. The Colts beat us the first time, 21–20, when we missed an extra point, and in Baltimore, 24–21, when Paul missed five field goals.

After the second Colt game nobody felt worse than Paul. We had outplayed the Colts and really felt we should have won. But with a minute and a half to go and leading 21–17, Paul had his fifth field goal attempt from the Colt 45 blocked, and Jerry Logan picked up the loose ball on about the Colt 20 and ran it to our 45. Johnny Unitas then threw long to Jimmy Orr, but the pass was overthrown out of bounds. We all breathed a big sigh because only a minute was left, but the sigh turned to screams of disbelief when Herb Adderley was called for pass interference against Orr. The ball was placed on our 5-yard line and Lenny Moore took it over the rest of the way the next play. Time ran out, and as we trudged to the locker room, some joker put a fake pistol in Paul Hornung's helmet.

When we got into the locker room, Paul discovered the pistol, picked it up, and put it to his temple. I yelled, "No, Paul!" and Jimmy Taylor called back, "Oh, let him, he'll miss!"

It was after the first Colt game when we lost 21–20 that the mental toughness that Coach Lombardi had been preaching and developing in me began to emerge. Before the season we felt that the Bears and Colts would be our toughest challenge for the Western Division title. On opening day we defeated the defending champion Bears, 23–12, in Green Bay. And the Colts lost to the Vikings. The next week we played the Colts. If we win, the Colts are 0–2, an almost impossible deficit to overcome. It was a great game, typical of the Colts vs. Packers. Both teams scored three touchdowns but we missed an extra point. We also missed two field goals deep in Colt territory. Late in the fourth quarter, our defense stopped the Colts and we got the ball in good field position. After a first down, we called time-out and I went to the sidelines to talk to Coach Lombardi. Because of the Colts' special defense, Coach told me to use a flood pattern left and to throw to Ron Kramer on the right side. With Ron's size and strength he should be able to break clear and take the ball into good field goal position or, with luck, to go all the way.

Back in the huddle, I called the play but a different pattern with McGee as the primary receiver and Tom Moore as secondary. I hoped to isolate the left cornerback on Max and Tom should have had a linebacker on him. I knew Tom could beat the linebacker so if I threw to him coming out of the backfield, he'd get us field goal position and, more likely, a touchdown. I thought the play had a greater chance than the Coach's to go all the way, especially against the special defense the Colts were in.

I took the snap, dropped back, faked a draw to Taylor, and turned to throw. Max was just making his fake, and I looked for Tom Moore and couldn't find him! He was shielded from me by the linemen. I looked quickly back to Max and he was covered! I knew the play was a bust so I threw toward Max but I intended it to go over his head and out of bounds. Just as I released the ball my elbow was hit by a Colt lineman and the ball became a dying quail without enough steam to make the sidelines, and short of McGee. The Colts right linebacker, Dan Shinnick, had intercepted and the ball game was over. I'd blown it!

When we got to the locker room, Coach Lombardi really blasted me in front of the whole team and I deserved it. When I got home that evening, I cried. But I vowed that I wouldn't let this loss, no matter what it meant, ever bother me again. And it never has. If anyone cost the Packers the title in 1964, it was me. And if I can point to one turning moment in my career, it was that play. Instead of letting it bother me, I dismissed it, as Coach did and the team did.

We finished that year on a rather sour note, encountering the Cardinals in the playoff game down in Miami. Perhaps they remembered our big game against them the year before in St. Louis, because they really laid it on us that day in Miami. We didn't look good at all. In fact, we looked awful, and we received some very harsh criticism in the papers—a point that Coach Lombardi has, from time to time, thrown up to us whenever he thought we were getting a little bit sluggish or lackadaisical in our play. One writer went so far as to say that one

of the reasons we looked so bad was the number of players
he had encountered who were eating hot cakes at a pre-game
meal. Although we were embarrassed by our performance, this
"hot cake" incident became a big joke in future dressing room
bull sessions.

Preparation for the 1965 season opened in mid-July. After
two straight second place finishes, Coach Lombardi had had
enough. He set the tone for the season at the first practice, telling us we had been away from the top too long.

Today I wear a championship ring on my right hand. On
one side of the ring is the word "dedication" and on the other
the word "character." Coach Lombardi used those two words to
describe the 1965 Packers in his press conference after we had
beaten the Cleveland Browns, 23–12, to win the NFL championship in 1965.

That was a frustrating and yet very rewarding year for the
Packers. Many adjustments had to be made throughout the season. Jerry Kramer, our All-Pro guard, was just recovering from a
near-fatal illness that spring. As a youngster in Idaho, Jerry had
stepped on a loose wooden plank in the barnyard of his family
farm. The board flew up and struck him in the abdomen, causing a seven-inch splinter to be imbedded. He was rushed to the
hospital and the wood removed. But in 1964 he suddenly started
losing weight and became quite ill. It was discovered that some
of the wooden splinters had not been removed in the original
operation; these had worked their way into his spleen and were
poisoning his system. After seven operations, he came to camp.
Though we were all pulling for him, only Jerry ever thought he'd
play again. We opened the season with him on the bench and
Dan Grimm, a second-year man, in his place.

Fuzzy Thurston, our other All-Pro guard, was sidelined
early in the season with a leg injury. Fuzzy may be the best
pass-blocking guard in football, and with him out and Jerry
Kramer out, it was tough for the offense to operate.

Forrest Gregg switched from tackle to left guard, and
Steve Wright, a second-year man from Alabama, took Forrest's
place. What had once been a cohesive, experienced line was now
a checkered quilt of veterans out of position and new men in
key spots.

But we somehow won. After our opening win against Pittsburgh, we met the Colts in Milwaukee. Always a big game, it
was especially so this year because the Colts were defending
Western Conference champions and favored to repeat. Zeke
came off the bench late in the game to replace me when I was

Fuzzy Thurston (63), an All-Pro guard and my
protector.

shaken up. He hit Max McGee, who replaced the injured Boyd
Dowler, with a 37-yard touchdown pass to put us in the lead
20–17 late in the fourth quarter. Then Willie Davis stopped Tom
Matte when the Colts were driving deep in our territory, causing Matte to fumble. Herb Adderley recovered. Herb had also
intercepted two Unitas passes, returning one for our first touchdown.

We won four more after that and went onto Wrigley Field
to play the Chicago Bears. The Colts had won all their games
except for the loss to us and, after a poor start, the Bears were
really coming on. We had beaten the Bears earlier in Green
Bay, 23–14, but since their loss to us, they had won three in
a row. They needed to win to stay in contention. And beat us
they did, by the score of 31–10.

We scored first in the first quarter. Midway in the drive,
I dropped back to pass, couldn't find a receiver open, and took
off when I saw daylight. No one will ever confuse me with a
scatback, but somehow I made about 30 yards before the roof

fell in. I didn't see Roosevelt Taylor, the Bear safety, coming from the side. If I had, I would have stepped out of bounds, but I kept going and Taylor really belted me near the sidelines. As I started down, about a ton of Bears fell on top of me.

I got up, walked toward the huddle, and suddenly was lying on the ground. I was helped to the sidelines, and Zeke took my place, leading the team to our touchdown as Jim Taylor scored from the 1.

The lead was short lived. Both offensively and defensively, the Bears were superb.

The next week was the low point of the 1965 season as far as I am concerned. In the game against the Lions in Green Bay I completed nine out of 12 passes for 107 yards, but as a team we ended up with −2 yards passing. I was dropped eight or nine times for losses, including a safety by the Lions and we lost the game, 12–7.

Though we were now 6 and 2 after the loss to the Lions, we were a full game behind the Colts who, after they lost to us, had gone on a rampage and won all the rest of their games. We were hanging tough basically because our defense was winning the game for us. They were coming up with the key play, stopping the other team at the appropriate moment, getting the ball for us and keeping us in the ball game. Without our defense that year, I know we wouldn't have won the title, because we would have lost too many games early in the season.

We were making small mistakes, the kind that is the most frustrating. On a running play, everyone would make his block, but one man wouldn't sustain his block long enough, and the man that he was blocking would bust up the play. In a passing situation, the extra one-tenth of a second needed to get the pass off wasn't available because something would break down in the pass blocking. Game after game and play after play we would be that one fraction away from executing perfectly, and that missing fraction was the difference between failure and success.

After the Lion loss the defense saved us in a game in Milwaukee against the Rams. The Rams completely stopped our offense, but Don Chandler got two field goals, and our defense held the Rams to one field goal, so we won, 6–3. Finally, in our next game we erupted to beat the Vikings, 38–13. But the very next game we traveled to the West Coast and came up flat as a pancake as the Rams dumped us, 21–10. Time was running out on us and the Colts had only one loss. They were having their problems, though, because the week that we beat the Vikings in Green Bay, 24–19, Johnny Unitas was hurt against the Bears in Baltimore and the Bears came on to beat the Colts, 13–0.

Now we were only half a game behind the Colts as we went into Baltimore for the big game of the year. If we beat the Colts in Baltimore, we would go ahead by half a game. If we lost, the Colts won the title.

Coach Lombardi decided to change the routine the week of the Baltimore game. Instead of practicing in Green Bay we traveled to the Washington, D.C. area and stayed in a motel near our nation's capitol. At this time, Fuzzy Thurston and Jerry Kramer had recovered from their injuries, Forrest Gregg had moved back to his spot at right tackle, and we were starting to get that old rhythm and execution down. As practice for the Colts game proceeded, we could feel the spirits of the ball club rise. The whole team was confident, and we entered Municipal Stadium in Baltimore on Sunday in an excellent mood. Before he sent us out on the field, Coach spoke to us and said, "I don't think I have to say very much. You all know the importance of this game, and I want you to know that win, lose, or draw, you have conducted yourselves in a manner that has made me extremely proud to be your coach this year. Go get 'em." There was absolutely no way we were going to lose that day.

The Golden Boy, Paul Hornung, had been injured much of the season, but his injuries had healed by this time, and Coach had set it up so that Paul would start the Colt game. He had one of his greatest games as he scored five touchdowns to lead us to a 42–27 victory in a fog-shrouded Baltimore stadium.

The next week San Francisco tied us 24–24 with John Brodie completing a pass to a substitute end with six seconds to go in the game. So it was back to Green Bay for a playoff game against the Colts for the right to meet the Cleveland Browns, the Eastern Conference winners.

With Gary Cuozzo hurt and Johnny Unitas out for the season, the Colts came down to Tom Matte as the quarterback. Fans all over the country sympathized with the Colts, assuming that they didn't have a chance to win. But believe me, that never entered the minds of the Green Bay Packers. We had great respect for Baltimore, especially for that fine defense, and we knew that with such receivers as Raymond Berry, John Mackey, and Jimmy Orr and runners like Lenny Moore and Jerry Hill and Matte himself, they were going to be a tough team.

We received the kickoff, and on the first play the odds against the Colts dropped to even. I threw a pass to Billy Anderson. As he caught it he was hit very hard by Lenny Lyles, and the ball was knocked free. Don Shinnick picked it up and rumbled down the sidelines toward our goal. I moved over to cut him off, hoping to knock him out of bounds, but just as I

got to him Jerry Logan, our old nemesis, threw a beautiful
block on me and Shinnick went in to score. Logan's block loosened
a number of my ribs on the right side so that I couldn't raise
my arm. Zeke Bratkowski took over. Finally, with a minute
and some seconds to go, Don Chandler kicked a field goal that
tied the game. In overtime, after Lou Michaels missed a 47-yard
field goal, Zeke took us all the way to field goal territory where
Chandler kicked the winning goal. The Packers had finally won
the Western Division title.

The championship game against the Cleveland Browns was
a study in execution. Our defense stopped the great Jimmy
Brown, holding him to around 50 yards rushing. The weather
conditions were bad, with snow on the ground, which late in
the game turned the field into a quagmire. But the great thing
about the game was the running of Jim Taylor and Paul Hornung
behind the blocking of our offensive line.

Our line was superb. Skoronski, Thurston, Bowman, Kramer,
Gregg, and Bill Anderson opened up huge holes in the Cleveland
defense, and our backs pounded through. My pass protection was
perfect. We played ball control in the third and fourth quarters and eventually won the game, 23–12. This was our third
championship under Coach Lombardi and in many ways one
of the most satisfying we had won.

The 1966 season was the greatest I have ever had as an
individual. It was the season where we were heavily favored
to win the NFL title and to win the Super Bowl. For the first
time in a long time the prognosticators were correct.

The war between the AFL and the NFL came to an end
in the spring of 1966 when the leagues decided to merge. Since
the beginning of the American Football League, the fans had
been demanding a meeting between their champion and the
champion of the NFL. The merger provided for such a game.

We on the Packers felt that if anybody was going to rep-
resent the NFL in that game, it should be us. Not only our
great tradition of 40 years of football dictated it, but the success
and stature we have had since the arrival of Coach Lombardi
said that we should be the team. But saying it and getting there
are two different things.

We opened the season against the Colts on Saturday night
in Milwaukee. Fans around the country had been waiting for
this rematch. Still fresh in their memories was the sudden-death
playoff in the previous year, the controversy about Don Chandler's tying field goal, and the fact that Johnny Unitas had not
played with the Colts in the game in Baltimore or the playoff
in Green Bay. Colt fans around the country and many other

fans were saying that if Unitas had been with the Colts in those games, they would have beaten the Packers. Nobody will ever know if they would have or not, but he was with the Colts in Milwaukee that Saturday night. We won the game, 24–3, as our defense intercepted two Unitas passes in the second quarter and returned them for touchdowns.

We lost only two games in 1966, one to the 49er's, 21–20, and one to the Vikings, 20–17. That Viking game was one of the strangest I have ever played in. It was almost a textbook example of ball control. The second half opened with the teams tied, 10–10. We took the kickoff and marched the length of the field with Elijah Pitts going in for the touchdown from the 2-yard line. Then Minnesota took the football and went all the way. They kicked a field goal and trailed, 17–13. We took the ball up the field, but their defense stopped us. They took over and marched down the field with Bill Brown going the last yard to win the game, 20–17. I had never been involved in a game where the offense would control the ball for eight or nine minutes, score, and then the other team's offense would control the ball for about the same time and also score.

Each season it seems that games with the Bears are crucial. It's the Green Bay-Chicago rivalry. No matter who is on top or who is favored, throw out the statistics, throw out the past performances. This game is something different. We had beaten the Bears in Chicago, 17–0, as our defense turned in a fantastic performance, stopping Gale Sayers and the rest of the Bear offense. But in Green Bay after our loss to Minnesota, the Bears came to play. I have never seen a more determined runner than Sayers that day. He was a tiger. He is such an exciting runner that every time he gets the ball you can feel the hairs standing up on the back of your neck, a prickly feeling of excitement like electricity running through your body. It was a typical Bear-Packer game and that means a lot.

We clinched the Western Division title for the second straight year in Baltimore, beating the Colts, 14–10, as Willie Davis caused Johnny Unitas to fumble on our 7- or 8-yard line and Dave Robinson recovered. The next week we finished the season in Los Angeles. I had been hurt in the Baltimore game and wasn't to play.

The Rams were battling the Colts for second place and were coming on strong. Many people felt that the Rams would beat us because we had nothing to gain. Also, they felt the Coach would not want to risk his front-line players in a game that didn't mean anything. We had the championship game against Dallas coming up a few weeks later.

They couldn't have been more wrong. I think the big reason we won can be summed up in Coach Lombardi's speech to us before the game. He said, "If you go out there today and give anything less than the very best you have in you, you're not only cheating yourself, you are cheating your team, your organization, your city, and your country; you are cheating your very Maker who gave you the ability to succeed. If you give Him anything less than the very best He gave you, you're cheating Him."

The last chapter of this book covers the championship games I've played in with the Packers. The 1966 season culminated in the exciting championship game against the Dallas Cowboys, which we were fortunate enough to win, 34–27. Then we opened 1967 by beating the Kansas City Chiefs in the first Super Bowl, 35–10.

It was a most satisfying season for all the Packers, and I enjoyed the greatest year of my career. I was fortunate to win a third passing title. On the surface that may seem like a great individual accomplishment, but in reality my success, like any athlete's, is due solely to the efforts of his teammates and coaches. I can illustrate this best by telling of the great benefit I and the whole offensive team have received from practicing daily against what we consider to be the best defensive team in football. Your passing game must improve when you're passing against Herb Adderley, the best cornerback in football; against Willie Wood, who, along with Larry Wilson of the Cardinals, is one of the best safeties in the game; against Bob Jeter, a very fast cornerback, and Tom Brown, a good, steady defender. Add three tremendous linebackers like LeRoy Coffey, Roy Nitschke, and Dave Robinson, and you can see why my passing improves.

I always had more difficulty throwing to my right on a down and out or sideline pattern than I did to the left. Constant practice against Adderley has vastly improved this part of my technique. I had a tendency on a fly pattern to "pull the string" too much and underthrow the receiver. Practice against Jeter and Wood cured me of this. After all, when your own defensive backs break up your passes in practice, the coach doesn't just shrug and tell you to forget it. You either do it then or not at all.

I'm sure our defensive line is as adept as it is to a large extent because it practices against an excellent offensive line and vice versa.

The success of the Packers has not been due to any one player or one group. It's due to all forty players and Coach Lombardi and his staff. This is a team, the finest group of people I've ever been associated with. I know that outside of my family, nothing will ever match the pleasure and satisfaction of being quarterback for the Green Bay Packers.

BART STARR—QUARTERBACK

Height 6-1, Weight 200 lbs.   Born January 9, 1934
University of Alabama
17th Draft Choice (1956)   12th Year in NFL

Starr's 11-Year Record

year	atts.	comp.	yds.	tds.	int.	Yds. Per Att. ave.	per cent
1956	44	24	325	2	3	7.49	54.5
1957	215	117	1489	3	10	6.93	54.4
1958	157	78	875	3	12	5.57	49.7
1959	134	70	972	6	7	7.25	52.2
1960	172	98	1358	4	8	7.90	57.0
1961	295	172	2418	16	16	8.19	58.3
1962	285	178	2438	12	9	8.55	62.5
1963	244	132	1855	15	10	7.60	54.1
1964	272	163	2144	15	4	7.88	59.9
1965	251	140	2055	16	9	7.58	55.8
1966	251	156	2257	14	3	8.99	62.2
Totals	2320*	1328*	18186*	111*	91	7.27	57.2

294 consecutive passes without interception (league record)

* Club Record

Championship Game Performance

year	atts.	comp.	per cent	yds.	tds.	int.
1960	35	21	60.0	178	1	0
1961	19	10	52.6	164	3	0
1962	22	10	45.5	106	0	0
1965	19	10	52.6	147	1	1
1966**	28	19	67.9	304	4	0
Totals	123	70	56.9	899	9	1

78 consecutive passes in championship games without interception; .081 per cent interception rate (1 of 123)
Most victories in championship play (4)—tied with Sid Luckman, Chicago Bears

** Dallas Only

Super Bowl 1967 vs. Kansas City

year	atts.	comp.	per cent	yds.	tds.	int.
1967	23	16	69.6	250	2	1

the
Green Bay
Packers

YESTERDAY AND TODAY

YESTERDAY

Webster defines the word *history* as a narrative of events. When the history of professional football is recorded, much of that narrative will revolve around Green Bay, Wisconsin, and its legendary Packers.

Since Green Bay and the Packers have become such a vital part of my life, I would like to tell the story of Green Bay and its team so that everyone reading this book can appreciate the years of tradition and history that extend back nearly a half a century for this fabulous football organization.

BIRTH OF A TEAM AND A LEGEND

On the evening of August 11, 1919, a score or more of husky young characters, called together by Curley Lambeau and George Calhoun, gathered in the dingy editorial room of the old Press-Gazette building on Cherry Street and organized a football team. They didn't know it, but that was the beginning of the incredible saga of the Green Bay Packers.

There had been some preliminary talk and planning, and that night's decision wasn't announced until two days later, but the big step had been taken. So August 11 is as good a birthday as any.

Actually, the initial spark had been struck a few weeks before during a casual street corner conversation between Lambeau and Calhoun. It was apparently one of those "why not get up a football team?" remarks, but once they got interested they wasted no time in contacting Green Bay businessmen.

25

First they talked Curley's employers at the Indian Packing Company into putting up some money for equipment. Because the team's jerseys had been provided by the packing company, which also permitted the use of its athletic field for practice, the club was identified in its early publicity as a project of the company. With this tie-in the name "Packers" was a natural, and Packers they have been ever since, although the corporation had practically faded out of the picture before that first season was half over.

EARLY DAYS

That first season the team won ten games and lost only one against other teams from Wisconsin and Upper Michigan. Games were played in an open field with no fence or bleachers, and interested fans "passed the hat." But the team was so successful by 1921 that Lambeau was backed by two officials of the packing plant in obtaining a franchise in the new national pro football league that had been formed in 1920.

Cash customers didn't quite pay the freight, and at the end of the season the franchise had to be forfeited. This was the first in a long series of troubles that the now famous team overcame, for in 1922 Lambeau gained other backers and bought the franchise back for $250. Troubles continued during that season. One game was rained out, and the insurance company wouldn't pay off because the official amount of rain was one one-hundreth of an inch short of that required in the policy.

Another storm late in the season when the Packers were scheduled to play the Duluth Eskimos proved to be the founding of the modern community corporation. A. B. Turnbull, general manager of the Green Bay Press-Gazette, told the Packers to play anyway. He then went out and helped organize the businessmen of Green Bay in the support of the team, and the Green Bay Football Corporation was formed.

THE IRON MAN ERA

With good financial backing, Lambeau began to pick up college stars from all over the country, plus some unknowns who were going to turn out to be "greats." And in 1929 Green Bay won the national professional football championship.

They repeated in 1930 and 1931 with a team featuring such all-time pro greats as Red Dunn, Verne Lewellen, Cal Hubbard,

Bo Molenda, Jug Earp, Mike Michalske, Johnny Blood, Bill Kern, Arnie Herber, Clarke Hinkle, Lavvie Dilweg, Tom Nash, Milt Gantenbein, and Hank Bruder.

In many games, 12 to 13 players would go for almost the full 60 minutes. These teams were hailed all over the country as some of the greatest ever.

THE HUTSON PERIOD

Trouble flared again soon afterward. A fan fell from the stands, sued, and won a $5,000 verdict. The insurance company went out of business. The Packers went into receivership and were just about to fold when Green Bay businessmen came to the rescue again, raised $15,000 in new capital, and reorganized the club.

About this time a rather slight, lanky end from the University of Alabama by the name of Don Hutson came to the club. From his first game on, Hutson became the terror of the league and the secret of Green Bay's next three championships. On his first play in professional ball, against the Chicago Bears, he took a pass from Arnie Herber and went 94 yards for the only score of the game.

With Herber and Cecil Isbell pitching and Hutson catching anything they threw at him despite all kinds of stop-Hutson defenses, Green Bay won championships in 1936, 1939, and 1944. All during the Hutson era they always finished in the first division.

RONZANI REGIME

After Hutson's retirement, Packer fortunes again went into a decline. The disastrous pro football war between the NFL and the All American Conference brought on another financial crisis after the 1949 season. In the midst of it, Lambeau resigned to take a position as head coach of the Chicago Cardinals.

Then began another major reorganization and rebuilding effort with Gene Ronzani of the Bears hired as head coach. Over $125,000 was raised in a giant stock sale all over the state.

Ronzani's teams improved each of the first three seasons until 1952. The Packers were in the thick of the title chase until the last weeks of the season. In 1953 the team played erratic ball, and Ronzani resigned with two games remaining on the schedule. His record with the Packers was 14–33–1.

BLACKBOURN TAKES OVER

The Packers overhauled their front office and coaching staff in 1954, hiring Verne C. Lewellen, all-time Packer great, attorney and businessman, as general manager. Reaching into college ranks for a head coach was the next step in the rebuilding plans. Lisle W. Blackbourn, a native Wisconsinite and Coach of Marquette University, was signed to a contract. During the four-year Blackbourn regime the Packers won 17 while losing 31.

McLEAN MOVES UP

Likable Ray "Scooter" McLean moved up from being an outstanding assistant coach to guide the destiny of the Packers for 1958. He resigned in December after a 1-10-1 record, the worst in Packer history.

FROM SANDLOT TO STADIUM

Procedures at Packers games have come a long way since the sandlot years of 1919-20 when the Pack was subsisting on the contents of George Calhoun's hat. Then there were no ushers, no majorettes, no band, and no public address system—the latter hadn't been invented yet. There weren't even any seats at first, and it didn't cost anything to get in.

When the Packers began their career in 1919, they played on approximately the same site as the now abandoned City Stadium, but with a mighty difference. Hagemeister Park, as it was called, was just a big vacant lot with a football gridiron marked on it.

There were no gates because there wasn't any fence. Spectators just dropped off the Walnut Street streetcar and walked over to the sideline or drove their own cars and parked about ten yards behind the ropes stretched around the playing field.

If they felt like it, they either sat in their automobiles or on top of them, but most preferred to get out and follow the play up and down the field. By moving as the play progressed, you always had a "50-yard line" location and were handy to any donnybrook that might require a little help. In fact, when things got exciting, the crowd sometimes spilled right onto the field, surrounded the scrimmage in a big circle and virtually took part in every play. Teams didn't huddle in those days, or the fans would have been in that too.

When the half ended, teams grabbed blankets and adjourned to opposite end zones where they relaxed and talked over the tactics for the next half. Nothing private about those huddles. The crowd formed a ring around the players, a practice encouraged since it made a handy windbreak. Fans weren't bashful about joining the discussions either, sometimes with surprising results. At least one early game was pulled out of the fire by a spectator's halftime suggestion.

In 1920 a section of stands was built—just a small bleacher with a capacity of a couple hundred—on one side of the field, and a fee was charged to sit there. The next year a portable canvas fence was erected around the whole field and a regular admission charge inaugurated.

When Hagemeister Park was dug up in 1923 to make way for East High School, the Packers shifted to the new baseball grounds out on the end of Main Street. This was called Bellevue Park because it was just east of the old Hagemeister Brewery, which was renamed the Bellevue Products Co. during Prohibition. Things were Big Time out there, with crowds of 4,000 to 5,000 storming the fences to boo the hated Chicago Bears.

The Packers used Bellevue in 1923-24, but it was obviously inadequate and too far out, lacking about every facility needed for football. Agitation to build a new stadium somewhere near the original site culminated in the erection of old City Stadium just back of the new high school.

The new plant was barely completed in time for the 1925 opening but was an immediate success, the Bear game that year drawing a record crowd of nearly 6,000. It was a typical small town park of its day, with wooden fences and stands on both sides between the 30-yard lines. A wooden railing surrounded the rest of the gridiron, along which the Knothole Gang stood or sat on the ground.

Seating capacity was gradually increased to 15,000 by 1934, with the end zones still uncovered. With the filling in of the area around the end lines, the ultimate capacity of 25,000 was reached.

One of the first tasks of the stadium builders was the creation of a good playing field, a job admirably done. Whatever qualities antiquated City Stadium may have lacked, one of the best turfs in the country wasn't one of them.

After World War II City Stadium gradually faded from its proud position as one of the favored fields in the National Football League to an inadequate and obsolete installation. As pro crowds increased it was impossible to expand the stadium any further.. With limited capacity, the Packers found it increasingly difficult to schedule top opponents at home.

September 29, 1957, was a proud day for Green Bay and its Packers. A modern million-dollar stadium with a seating capacity of nearly 35,000 was dedicated. (Since that time, the capacity has been increased.) The people served notice on the football world that they intended to support and keep their "Packers" in Green Bay for as far as men could see into the future.

The Packers solidified their future in the National Football League by hiring a dedicated football man, Vince Lombardi, as head coach and general manager. Lombardi was signed to a five-year contract after a widespread search for the right man to place in complete charge.

In his first year Lombardi led Green Bay from its worst record in 40 years to its best finish since 1944, when the Packers had won their last championship. He was unanimous choice as Coach of the Year in his first season as Packer head coach.

VINCE LOMBARDI—HEAD COACH AND GENERAL MANAGER

When Vince Lombardi came to Green Bay in January of 1959, he prefaced his arrival with the statement that he was "no miracle man," but within one year he had won a divisional title. From a 1-10-1 record in 1958, Lombardi forged a 7-5 season in 1959 and a year later won the Western Division crown. The world championship title followed in 1961, 1962, 1965, and 1966.

Lombardi played his collegiate football at Fordham University, where he was a 185-pound guard and one of the famed Seven Blocks of Granite. In 1949 he was named assistant to Earl ("Red") Blaik at West Point. Lombardi maintains that his experience under Blaik was invaluable.

He left West Point in 1954 to join the New York Giants under Jim Lee Howell as offensive line coach. In 1959, he came to Green Bay and has since forged a football dynasty that in eight years has produced 123 wins, 35 losses, and 3 ties, good for four championships, one divisional title, and the first Super Bowl victory. His record is tops in football today.

Coach Vince Lombardi, Green Bay Packers.

TODAY

While the Packers own probably the most unique tradition in professional football, to me and my generation the story of our club revolves around one man—Coach Vince Lombardi. Putting it simply, I think the world of this man. He has changed me completely and has literally made me what I am today as a football player. In fact, as I will touch on later, he has been a driving influence in my every way of life. He is a very forceful, dynamic individual, extremely intense, well organized at all times and a thorough, tough, strict disciplinarian—a perfectionist!

You will read more in the following pages of his philosophy that WINNING IS NOT EVERYTHING, BUT MAKING THE EFFORT TO WIN IS. As a result, we continue to make that effort to win, regardless of the effort required.

The Packers have possessed an outstanding coaching staff ever since the day Lombardi came to town. An example of this is the fact that three of his fine assistants have gone on to other clubs. Three years ago Bill Austin went to the Rams in a key spot and moved up from there to be head coach of the Pittsburgh Steelers.

Then, when the Atlanta Falcons were founded in 1966, Norb Hecker was appointed head coach. Norb took with him, as his number one assistant, Tom Fears, end coach of the Packers.

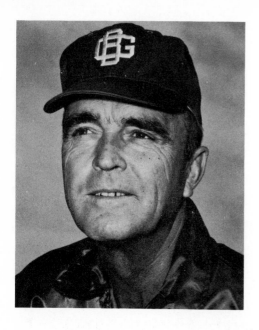

Coach Phil Bengtson, Green Bay Packers.

One year later the New Orleans Saints joined the NFL, and who did they select as their first head coach? Tom Fears.

Undoubtedly, one of the reasons other clubs respect Lombardi's staff so highly is that they know the type and amount of training these men receive from him. Other clubs are quite aware of how closely our coaches work together and the hours upon hours of extra time they devote to their jobs. These coaches pay the price of winning right along with the players, for they must be thoroughly organized and well prepared at all times. This makes their price of winning very expensive. Our coaches sacrifice many hours from their families in order to mold us into the team that will reflect their efforts. There is no other way in Lombardi's creed. Dedication is deeply engrained in our ball club because we see how hard our coaches work for us, and we naturally want to work that much harder in an effort to match their contributions in our behalf.

The Packers staff today has been changed slightly. Dave Hanner has joined us in the past two years and helps Coach Phil Bengtson with the defense. Bengtson, a former tackle at the University of Minnesota and later line coach for the University of Missouri, Stanford, and the 49'ers, is really a master on the defensive phase of football.

In addition, when Jerry Burns left the University of Iowa as head coach, he succeeded Norb Hecker, and Bob Schnelker of Bowling Green became end coach when Fears departed for Atlanta with Hecker. Schnelker had played for Lombardi with the Giants and came to us from the Los Angeles Rams. He has already made many outstanding contributions to the Packers and has helped me greatly with the techniques and philosophies on receiving which are included in this book. Ray Wietecha, who succeeded Bill Austin as offensive line coach, and Tom McCormick, our most recent addition as offensive backfield coach, round out the staff.

From the time Lombardi first came to Green Bay, along with his staff, it was quite apparent that this was going to be a thoroughly disciplined ball club, highly prepared, mentally and physically tough, and ready to pay whatever price necessary to become champions. You knew immediately that Lombardi was a dedicated individual, sincere and possessed of a burning desire to succeed, and that he would accept nothing less than the best effort of everyone. As a result, I think every one of us on that squad began to push ourselves into utilizing our full capabilities right from the beginning. We knew this man would settle for nothing less than our maximum, and we automatically reacted accordingly.

His coaching system is simple. In fact, he has told us on many occasions that he feels it is so simple, it must have been designed for simple-minded people! The Lombardi system is built around execution. There is nothing particularly fancy about it. We don't attempt to do a lot of nifty ball handling or try to fool the defense a great deal. We merely attempt to establish a sound, fundamental game where one fellow is pitted against another, and it becomes his responsibility to just root the opposition out, block him any way possible, and let the back adjust.

Coach Lombardi collaborated on an outstanding book not too many seasons ago which was entitled *Run to Daylight*. This phrase was coined because our running game is built around running to wherever the hole is created. The offensive linemen

If you look closely at this photo, you will see the "adjustment" the back made. He was diving toward Forrest Gregg (75) but as the hole developed inside, note how his body leans and the right leg is about to enable him to slip through. Jimmy Taylor (31), the runner, is very good at "running to daylight."

block the defensive linemen any way possible, and the offensive back must be prepared to break through wherever the hole develops.

Ours is a system in which we try to blend passing with running. If statistics are checked down through the years since Coach Lombardi has been in Green Bay, the passing and running phases of our game will probably balance out almost even, with no single year varying more than 20 or 30 plays. We make a real effort to balance this out because we know that you cannot win consistently without a balanced attack. In addition, we also know that if you do have a well-balanced attack, you possess a far better possibility of controlling the ball. Normally, controlling the ball means controlling the ball game and, thus, winning. This is Coach Lombardi's theory—you must control the ball as much as possible, for there is no way the other team can score when you have the ball. Every team in the National Football League today has great capabilities in scoring, and probably the best defense lies in restricting the opposition from getting the ball.

The Lombardi system continually stresses a minimum of mistakes. Mistakes on the football field will beat you, and he continually pounds away at us that we cannot afford to make mistakes. Let the other team make the mistakes, he preaches. A mistake is a deflating disappointment for your club and an inflating situation for the opponent. As a result, your playing code is to minimize your mistakes and never allow your opponent to capitalize on your error and beat you on something you gave him free.

Coach Lombardi's mental and physical approach to the game is as follows: physical toughness by you will make the opponents weaken, and mental toughness by you will make them crack. Like so many of Coach Lombardi's philosophies, he preaches them to us continually, and you will find me referring back to them on numerous occasions throughout the following pages. The Packers always attempt to be in as good physical condition as possible—both in season and out. When we report to training camp, we start off with a very fast tempo. If a player is not in good physical condition, he is left far behind right from the start.

All of us got a big kick out of Tom Brown when he came to us from baseball a few years ago. Tom, who is one of our outstanding defensive safety men, had been playing baseball all summer prior to coming up to our training camp. The day he reported to the Packers his tongue hung out like a red necktie, and the rest of us broke up laughing at him. Here was a guy who had been playing baseball all summer long, and by the end of the first 20 minutes of Packer drills, he was completely out of gas. It proved a great point to us.

Along with this penchant for being in top physical condition at all times, Coach Lombardi has another saying—you have to play with your little hurts. Of course, what he means is that when you have a squad of only 40 players, it becomes necessary for every man to be mentally tough enough to play although slightly injured. In fact, he would prefer many times that you play even when you are more than slightly injured! He means that you must be mentally geared to overcome a certain amount of pain and keep going because the team cannot afford to be without you if you are at all able to play.

Along with this, he harps continually to the reserves who back up the first liners that they must be ready to go at all times. He demands that they put in the same preparation, the same dedication, the same tireless practice, and every other element that goes into preparing for every game so that if something does happen to one of the starters, the substitute is ready to step in and do his job.

This is a rugged task to ask reserves to get mentally geared to, but it is another of the many basic demands which Lombardi puts on our squad. Every one of us accepts this attitude psychologically as part of our jobs, and we attempt to act accord-

One of our fine team physicians, Dr. James Nellen, displays the "hardnosed" attitude so typical of Lombardi by completely ignoring a grimacing Tom Moore, who played several years with Green Bay before joining the Los Angeles Rams.

This shot reflects the loneliness of a quarterback when things go wrong. In 1963, when I broke my hand, John Roach (photo) substituted for me and played very well, but the Bears still won.

ingly. These are the little things that are a part of the Lombardi system which has paid off so handsomely for us in championships won. There are numerous examples of this ability of back-up men to come on strong when injuries have been suffered by the first liners.

In 1963, when I broke my hand against the St. Louis Cardinals, we won three out of the next four games—and they were tough games too—with John Roach at quarterback. John was mentally and physically ready to move in, and he did an outstanding job for us in taking my place. In the last two years I got hurt a couple of times, and Zeke Bratkowski came on like a storm. Zeke is a classic example of someone stepping in who has not played much all year and being completely geared to take charge of the team when he is needed. Two years ago, Zeke filled in for me in the playoff game against the Colts. If we had not won that one, we would not have made it to the championship game.

Coming down the stretch again in 1966, Zeke had to take over for me in a crucial game with the Colts, and once again he led us home in front. Max McGee is still another good example of a performer who has played very little the last two years but is always ready when needed, as in his great performance in the Super Bowl.

There is no way you can praise players like Zeke Bratkowski, John Roach, and Max McGee highly enough for their frustration of sitting on the bench for many games and then being able to perform so completely and expertly when they finally get the emergency call for duty. This is possible only because they have accepted Coach Lombardi's theory of always being prepared regardless of whether or not you gain the opportunity of exploiting your preparedness.

Here is a shot of one of my favorite teammates through the years, Max McGee. Max has done outstanding reserve work for us the last two years, ready to give a superior performance whenever called upon.

While this situation is particularly applicable to the Packers, other teams' second-line players have also performed exceptionally in emergency roles. Most good football teams have a good bench or an outstanding selection of reserves. For instance, Gary Cuozzo stepped in and replaced John Unitas for Baltimore a couple of years ago. Then, when Cuozzo was injured, Tom Matte shifted over from halfback and did a remarkable job against us on a makeshift basis. These are the marks of real athletes, and I want to salute them.

In the last seven years, Coach Lombardi and the Packers have attained a record that is unmatched by any team. We have won five division titles, four NFL championships, the first Super Bowl crown this last January, and have added two second place finishes in our division and a playoff bowl victory in Miami. History shows that this is a great record, and I am sure that everyone in the Packer organization is extremely proud of it, from Coach Lombardi on down.

As mentioned before, we approach each season and the start of training camp with one basic idea in mind—to win the championship that year. I can remember Coach Lombardi's words in 1965, the first words that he uttered in greeting the training camp: "Gentlemen, our objective for 1965 is to be champions of the NFL again. We have been out of it for two years and that's long enough!" Though we had some hardships that year and were down at times, everyone on the ball club wanted to win as much that season as on any ball club with which I have ever been associated.

His opening statement was virtually the same in 1966, when we went all the way to the first Super Bowl.

Though shown here in an unhappy situation, Tom Matte of the Colts performed well in a reserve role as quarterback.

physical condition and individual drills

3

There is only one way you can play football. That is to be physically and mentally prepared. Not only prepared, but peaked to the finest physical condition possible. There are many basic drills to help you reach top condition.

Every workout should begin by merely loosening up. Never start any type of heavy exercising until you are thoroughly warmed up. Otherwise, you are asking for pulled and strained muscles.

Exercise 1

The "side straddle hop" is a favorite among athletes for quick, brisk warmup. A. Begin with upright stance, hands by sides. B. On count of one, hop to spread position shown, with hands touching above head. On two, return to original position and repeat.

A

B

A

Exercise 2

Another good exercise for stretching muscles. **A.** Begin in upright stance. **B.** Lean over, legs straight, and touch your toes. **C.** Come up, slap the midsection. **D.** Reach as high and as far back as you can, then return to original position and begin again.

B

C

D

A

Exercise 3

The "windmill" is an excellent warmup exercise that stretches the upper body as well as the backs of the legs. A. Begin with an erect stance, feet spread, and arms out to the side. B. On count of one, lean over, keeping legs straight, and touch the right hand to the left toe. On count of two, return to the original position. C. On third count, repeat maneuver, this time touching the left hand to the right toe.

B

C

A

Exercise 4

Rotating the body helps to loosen the upper trunk. **A.** Begin in upright position, hands on hips. On count of one, lean forward from waist. **B.** On the second count, lean to the left. **C.** On the third count, lean to the rear. **D.** And on the fourth count, lean to the right. After a few of these, stop and repeat exercise by "windmilling" in opposite direction.

B

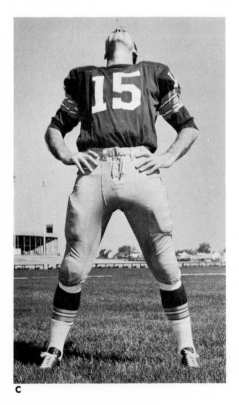

C

D

Push-ups are excellent—particularly for a passer. They do a wonderful job of developing the shoulder and arm muscles. Push-ups on the fingertips are equally beneficial for developing strength in the hands.

Exercise 5

The simple push-up always has been and always will be a fine conditioning exercise (A & B).

A   C

B

Exercise 6

This is a sequence of the "six-count burpee" which is a good exercise for stamina, as well as the arms, since push-ups are involved. A. Exercise begins with player standing erect. B. Assume half squat, knees outside elbows. C. Kick legs back and keep them straight. D. Lower body and raise it as in normal push-up. E. Bring knees back to elbows. F. Stand erect.

Surprisingly enough, your stomach muscles contribute to your throwing; sit-ups help you build strength in this region. In addition, your abdominal muscles must be strong in order to absorb the pounding every passer takes when releasing the ball with his hands up high. These muscles perform still other service to your anatomy in helping move your body into position to throw.

Exercise 7

Sit-ups are always good and are usually done with legs flat on the ground or with the knees bent. **A.** These demonstrate the sit-up with the legs flat on the ground. **B.** On count of one, raise body up, touching the right elbow to the left knee. On *two*, return to prone position. **C.** On *three*, raise body again, this time touching left elbow to right knee.

A

B

C

Exercise 8

A. Start with feet on the ground. B. Raise feet about six inches; pause. C. Spread feet slowly; bring together and back to starting position.

A

B

C

Any exercise that places tension on the abdominal area is recommended for developing these stomach muscles. Leg raises are especially effective. Perform these by lying on your back with your feet on the ground, and then raise them about six inches, pause, and spread your feet slowly. Bring them back together again and lower them to the starting position at a deliberate pace.

Exercise 9

The following is another good stretching and conditioning exercise. **A.** Begin by lying on your back, feet flat on the ground. On count of one, throw your feet over your head, touching the ground on the other side. **B.** On count of two, assume a position of "bicycling" with the feet. **C.** On third count, bring the feet to a forty-five degree angle with ground and hold. **D.** On four, lower legs to six inches; keep legs straight. **E.** On five, open and close the feet on command.

A

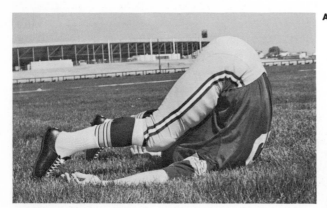

B

C

D

E

A

Additional exercises that are good for stretching and strengthening are number 10, the wood-chopper; number 11, the hurdler's stretch; and number 12, the running stretch.

Exercise 10

The "wood-chopper" is a great exercise for stretching the back and hamstring muscles. A. Begin by standing with feet spread, hands on hips. B. On count of one, lean over, legs straight, and touch the ground. C. On count of two, touch the ground with the feet farther back. And on the count of three, reach even farther back and try to touch the ground. Return to original position.

B

C

Exercise 11

It is imperative to keep the hamstring muscles loose and properly stretched before beginning strenuous running. **A.** One of the best exercises for stretching these muscles is the "hurdler's stretch" in which the player sits down, one leg stretched in front and the other behind. **B.** He reaches as far out over his foot as possible. **C.** After a few of these, change legs and repeat.

Exercise 12

This simple exercise is very good for the groin muscles. Stand erect, feet slightly spread. Step or stride forward, bending knee of front leg until knee of rear leg touches the ground. Return to starting position and stride off on opposite leg.

As a quarterback, you don't have to be concerned with running great distances at top speed, but if you can cover up to 10 yards in good time, this certainly is in your favor. Quick speed will be especially helpful in retreating quickly to set up for passing.

One drill you should employ is the basic maneuver of getting away from the center. It isn't necessary to have a center. Just hold the ball in the position you receive it from center, turn, and run back. This exercise furnishes you the opportunity to drill on several facets at the same time.

You can practice keeping your hands relaxed on the ball and not becoming tense as you run back to set up. Work on having your head turned, looking over the defense as you move. And concentrate on those short, choppy steps in scooting back into passing position just as rapidly as possible. You can accomplish all of these without a center.

Another fundamental you can practice in your final stages of setting up is being relaxed as you step forward to deliver the ball. This will become an automatic maneuver too with practice.

Strive to develop agility. Work on lateral movements, quick starting, stopping, spinning, turning, and recovering from being off-balance. Don't slight anything that might help you perform your basic maneuver as a quarterback.

There are all sorts of drills, and you may need to improvise some of your own. The main item is to be prepared for any type of emergency that might arise in a ball game. If you discover some move that helps you particularly, work just that much harder on it and develop your ability to perform it just a little bit better.

AGILITY DRILLS

Agility drills are excellent for learning to change directions quickly. Many times it becomes necessary for you to change directions spontaneously when setting up to pass and the pocket breaks down. Or, if a runner breaks assignment in the backfield, you may have to improve and take off in an entirely different direction. You must be able to move in all directions, maintaining good balance—and be quick about it.

ENDURANCE

Running up and down stadium steps, or any type of stairs, is excellent for endurance. I mentioned earlier that it is important for the quarterback to be in as good condition as anyone else on the club. Don't kid yourself into thinking you can get by without being in razor sharp condition.

The first time you start to tire, your passing will show it immediately. I have experienced this many times in hot weather, particularly in the Cotton Bowl during preseason games in Dallas. I'd be going great for about three quarters and then just poop out in the fourth quarter.

My passing would show the effects of fatigue right away. I would be sharp up to a point, and then I would actually feel myself sliding downhill. I was falling somewhat short of my capabilities because my legs were tiring. I was getting that rubbery feeling because I was not yet in good condition for the season.

Of course, you can play yourself into condition too, but you should strive to get into as good condition as possible· by the time that first game rolls around, whether it be a league game or just an exhibition.

HAND DEVELOPMENT

This doesn't deal with strength or endurance, but let's take a little additional look at development of the hands. An excellent drill for potential quarterbacks is to practice handling a basketball rather than a football.

The reason is this: If you handle a basketball, take it from a real or imaginary center, move around, run back from the center, slide up and down the line of scrimmage with it and pretend to hand it off, you'll find that when you go back to a football, it will feel about the size of one of those ten-cent ones that you buy for your kid brother.

The ball will feel much smaller than normal and you'll be able to handle it with half a hand. It's a psychological thing—strictly mental—but it's worth giving a try. It's worked for me. If you handle any object that is larger or heavier than the actual thing, you will always do a superior job with the original object. This is the same principle as a baseball batter coming into the on-deck circle swinging a heavy bat and then tossing it aside for his regular bat, which then feels like a straw by comparison.

Prior to going to training camp in the summer, I also make use of a weighted training football. I practice lobbing it just to strengthen my arm. I have found that it gets my arm in good shape before starting the year, and as a professional player, I can tell you that your arm must be in excellent shape to stand up under the long season of throwing.

Exercise 13

A

B   C

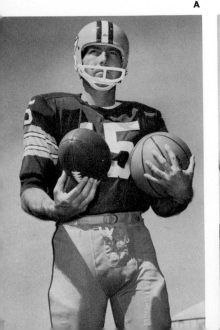

Many players develop sore arms during training camp, or somewhere along the course of the long schedule, because they never reached the point of being in proper condition.

DIET

Like most professional football players, I follow a common sense diet—both during the schedule and in the off-season. Don't become lax in your eating habits during the off-season, because weight will slip on easily that will come off reluctantly.

Personally, I eat lots of fruits, vegetables, and salads along with plenty of good red meat. I make it a point to stay away from starchy, fatty foods, even though I probably could afford some extra pounds.

To me, it is a mistake to try and keep myself at a heavy weight just because I am not one of the bigger quarterbacks in the league. In fact, I'm not even concerned about losing a little weight as the season goes along because I've found I really function better when I get myself in the best possible condition. I'll report to training camp at about 200 pounds and gradually work my way down to about 190 by midseason. That's really my best weight, and I'll try hard to hold it there throughout the balance of the year.

I have learned over the 11 years I have been playing that it pays to play just a little bit lighter each year, and I have been coming down slightly each season to my present 190-pound minimum.

Young players should shy away from any form of greasy, heavy, or fatty foods that are hard to digest. Use your head at the table, the same as you do on the field, and if in doubt on the proper food to eat, consult your team doctor. He will come up with the right answer for you.

I am not confused as to the sport I prefer to play in these photos, but I wanted to show how "comfortable" you can make a football feel by handling a basketball briefly each day. Young quarterbacks should even be encouraged to fake with a basketball, both one- and two-handed, as shown here, and generally move it around for a period each day. When the basketball is tossed aside and the football picked up again, the latter feels much smaller and completely manageable by comparison (A). B. Two-handed fake with basketball. C. One-handed fake with basketball.

qualifications
of a
quarterback

We have touched on some of the qualifications of a quarterback in the story of my life, for I have applied most of these toward my own approach to the game through the years. The following qualities are those which I feel every successful quarterback should possess.

DEDICATION

As good a place to begin as any in quarterback qualifications is that of dedication. If you are going to get the job done in any field of endeavor, you must be totally dedicated to the task. You must possess a burning devotion and desire to succeed at it, or you will not succeed. So, in quarterbacking and leading your team, dedication to getting the job done must go to the top of your list.

You must learn quickly that this positive approach to the game automatically will rub off on your teammates. Since you are calling the signals and running the team, the other players can sense this dedication and they, in turn, will pitch in with you to get the job done. There never has been a winning club in football without dedication on the part of the quarterback and the rest of the team.

RESPONSIBILITY

A good quarterback must enjoy the responsibility that goes with his work—and there is a great deal of responsibility involved. The quarterback is handling eleven people, manipulating them, maneuvering them, and applying his knowledge of their strengths and weaknesses against an opponent equally desirous of winning. When game time rolls around, you know your team's strengths and weaknesses and also those of your opponents. You have worked all week in getting ready for the ball game, and you have spent extra hours with the coach and with the players in order to be prepared.

It is your job to coordinate the ideas of the coach and transmit them to the team. You are quite conscious of the responsibility wrapped up in you as a quarterback of the team, and you must enjoy carrying this responsibility,

Some players can get all fired up on the field, lose their tempers, and even take a poke at someone. Under no circumstances can a quarterback afford to lose his composure. You must be able to think on your feet at all times. Develop an extremely high boiling point, as there is no other way for you to be a successful quarterback. You must have yourself and your team under control at all times. This is your job, and you must have pride in the responsibility that goes along with it.

STUDIOUSNESS

If you are not willing to put in many extra tedious hours in study, then you should never try to become a quarterback. You must genuinely want to become a student of the game. Many hours are required for studying plays, diagrams, charts, frequencies, movies, scouting reports, and everything else that goes into making you and your team a more successful operation.

The evolution of defense has made football a more complicated game. To pilot your team against the intricacies of defenses that have spent as much time learning your offense as you have their defenses, then you must be willing to give that extra effort to stay one step ahead of them. You must learn to absorb football facts like a sponge. Extra time, extra effort, and extra energy are required for you to do your football homework.

CONCENTRATION

The element of concentration in a quarterback is strictly a matter of development. In golf there is an age-old argument about which weakens first in a player—his legs or his concentration. The matter of concentration is probably even more important to a quarterback than to a golfer, for he must be able to maintain his composure and think clearly and completely under all conditions.

The ability to concentrate on your target, regardless of how heavy the traffic gets around you, is a must for a good quarterback. You must never let the pressure of opposing players rattle or upset you.

I have worked very hard down through the years to perfect my concentration in all circumstances. This is a matter which everyone must develop within himself. Coaches cannot teach you concentration. It's strictly up to you. I strongly encourage every young quarterback to develop the best possible concentration and learn to extend it over the longest period of time possible.

A few years ago, when we were on the West Coast getting ready to play the San Francisco 49'ers, we had been working out

One of the big young "bombers" in pro football, the Rams' Roman Gabriel, takes a long stride in preparation to heaving one. This is an excellent example of concentration on the quarterback's part. He doesn't even know those four guys are anywhere near him.

about 30 minutes when we began to make a few mental errors. Finally, Coach Lombardi almost blew his top. He pulled us all over to one side of the field and said, "Look, fellows, I want to tell you one thing. I don't know if you are aware of this or not, but in kindergarten a youngster's period of concentration is about one to two minutes. From this, it steadily increases. Now, I don't know what your level is, but right at the moment I don't think it is much beyond the kindergarten stage." There were a few chuckles, but he got his point across, because we realized we were not concentrating thoroughly the way we should have, and our plays had slipped into a very sloppy state as a result.

Because of the noise, pressure, and excitement of a football game, you must always be on guard never to surrender your powers of concentration. It is amazing that when you do lose your concentration even for a split second or for a single play in the course of a game, nine times out of ten a mistake will occur.

It's my firm belief that pass interceptions are the direct result of lack of concentration. Many times, of course, interceptions are pulled off as the result of a great defensive maneuver, but quite often a quarterback loses his ability to concentrate and ends up throwing the ball into a crowd. A pass interception occurs simply because he has lost his concentration just long enough to put the ball in the wrong place.

GOOD MEMORY

A quarterback must possess a good memory, for he is called on to remember events that happened in previous games under similar circumstances and situations. He must recall ideas from scouting reports, game movies, his own notes on various teams, and, of course, the game plan.

I'm not sure anyone is born with an excellent memory. However, I am sure that a good memory can be developed by almost anyone who is willing to concentrate and is dedicated in his duties. If you are a dedicated person—and if you're not, you shouldn't aspire to being a quarterback—and are blessed with even normal intelligence, you can mold a good memory just by working at it.

Concentration, dedication, desire to study football as a subject, and the acceptance of responsibility all combine to feed facts into your mind so that you ultimately develop a knack for pulling out thoughts at the proper point in a game.

PHILOSOPHY AND ATTITUDE

My philosophy on the game has become the same as my philosophy of life. It is really very simple. It narrows down to the basic analogy that you get out of life, and out of football, exactly what you put into it. When a person realizes this and applies himself accordingly, he is sure to succeed because he then possesses the most fundamental key to success—proper attitude.

If you have this attitude, you then will establish a goal for yourself and for your team. Once the individuals have established their goal, then these form into a team goal. The two go hand in hand because dedicated individuals strive to make the finest contribution they can to the success and goal of the organization. Coach Lombardi makes sure this goal is established very early each season. For example, when we first came to camp last summer, his opening remarks were to the effect that our goal in 1966 was to be the champions of the National Football League. Frankly, this is an annual goal with us, but Coach Lombardi re-establishes it in the first meeting of each season—pointedly and emphatically. With the merger of the two professional leagues, I am sure that our goal, from this point on, will be to repeat as champions of the combined leagues.

In order to reach any goal, you must take sound fundamental steps to get there. This is an area where Coach Lombardi excels the most and where I have been most impressed with him as a leader. If a single word summarizes his ability to mold winning football teams, it is the word *preparation*.

If you are going to build anything that will stand for a long period of time and survive all elements that may be fighting against it, it first is necessary to build from a sound, firm foundation. This is the basis of operation applied by the entire Green Bay Packer organization, and every member of the coaching staff and team strives diligently to be completely prepared at all times.

Let's review quickly our interpretation of the word *preparation* as it pertains to an upcoming football game. We feel that preparation for any contest encompasses a complete, thorough working knowledge of our opponent. It is our responsibility to become so well organized for this particular game and so well prepared for it that we will leave nothing to chance when the opening whistle blows.

Obviously we are going to be surprised from time to time, as that is where the cat and mouse element enters into football.

However, we try to be as thoroughly prepared as possible so that when our opponent does confront us with something we hadn't anticipated, we are prepared to make a countermove to offset it. Proper preparation will hold these surprises to a minimum.

Next, the desire to practice must be deeply engrained in every one of us on the team. As the old saying goes, we must be willing to pay the price. This is much more important to success than most people realize. I have seen many football players who were endowed with a great deal of natural ability but were not mentally geared to pay the price of blood and sweat on the practice field. Such players are not willing to make the necessary personal sacrifices to attain success. They just don't realize that anything worthwhile—anything of genuine value—requires sacrificing and the giving up of many things in life. I feel most deeply that the price of success is hard work, pure and simple, and those who have attained the proper attitude are willing to work and make the necessary sacrifices.

In this area of practice for perfection, there are many fine byproducts that arise such as poise, confidence, teamwork, and loyalty.

POISE AND CONFIDENCE

You gain poise and self-confidence because practice sessions are designed to be successful experiences and as you succeed in something, you normally become self-confident. Your poise grows. You learn to stand on your own two feet and automatically make good, quick, firm decisions under pressure.

Anyone can make a decision if he is given time enough or the pressure is removed. However, it becomes our job to learn how to make decisions quickly under the intense pressures of key game situations, and we can never afford to become frustrated.

Your self-confidence grows right along with your poise. Once again, the success you enjoy in practice breeds self-confidence until you sincerely feel you can accomplish almost anything. This is the way it has to be if you are to develop the proper mental approach to the game. This self-confidence is gained on the practice field, and you carry it right through game time. You have been successful in practice, and you have no other thought but that you are going to be equally successful in the ball game. One eminent author has referred to this as "positive thinking."

Of course, there are occasions when you are defeated regardless of how well you are prepared, but you must accept

Joe Schmidt became very close to me in the 1962 Thanksgiving Day game. I saw quite a lot of Joe and his playmates, Karras, Brown, *et al.*, that day.

that with the proper attitude as well. You must remember that defeat is a part of life and that the greatest insurance salesman in the world doesn't sell a policy on every call. You must learn to accept these defeats and convert them into victory by coming back even harder the next week.

A quarterback can never afford to lose his poise, regardless of the situation. He can't become involved in a heated argument or get upset by any turn of events in the game. The minute a quarterback loses his poise or self-confidence—and it's amazing how closely the two go hand in hand—he has a tendency to lose his concentration. Then he's really in trouble.

The only time I can remember letting something "bug" me and really losing my poise in a game occurred in Detroit in 1962. Thank goodness it was near the end of the game and had no bearing on the outcome.

It happened that in 1962 we had won ten consecutive games, and we breezed into Detroit on Cloud Nine for the traditional Thanksgiving morning game. The Lions weren't only ready for us. They annihilated us.

There was less than a minute to play, and as is the case many times when you are losing, if you can't take it out on anyone else, you tend to blame the officials. Referee Red Pace came down the sidelines near the bench, and I decided I was going to give him a piece of my mind and relieve some of my frustrations for the day.

As he went by I yelled, "Hey, ref, if you give us any more of those stinking, lousy calls you've been handing out all day, I'm going to reach out and bite that big, fat head of yours right off."

Pace stopped, looked at me, and replied, "Starr, if you do, you'll be the only quarterback in this league with more brains in his stomach than he has in his head!"

Our bench broke up with laughter even though we were getting our heads kicked in, and that cured me of losing my poise.

TEAM CONFIDENCE

We spoke earlier of confidence being an absolute essential for a quarterback. Over and above your own personal need for self-confidence is the requirement of instilling this in your team. The other players on a club can feel the confidence of the quarterback. It rubs off on them.

With that confidence bubbling over and oozing into the whole team, a quarterback can call the worst play in the world, and a confident club will make it work. The players' confidence in the quarterback and his ability seems to furnish the incentive to make the team turn bad plays into good ones. It gives them momentum that's hard to stop.

Coach Lombardi has a slogan that he uses often: "Confidence is Contagious." This idea is one of the Packers' secret weapons. We live by it.

AN ANALYTICAL MIND

Another essential for becoming a good quarterback is the developing of an analytical mind. You must have the ability to

spot defensive changes, defensive weaknesses, and other altera-
tions that may have been made by your opposition since you
scouted it or played it last. The other team may have changed
tremendously since your scouting reports, your last movies, or
your past experiences, and it may be playing you quite differently
this time.

If so, the quarterback must be capable of spotting these
changes immediately and adjusting accordingly. Here is where
many of the qualities we have just discussed must come into
action for you. The poise, confidence, dedication, willingness to
accept responsibility, concentration, memory, and analytical mind
must all be marshalled to give you the ability to spot the changes
and make the proper maneuvers to counter them.

Norm Van Brocklin has a great reputation for possessing a
sharp, analytical mind, which he gained while a quarterback with
the Los Angeles Rams and Philadelphia Eagles, before becoming
coach of the Minnesota Vikings. There is a legend in the National Football League that Norm actually would go into the
huddle and many times create a play right on the spot, practically
drawing it on the ground.

You might expect that approach more from a sandlot team
than from a finely honed professional club, but the players on
these squads are highly intelligent and can adjust right in the
huddle and apply a little individual twist to a regular play to
outmaneuver even the best conceived defense. A classic example
of this is a type of pass that since has become a regular part of
a lot of teams' repertoires but which at that time was a real
novelty.

Back in 1960 when Van Brocklin was leading the Eagles
to the Eastern Division championship, they faced the New York
Giants one Sunday in Yankee Stadium. Van Brocklin noticed
that every time he ran his halfback up the center and folded
(put the center back on the defensive tackle and pulled the
guard behind the center to fold on the middle linebacker), linebacker Sam Huff stepped up and filled the hole.

When Van Brocklin would give the ball to the halfback
diving up the middle, his fullback on the opposite side would
simulate a dive over there. Huff got to the point where he would
ignore the fullback faking and would concentrate on the halfback. Van Brocklin faked his halfback into the line as on another
trap play. When the trap was faked, Huff took the bait and
allowed the fullback to escape free downfield.

Since the fullback was Huff's man and was running free,
Van Brocklin decided to fake the ball up the middle to the half-

back, backed up, and tossed a pass to the fullback. Huff was completely out of position to cover the fullback, who gathered in the ball and went all the way for the score that won the game.

This was typical of Van Brocklin, and it was typical of an analytical mind taking advantage of a defensive weakness on the spur of the moment.

ABILITY TO ADJUST

Possibly we should extend the matter of an analytical mind a step further and add the ability to adjust once the situation has been properly analyzed. This calls for quickness and aptitude as well. It would be worthless for a quarterback not to follow through on his analysis once it has been established.

VAN BROCKLIN IMPROVISED PLAY

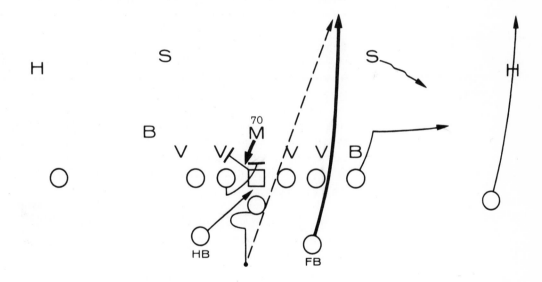

1. Van Brocklin faked his halfback into the line as on another trap play.

2. When Van Brocklin faked the trap, Huff (70) took the bait and allowed the fullback to escape free downfield for an easy completion from the quarterback.

The quarterback must have flexibility in thinking and alertness in acting upon his decision. He cannot afford to go into a game with a fixation on his plan alone and not be willing to accept the fact that a change may be called for in strategy or tactics at any time. He must be capable of changing his attack at any point he senses the defense is ahead of him, rather than letting the opposition put him in a bind that he may not maneuver out of before time runs out.

Many of these factors are closely aligned, but I would like to touch briefly on the matter of judgment. The quarterback certainly must possess an abundance of just plain "horse sense" out there on the football field. He must exercise sound judgment at all times, and that extends all the way from selection of plays to call in certain situations right on through the proper moves to make when the clock is running out.

How does a quarterback develop a sense of judgment? Is he born with it, or is it made? The answer to these is incorporated in the previous points we have covered in the qualifications of a quarterback. Proper preparation for the game and application of the proper principles of quarterbacking will develop sound judgment in signal calling. Good judgment can result only from a sound base of operation.

An excellent example of the application of many of these points is when and when not to call an audible at the line of scrimmage. The best laid plans in the world may be shot down in a split second by a shift in the defense that moves its strength right into the teeth of the play you have called in the huddle.

The defenses in football have advanced to the point where they mask their intentions right down to practically the moment of the ball being snapped. Once the quarterback realizes his call has been nullified by the defensive move, he must be capable of changing his signal immediately and substituting the proper play to challenge the opposition's move.

There is no time for pondering at this point. All of the factors that make up a good quarterback must function rapidly and effectively or the play will be dissipated. Ample preparation is your best answer at this stage.

A TOUCH OF DARING

If there is a noticeable shortcoming in my makeup as a quarterback, it probably comes under the heading of desire to gamble. However, in recent years I believe I have become much more daring, probably because I have matured and acquired the necessary self-confidence. This really is desirable in a good quarterback. Not only does a touch of daring make your offense more effective, but a quarterback who is willing to take this occasional gamble shows his teammates that he possesses the necessary ingredient of self-confidence.

The other players know in an instant that if the quarterback didn't have the courage to pull off a daring maneuver occasionally, he would never attempt it. As a result, when he does hit with this surprise, his team strikes out just that much harder to make the play successful. We pulled off a couple in recent years that have worked extremely well.

In the first Baltimore game of 1965 in Milwaukee, we had fourth and about a foot and a half to go for a first down on our own 12-yard line. We decided to go for it. Frankly, I was a bit surprised that Coach Lombardi agreed to let us try for it when we were backed up that close to our own goal, but something had happened in the course of the preceding two or three plays that probably influenced his decision. We called a play that had been very good for us up the middle. It was a quick trap for short yardage, and I knew they were going to be in a gap-type defense where we could break through.

I called the play and didn't tell anybody that I was going to run it. Our line did an amazing job of breaking through, and Elijah Pitts, who was in at halfback for us at the time, dashed up the middle. He made a beautiful fake, and I am sure that one of the reasons it was such a great fake is because he thought he was going to get the ball. Instead of handing it to him as he went by, I just faked to him and sprinted out to my right, on the weak side. We were in a left formation and Boyd Dowler, who was split to our right, came slanting down looking inside a bit to help us screen any defender back in the secondary.

The defender never even saw me until I was outside and running, and I must have made 20 or 25 yards before I got caught. I called the play this way because I felt I would get a better fake from Pitts if he didn't know that he wasn't actually going to get the ball. Thanks to his faking, the defense was drawn to the inside, and it worked out very well.

Another time, against the Minnesota Vikings in Minneapolis, we ran the same play from the same formation except that we did call the bootleg out—the fake, and then the roll to the outside. This was on third down with very short yardage and they were ganged up in the middle. Our back again made a great fake, enabling me to get outside and scoot for a fine gain.

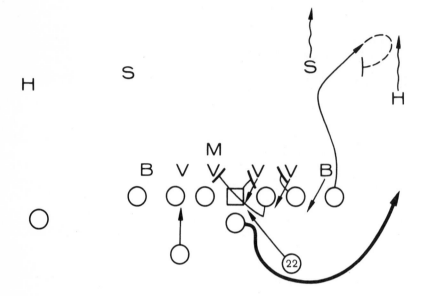

1. Elijah Pitts (22) faked well into the line (he thought he was getting the ball) enabling the quarterback to run outside all alone.

These plays aren't necessarily very daring, but they're a little more daring for me than in the past, and I think I continued this trend even more during the 1966 season, which was my best ever.

When anyone speaks of a daring quarterback, this always brings to mind Johnny Unitas. Johnny is the greatest quarterback in football. He's built a great deal of his reputation on being a gambler, having the knack for pulling the unexpected. It actually boils down to the fact that Johnny is completely self-confident out there on the football field. He truly possesses that rare ingredient of poise. Nothing ruffles him. As a result, when the occasion calls for taking the gamble, he feels he can make it work—and he does, in most instances.

When a quarterback like Johnny Unitas goes for the gamble and gets away with it, he really upsets the opposition. He just destroys it! It is really demoralizing, and many times a team loses a game because it never fully recovers from being shocked by one of these plays.

COURAGE

Football is a game of courage. Without the courage to hold on to that football until the last split second before turning it loose to his maneuvering receivers, a passing quarterback would be out of business. He knows he is going to be slapped right on the seat of his pants with little chance of defending himself, but he must have the courage to pass the ball first and never worry about his own self-defense. Otherwise, he is playing the wrong position—and he won't be playing it long.

Television's isolated camera has made a point on occasion of following the quarterback's action after the ball has been thrown. As a result, a lot of fans who never saw the quarterback getting knocked down because they were following the flight of the ball when it was released have come to realize that there are some pretty rugged shocks being absorbed by that quarterback as he turns the ball loose.

Getting knocked around quite a bit is part of the trade of a quarterback. When you're passing, you have to expect to be crunched by some big lineman charging in on you, but it takes extra courage because you cannot defend yourself or retaliate.

The rules protect a passer from being hit after he has released the ball, but there are enough borderline cases in the course of a game to keep you flat on your back a good part of the day. The officials do a good job of making this judgment call on whether or not the passer has released the ball before he is decked, but that doesn't protect him from taking the pounding. He simply must possess sufficient courage to stand back there and accept his beating as part of his job. You might call it an occupational hazard.

This brings us back to accepting responsibility. If the quarterback wants the responsibility of running his team, he must possess both the physical and mental courage, knowing full well he is about to be knocked down and fallen on time and time again. The mental approach to the position is equally important in playing quarterback—and many times, I believe, even more so.

the
mechanics
of
quarterbacking

Sammy Baugh once said, "The easiest position in football is the quarterback in the T-formation. All you do is hand the ball off and pass." And if the T had been popular when Sam started, he probably would have played until he was fifty. But when the Redskins switched from the single-wing to the T, Sammy Baugh had to learn the mechanics of being a quarterback. All quarterbacks today, from peewee league to pro, have to learn the basic mechanics of quarterbacking. And the better they learn the fundamentals, the better they become as quarterbacks.

As we get into the mechanics of quarterbacking, the big point I want to stress is comfort. The most comfortable position is to place the feet about shoulder width apart, pointing the toes pretty much straight ahead. Some may prefer to point the toes slightly in or out, but I think straight ahead (parallel) is best. This gives you a good comfortable beginning base for your stance. The weight should be on the balls of the feet, not back on the heels, so you can move readily from side to side and push away to the rear or straight ahead.

Remember, weight on the balls of the feet, heels just slightly touching the ground. Here again, you'll have just enough tension in the legs to make them respond to a quick movement. The knees are only slightly bent, so the body is still generally erect. The hips are parallel to the line of scrimmage, also parallel with your feet. The body is leaning slightly forward but fairly erect. In other words, you aren't stooped way over so that your head is down and you have to lift it in order to look. The body is erect enough for you to look out comfortably and turn your head from side to side. The head has to be up so you can scan the defense and so your teammates can hear your signals readily.

75

I mentioned weight distribution a moment ago. Most of the weight should be on the balls of the feet. You might sometimes use a little waggle back and forth with one foot or the other—like a golfer's waggle—as you are positioning yourself to get comfortable. Some players almost do a little shuffle until they get their body into a comfortable feeling, weight-distributed position.

To review, strive for comfort, and make notes of the points numbered in the accompanying photos.

Your practice procedure from here could consist of many things. If you want to work on hand-offs, you should practice moving laterally, up and down the line of scrimmage, backwards on draw plays, out to the side for fullback off tackle plays, quickly to the rear for sweeps and end runs to the halfback.

These three photos show the proper stance of a quarterback from all angles.

This picture shows the stance of the fine young quarterback Bill Munson of the Los Angeles Rams.

This is a staggered stance used for years by Y. A. Tittle. Since he always assumed this stance, it was never a tip-off for any particular play.

SIGNAL CALLING

In order to put your team in motion, you need the art of signal calling. A quarterback should have a good, clear, crisp voice. His basic confidence, his desire and determination, his willingness to accept the challenge of responsibility come out in the type of voice he has on the field. My wife has said that I am pretty much a Dr. Jekyll and Mr. Hyde. I'm not very loud around the house, but in the 50th row of our stadium she can hear me as if I were just across the room.

Maybe this is true. I do try to call signals loud and clear. I feel that when the team hears me call the play with authority in the huddle, come to the line of scrimmage, and really zing those letters and colors and code words and counts out, they have a feeling of reassurance and a lot of self-confidence.

If your head is up and you are scanning the defense, as your eyes shift from different players, up and down your own line, you are able to check things out, and you can call your

Left: This rear view of my stance points up the feet comfortably spread, knees slightly bent, head up—surveying the defense.

Right: A quarterback barks out his signals so everyone can hear.

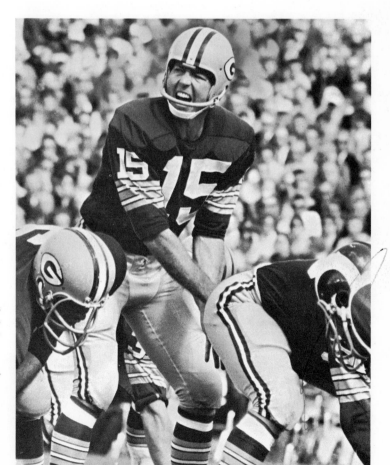

signals authoritatively with a great deal of gusto. Whatever type of count you have as a team, be consistent. Be authoritative in your calls, and establish a consistent calling and method to your cadence, so that your team will become confident with it.

I don't think many people realize that when one quarterback has to leave a game and another one comes in, a team may suffer a couple of off-sides shortly thereafter because they have to adjust to the new quarterback. No two people are alike, and though you use the same cadence and the same calls, all quarterbacks have certain variations. They may have little differences in their tempo, and the team is upset or off balance for just a few plays until they get settled down and get into the rhythm of hearing the new quarterback. If you are the quarterback of the team, be consistent, so that the team will develop complete confidence in your cadence and will respond by firing off on that count.

AUDIBLES

There are all sorts of ways of identifying plays today. Some teams like to number a back in a hole, some by series, some by code words or just by descriptive terms. Most teams, I think, prefer to call their plays with numbers so they can change the plays on the line of scrimmage. Some pass plays, though they may be descriptive in nature, such as a wing post or an "X" corner, many times also have a number with them. With such a system, if you want to audibilize or check-off to another play on the line of scrimmage, you can do so and go to almost any play you have in your attack.

I mention audibles and automatics or check-offs now, because there has been extensive use of audibles for several years as a result of the shifting defenses that have become so prevalent in modern football. A team, whether it be college, pro, or high school, should have a simple system of automatics. When I say a high school team could make use of audibles, I am not being facetious, if you develop a simple system so that it could be effective.

Because defenses are so good today, you are often confronted with the possibility that the play you called in the huddle will be nullified. Let's say you called an end run, and at the last minute they shift their defenses so as to stymie this play. In so doing they probably have left themselves open for a counterattack someplace else. If you can go to an audible or an automatic or a change-up or a check-off (whatever you want to call it) you probably have a better chance of succeeding with the change-up than you did with the original play. This is the only reason for having it—to counteract the defensive move and to come up with a better play yourself.

Obviously, there are two basic plays that you go to in an automatic: a run or a pass. We like to go to either, but most of the time when we automatic, if there is any amount of yardage at stake, we will pass. By yardage I mean anything over four yards. Rather than take the chance of a running play failing, we will throw the ball. So we end up checking most of the times to a pass. Here are three of the most common ways to get into an automatic. I have used all three with the Packers.

Number one is to have a live color. Let's say that in a particular game your live color for automatics is blue. At the line of scrimmage the quarterback starts his count with the color. If he says red, yellow, or orange, the team knows there is no automatic and that the play called in the huddle will be run at the line of scrimmage. However, if the quarterback comes to the line of scrimmage and calls out blue, the play called in the huddle is no longer on. The next play he calls at the line of scrimmage will be the new play.

Now the quarterback says "Blue—84." This might mean a pass or a running play. He can call anything he wants by just calling out that live color of blue. Then the ball is snapped according to whatever arrangements they have for their automatics. If the count given in the huddle is two, then the ball is snapped on two, even though the quarterback has changed the play.

However, let's say the count is on three, and in their system all automatics mean the snap of the ball is on one or on two. When the team hears the automatic, they realize that the snap number changes. I frankly don't think this is a good idea because the linemen and the backs have enough to think about without changing the count number. I think the count number should remain the same as in the huddle, because this is one less thing to have to remember.

The second way to get into a check-off is to repeat the snap number. This is a very good way and some teams prefer to use this. Let's say you called a play "29 on 3" in the huddle. You come to the line of scrimmage and say "2—47," or whatever you're counting up there. Since you didn't repeat the snap number, which is 3, the play you called in the huddle is still on, and the linemen pick this up right away.

But, assuming the snap number is 3, you come to the line of scrimmage and say "3—47." Then you have alerted the team right away by repeating the snap number 3 that 47 is to be the

new play. They also assume that in this system you will snap the ball as called in the huddle.

The new play 47 is on 3. You start counting and run the new play. Or let's say the snap number is 1 and you walk to the line of scrimmage and say "1–75"; the new play becomes 75, and the snap number is on 1. That's another example of getting into this type of automatics.

A third way is to repeat the number of the play called in the huddle. This is also a good way, though I don't think this is as good as the previous methods. Say you call a play "22" in the huddle. You walk to the line of scrimmage and say "22," repeating the play you called. This alerts the team that you are no longer going to run that play. You repeated the play number and you are going to something else, and your second number would then be 58. You say "22–58," and then whatever you say after that.

Here again the count number is determined by what your automatic system calls for, whether it remains the same as in the huddle or whether you change whatever you change to an automatic.

So, here are three different methods by which you handle an automatic. All of them are good, and it's really just a matter of choice as to which the coach thinks is the most effective.

Here are the basic types of plays that the Packers go to in an automatic. I mentioned we either go to a run or pass, but specifically we go to quick hitting runs or trap-type plays that take advantage of gap defenses where the linemen are charging hard and you can trap them easily. Occasionally we go to a sweep play where everybody is pitching to the inside, and we can turn the corner easily. Or we will pass, usually a quick slant in or down and out.

Since Coach Lombardi has come to the Packers, we have used audibles extensively. In fact, the first two or three years that he was here, we made a living off them, because I felt at that time that the defenses tipped their hands a great deal. We were able to take advantage of them much more than we are today. Teams disguise their defenses a lot better today than they formerly did. We still use audibles a great deal when we have the occasion, because you shouldn't try to butt your head against a brick wall.

They can't conceivably defend against everything you have. So, if they give you something out of the ordinary, they leave themselves open someplace else. If you can analyze the situation quickly and come up with a good automatic, many times you can hurt them because they don't realize that you have taken advantage of this defensive weakness.

RECEIVING BALL FROM CENTER

You have to be able to receive the ball from center comfortably, accurately, and confidently.

The placement of the hands is quite important, for this exchange between center and quarterback should become automatic. It is something that should not have to be thought out. As you can see from the illustration, I have my right hand up, my left hand down, the fingers spread slightly. The hands are in a relaxed position. Thumbs are together. The right hand is placed under the seat of the center, applying a firm pressure against him. This gives him a target, something to shoot for, snap the ball to.

Above: The quarterback seen from the front, with center over the ball. Points to consider: (1) Feet are comfortably spread (about shoulder width) and parallel to each other; (2) Knees are slightly flexed; (3) Body leans forward slightly from waist; (4) Arms are extended but not stiff. *Top right:* The quarterback seen from the side. (1) The right hand is under center just far enough to receive the ball. The left hand is touching the right along the thumb line, hanging relaxed to form a "backstop"; (2) Head is up, to survey the defense. *Bottom right:* If the ball is to be snapped to anyone other than the quarterback, then the quarterback must assume this stance and not extend his hands under the center as usual.

As the center brings the ball up, his natural motion should turn it slightly. I have seen some centers turn it all the way around, but if you just let him snap it naturally, the ball will make about a third of a turn, and it will fit perfectly into your hands. If you'll have him snap the ball from the ground with the laces pointing up—looking right at him when he snaps the ball—the laces will come into contact with your hand in such a way that with a slight adjustment you'll be ready to throw a pass.

Two views of the proper position for the quarterback's hands to receive the ball from the center. Fingers are comfortably spread but relaxed. Left hand acts as a "backstop" against errant snaps.

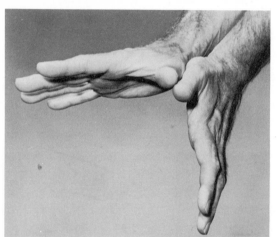
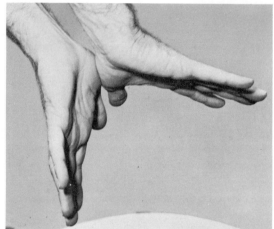

Front and side view of the ball immediately after the snap from center. With the center making a slight turn of the ball on the snap, observe how little adjustment is necessary by the quarterback to assume a passing grip. Placement of laces results from the ball resting on the ground, laces up, prior to exchange from center.

Both hands are on the ball as it comes up from the center. You trap it with your hands. You'll notice also in the picture of the stance that the elbows are in close to the body. The arms are slightly extended but loose. They aren't stuck out like a piece of board. They are comfortable.

One practice procedure the quarterback should get into the habit of doing is riding with the center's motion. Because the center has to move forward and laterally as he snaps the ball, your hand has to go with him. In other words, you can't be pulling away as he goes forward, or the ball will go straight up in the air. A great deal of coordination between the quarterback and the center is needed. You should spend a good amount of time with your center, until you become thoroughly confident. There is really nothing worse than to walk to the line of scrimmage, call a fine play, have your team all set to go, and then blow the whole thing by not even getting off a good snap.

Any time you practice, a great deal of conscious effort should be made to improve your weaknesses. If you are weaker at moving to your left than you are to your right, then work more on moving to your left. Don't work on the easy things that you do well, but on the ones that you don't do well. If you tend to ignore the things you can't do well, you'll never be able to do them. In a like manner, if you just continue to strengthen the things you do best, you are getting a false picture of yourself. As a result, you will tend to lack confidence in the areas where you are a little bit weak. Believe it or not, you're aware of your weaknesses, and your mind reacts accordingly. The best way to feed it positive thoughts is to have it well conditioned so you can go left, right, backward, or forward to perform any phase of quarterbacking automatically. Through having done it so much, your reflexes will take over, and you will go through the maneuver without a hitch.

The ball has just been received from the center.

WHEN DOES THE CENTER SNAP THE BALL?

This depends a bit on the type of cadence. If you're using a cadence in which the ball is snapped on the first, second, or third sound and you are saying, "hut one, hut two, hut three," he might actually start the snap on the "hut" part of your count. As you complete the count "hut three," on the "three" the ball is in your hands and the line is gone, because they are moving on the "hut" count too.

However, if you are using a count like a sound, you walk up the line and say "hut . . . hut . . . hut." Then the center has to have really good reflexes. As you say "hut" the third time, he has to snap the ball instantly to you, and the line, of course, charges also.

Many teams today use a nonrhythmical count. By that I mean there is no pattern to it. The quarterback might say in the huddle, "Okay, on three this time." He might say, "hut . . . hut . . . . . . hut" (with a long pause between the second and third "hut" or between the first and second). This keeps the defense honest. They can't guess with you in any rhythm or count.

There are pros and cons on the different systems. Some coaches seem to think that with a rhythm count such as "hut one, hut two, hut three, hut four," you get into a good rhythm. Others feel that by conditioning yourself to sit there and hold until you hear the sound to explode, you keep the defense on edge, because he is just waiting. He can't guess the feel of the rhythm either. He's just sitting there.

So, there are all sorts of ideas as to the best counts to use. With any system, the center has to do a lot of work and have good reflexes in order to get the ball to you on the proper count.

I might mention here that the Green Bay Packers have an excellent cadence drill. After we have gone through our calisthenics, our first drill of the day is a team drill. We fire off, reacting to the cadence, by coming off the ball as quickly as we can for a few steps.

This practice gets right back to many of the things we talked about. First, it represents the idea of team work—we are doing things as a team. We're doing fundamental things, we're preparing, we're practicing, we're developing pride in coming off the ball well. The defense reacts to the ball on a snap too. They react by sprinting off a few steps. A team should have a drill like this in their practice procedure.

Since we have been discussing stances, exchanges, etc., let's have a look at the fundamentals of the center's stance.

THE ROLE OF THE CENTER

The first thing we teach our centers is to get a good basic stance with their feet. Most of the college centers today are leaning forward on the ball. Their hands are extended and all their weight is forward.

In pro ball we do it a little differently. We sit back. A center in a two-point stance is more or less sitting back on his haunches, and the ball is just naturally placed right in front of his nose—a little forward of his head. All he has to do then is place his right hand on top of the seams of the ball. We keep the seams straight up, just as the passer would have it. The center then puts the thumb of his right hand on the ball, and it is strictly a one-handed snap.

We don't have any pressure forward or backward. It's an even stance—one where the center can move backward, sideways, or forward.

All he does with his left hand is place it on the ball so he has some place to put it. Rather than keep it on his knee, which many teams have their centers do, we have our center put both hands on the ball. The left hand is strictly there to even out his weight. He just crumbles up his knuckles and places them right on top of the ball. Everything in centering is done with the right hand.

On the snap, he keeps his arms stiff and brings the ball straight up like a swinging pendulum. By keeping his arm stiff and swinging it like a pendulum between his legs, the center gets the ball to the quarterback at a quarter turn.

The center seen from the side. Note left hand resting on ball.

With the quarterback's hands behind the center and his right hand on top, this type of pendulum swing by the center gives him the ball with the laces right across his fingertips. Now he can lift it up and throw it immediately if he prefers. Otherwise, he has good control of the ball in making his fakes and handing the ball off.

Let me recap. It's even distribution of weight for the center—not too far forward, not too far back. Everything in the snap is done with the right hand and a stiff arm. He swings it like a pendulum. This automatically turns his arm a quarter turn and puts the ball with the laces up into the fingertips of the quarterback.

STARTING THE PLAY: HAND-OFFS, FAKES, AND LATERALS

Let's consider now the handling of the ball on a running play. You have spent a great deal of time working with your center, so the exchange is fundamentally sound. On a running

Note the concentration of the quarterback on the target area of the runner. Left hand is just being removed as quarterback prepares to hand off to the fullback. The eyes of the fullback (31) are focused on blocking ahead, not on ball. 1966 championship game against Dallas.

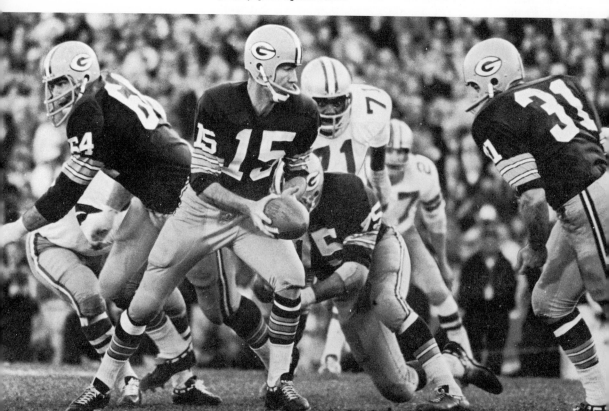

play the responsibility for a good hand-off is solely with the quarterback, because the back who is to carry the ball must have his eyes on the hole to see how the blocker in front of him is going to handle his opponent.

As you take the ball from center, it should immediately be brought close to your body. In other words, as you receive the ball from the center, your hands should quickly come back toward your midsection, elbows in close, hands bringing the ball in tight quickly. This prevents any offensive or defensive players from brushing the ball. If it were being handled loosely, out from your body, it might be knocked away, causing a fumble.

If you are going to make a handoff by a spin or turning away from the line of scrimmage, remember to keep your body between you and the defense. Make them come through you in order to get to the ball. If the ball is to one side as you are making a hand-off and you can't protect it, the defense has a good shot at it and this could cause a fumble. So, when possible, keep your body between the defender and the ball.

As you start to hand the ball off to the back who is going to receive it, move as in passing with short, quick, little sliding, shuffling steps, pick up the back, and immediately focus your eyes on the target area of the back you are going to give it to.

If you are to hand off a dive into the line of scrimmage, then you want to move, as quickly as possible, somewhat forward down the line of scrimmage so this back cannot beat you to the hole.

The quarterback's elbows are being drawn toward the body to pull the ball in and protect it.

DIVE PLAY

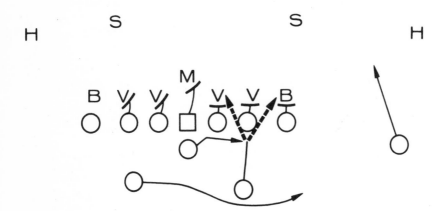

The actual contact of placing the ball in the runner's mid-section is firm and crisp but not necessarily hard. You want him to receive the ball comfortably but firmly. Slip it into the mid-section where, when he receives it, he has good control over it and doesn't have to spend time fumbling and juggling the ball in order to take off with it.

The Hand-off. The quarterback should pull the ball close to his body immediately upon receiving it from the center. This prevents accidental dislodging of the ball. Also, he should keep his elbows tucked in close to his sides.

Never "crowd" the runner, but at the same time try to avoid extensive "reaching" with the ball. Hand-offs are perfected by practice. With sufficient drill, hand-offs to ball carriers become an automatic operation

A hand-off about to be made in the 1965 championship game. Observe how the quarterback's eyes are on the back's midsection. Note the simulated pass protection drop of the left tackle (76) in order to get the defensive end to inch toward the outside.

A clear picture of me about to give the ball to Paul Hornung. Notice that the elbows are close to the body, the ball tucked in closely, and where the eyes are trained.

This photo illustrates several points: (1) The quarterback is carrying out a good "bootleg" fake by continuing to look at the running back. The quarterback's right arm "flowed" with the back on the hand-off; (2) the hand-off has just occurred and Elijah Pitts of the Packers is adjusting it for security; (3) Pitts' eyes are already on the area where the play is designed to go.

FAKING

Good faking should be an integral part of every play to insure proper "follow through" and create more deception in the backfield. Most defenders are looking at the quarterback and trying to follow the ball. So, as soon as you hand it off, if you stand and relax and watch the play, you show them right where it's gone. They see it quickly enough anyway, but if you are carrying out your fake in the backfield properly, they may be looking at you for just a split second longer than they otherwise would, enabling the running back with the ball to gain an extra advantage. The situation is much like play action passes when you attempt to freeze the defense momentarily for that little added protection. Even in the professional ranks, the coaches are continually reminding you to carry out your fakes.

The following posed photos depict the two basic types of faking between a quarterback and a runner with the ball and

Faking hand-offs becomes an intricate part of a quarterback's duties. Whether utilizing the two-hand (with the ball) or one-hand fake to the runner, the quarterback must be ready to continue his play without hesitation, whether it is a hand-off to another back or a retreat to throw the ball. When the ball is being held with both hands, note how the quarterback's elbows are tucked in at the sides and the ball is carried close to the body.

In the empty hand fake, the ball may be hidden down by the side as shown here, or it may be hidden in the mid-section.

An excellent example of the ball being hidden in the quarterback's midsection is demonstrated here with this "bootleg" fake. This photo shows the one empty hand faked into the runner while the other hand cradles the ball close to the body to help hide it from the defense.

The quarterback makes a bootleg fake after the handoff. Observe how the quarterback is scanning downfield to see what the reaction was to the play.

with the hand. The action photos show good faking under game conditions.

At the same time, you may pick up some sort of information in carrying out a good fake. A receiver may come back and say, "Look, run that same type of play. When you do, my defender has a real tendency to come up quickly, thinking it's a running play, or else he tends to relax a little on me out there. Why don't you throw me a pass off this same type of action?"

Many times a smart receiver will come back and tell you this. You may not have this particular pass in your repertoire, but there is nothing that prevents you from doing it, because all pass protection is basic. You can often improvise on the spot.

If you will concern yourself with good faking, you are going to eliminate a lot of fumbles too, because you will be "looking" the ball into the back. When you are careless and not too concerned about your faking, fumbles often occur.

Fran Tarkenton displays an excellent bootleg fake after handing off the ball. *— but notice how the linemen are all headed for the ball!*

IMPROVISING A PLAY

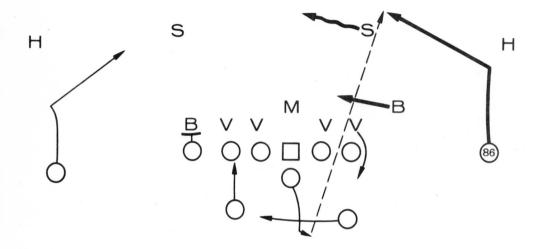

1. A few years ago, our split end Boyd Dowler (86) noticed that every time we ran a sweep to our left, the weak-side safety and linebacker were very quick to leave their positions.

2. Though we didn't ordinarily use this pass, we later called this play, faked it, and hit Dowler in the area vacated by the safety.

Right here, let's place special emphasis on faking for high school and college quarterbacks. Learning to fake well is a tremendous asset, because you can literally fool your opponent, particularly at the high school level. Even in college you can often fool him too. It's pretty tough to fool them in professional football because these players are the cream of the crop, and they have seen just about anything you can throw at them. However, sometimes in a professional football game, you'll see people get faked out of position.

You'll find that if you learn to fake well, it's almost like having an extra blocker or two. You should work with your coach as to the method he wants. You may want to use one or both of the methods we discussed here—both hands on the ball, the riding type method, or faking with the open hand and hiding the ball with the other hand near the midsection.

Use the method that is best for the particular play at the time. The idea is to learn to fake well and to be an actor. Have some imagination, and you'll find it will really pay off. You'll fool your opponents many, many times.

Two of the most deceptive ball handlers in the game were Eddie LeBaron and Babe Parilli. LeBaron was the pint-size quarterback for many years with the Washington Redskins who finished up with the Dallas Cowboys after Dallas came into the league. He was a tremendous faker, and I think he developed this faking ability to the point where it gave him an added advantage over the larger men. He froze the defense, enabling him to either throw a pass or to pull off some maneuver that completely crossed up the defense.

The finest faker that I have ever seen was a fellow by the name of Babe Parilli. Most people may find this quite a surprise, but Babe was my idol for many years.

I had the pleasure of working out with Babe for two weeks prior to my senior year in high school in the summer which preceded Babe's senior year at the University of Kentucky. Charley Bradshaw and Bill Moseley, who was the head coach at my high school in Montgomery, ran the same type of offense as Kentucky because they had played under Bear Bryant and were following his offensive theories completely.

I went to Kentucky that summer and learned more about quarterbacking in two weeks from Babe than anyone had ever taught me in my life. Many of the things that I still practice today are fundamentals which Babe taught me in those two weeks.

Babe had extremely fast hands. He possessed the ability to keep his elbows tucked in fairly tight to the body so as not to show the defense the ball at any time. He would assume a position with his knees slightly bent, looking just like a master card dealer leaning back on one of those little seats that you take to golf tournaments. Just the hand was shuffling out from side to side. I have never seen anyone who could fake more deceptively than could Babe. I don't know if in coming to the pros they changed his style slightly, or if he found it not as feasible to be quite the faker he had been in college, but he never was the real sleight-of-hand artist here that I had once known him to be.

He used all the types of fakes discussed—the dead fake where you put the ball in with both hands, ride it, and pull it back quickly; where you would fake maybe to the first back with the ball, to the second back with the hand, and then retreat to pass; or where you would make just an open-hand fake with one hand.

POINT OF FAKE

The point of fake occurs just as you make the simulated hand-off. You and the running back try to make the fake look as much like the hand-off as possible. The receiving back doesn't try to overdramatize the move or overemphasize to the point where the "fake" is just that. He merely tries to come in cleanly, faking just like he's getting the ball and diving into the line of scrimmage. In order to fake well as a quarterback, you must have good support from your running backs.

One of the finest fakes I have ever seen a back pull off was executed by Tommy Moore in Green Bay a few years ago. I made a quick fake up the middle to him, and Tommy leaped into the line of scrimmage as if he had the ball. As a result, I was able to sprint out around the other end on a bootleg type play, simply because Tommy made a tremendous fake.

These matters of laterals, hand-offs, faking, and the many other facets of ball handling in the backfield by the quarterback are of such vital importance that we asked Coach Jerry Burns to add his knowledge in describing the proper procedures for the runnning backs or receivers in these phases of the game. A most astute coach, who developed several of the outstanding collegiate quarterbacks in football while serving as head coach of the University of Iowa, Jerry has included instructions for the other backs in the following pages of this chapter.

The Burns line of thinking for backs is as follows:

A lateral pass seldom nets the yardage of a forward pass, but let one backfire and you must pay a horrible price. As a result, a quarterback just can't afford to execute a lateral pass in any manner other than the proper one.

So, learn your fundamentals well and then work at them until a lateral pass becomes almost an automatic maneuver. Practice will teach you the correct moves with the ball and establish the speed and actions of the backs to whom you will be pitching.

There are two basic types of lateral passes—the two-handed dead or floating type of pass, and the one-handed spiral pass. This first type of pitch-out from the quarterback to another back is nothing more than receiving the snap from the center, turning immediately, stepping in the direction of the intended flight on the ball toward the back, and letting the sweeping motion of the arms carry the ball out to him. There is no attempt to spiral the ball at all—it's just a soft, floating pass.

This can be a very quick pass because you don't have to shuffle your feet or pull the ball back toward your body or readjust the hands for the spiral. You must toss the ball out to him. It is a simple pass for a back to receive because it does not have any spinning action on it, and this enables the back to catch it rather easily. The spiral pass pitch-out is also used and can be very effective, but it is a little harder to handle.

The one big thing to guard against here is rushing the toss so that you mislead the back by throwing it low, high, or way out in front of him. You just lead your back, and with a little practice, you will be surprised at how softly—yet quickly—you can deliver the ball to him. A lateral usually is used on a quick

The two-handed "toss" or "pitch-out" is demonstrated here. This method is suggested for younger quarterbacks until they can completely master the one-handed technique. The ball comes to the runner from the two-handed toss in a "dead" or floating motion and, under most conditions, is more easily handled than the spiral toss.

The one-handed toss, or pitch-out, is pitched to a runner in this manner. It is spiraled and is really just an underhand flick. With proper practice, this is not a difficult maneuver to master. When pitching out to a runner, try to give him a slight lead and have the ball arrive approximately waist-high.

The quarterback reverse spins to his left and dead tosses the ball to the fullback on a quick outside play. The quarterback's eyes are fixed on his target.

I had the pleasure of playing in the 1967 Pro Bowl game with Gale Sayers of the Chicago Bears. He destroyed my whole sense of timing with his tremendous burst of speed on pitch-outs.

PITCH-OUT

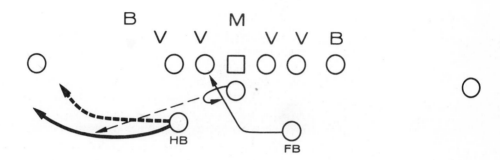

1. The halfback gets to his outside as quickly as possible, yet under control, with enough "belly" in his route to give the quarterback a better target.

2. If the halfback runs too shallow or flat (broken line) he gives the quarterback a poor target and crowds his blockers too closely.

pitch-out to a halfback who sprints out to one side or the other, or as a toss type play back to the fullback who is running wide. The back's maneuvers on these outside pitch-outs amount to sheer speed, because on most of these plays there is some defensive player he must just plain outrun.

The first thing we coach our backs on starting this play is to come away from the line of scrimmage. The receiving backs can't close down the angle between the quarterback and themselves because this puts too much of a premium on the accuracy of the quarterback.

FOOTWORK

In regard to the footwork of the back on receiving the lateral pass, the first thing we tell him is to make a fall-away step. His outside foot is a lead foot, but it is pulled away from the line of scrimmage. In this manner, he is able to get started running and still be in a position to "make a belly" away from the line of scrimmage so the quarterback will have a good target to aim the ball. By making this one step away from the line of scrimmage initially, he also can turn to look back for the ball and be in a position to come up and catch it if the quarterback puts it in front of him.

RECEIVING

Our backs are taught to receive the ball exactly the way our ends receive it. It becomes a matter of looking the ball into their hands like receiving any kind of a pass after the quarterback has flipped it. We tell our backs to use both hands and never try to handle the ball with one hand. The position of the ball as they receive it, of course, depends on which of the two types of passes the quarterback has used—the two-handed flip or the one-handed spiral. The one-handed spiral lateral is just like receiving a forward pass because it has the same amount of speed and zip as a short pass.

On our hand-offs from the quarterback with the play into the line, we emphasize that the back never looks' for the ball. He also never reaches out and snatches or tries to grab the ball from the quarterback. It's up to the quarterback to put the ball into the back's stomach. We have two methods of taking the ball.

Our fullbacks use what the majority of college players are accustomed to—taking the ball with their inside elbow up and their outside hand as the stop. Their outside hand rests down on their hip, fingers spread, and the quarterback sticks the ball under the elbow into the stomach. The back then closes his elevated arm and elbow down over the ball and traps up under the ball with his outside hand.

Again, in all of these the fullback is not looking for the ball. He's to be concentrating on the hole, and the quarterback is responsible for getting the ball into his stomach.

On the halfback hand-offs, our halfback takes the ball with his inside arm back out of the way, and his outside hand again is about hip-high, with his wrist in close to his hip. His hand forms a stop on the far side of his body as the quarterback makes the hand-off. The quarterback then puts the ball in the stomach, and the inside hand, which is kept back in order to give the quarterback a clear shot at the stomach, then comes forward and grabs the ball, along with the outside hand used initially for the stop.

The Hand-off. This photo shows not only proper technique by the quarterback in handing the ball to the runner, but also how most runners with the Packers normally receive the ball. Note the receiver's outside hand comes up by his waist to act as a stop for the ball. The inside arm is held back out of the way so as not to interfere with the placement of the ball.

A common way to receive the ball on hand-offs is for the receiver to raise his inside elbow. This allows room for the quarterback to place the ball in the receiver's midsection. In draw plays and similar situations, we also use this style.

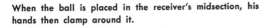

When the ball is placed in the receiver's midsection, his hands then clamp around it.

This technique is hard to get across to backs who have been using the "inside elbow up" technique through their college career. One of the matters we emphasize in keeping this inside arm down and back out of the way as the quarterback puts the ball across in front of this arm is that you must be really conscious of it until you've mastered the technique. In each practice session where new backs are having trouble trying to learn this, we make them hook their thumb in their T-shirt as they come forward. This almost makes them take a one-handed hand-off until they get the idea that the quarterback can make the hand-off without them having that elbow up.

One different type of hand-off we use is that on our draw plays. The quarterback, of course, is trying to make it look like a pass. The receivers are going out downfield, so he has to be

The Draw. On draw plays where a pass is faked, the quarterback starts off by retreating as if to select a receiver. He then turns and hands the ball off to a back on a draw maneuver. Note how the halfback appears ready to block for the passer.

As the quarterback delivers the ball, observe once again how he "looks" the ball into the runner's midsection to assure a proper hand-off.

Following the hand-off, the quarterback continues to his rear, carrying out his passing fake as effectively as possible to help insure the success of the draw play.

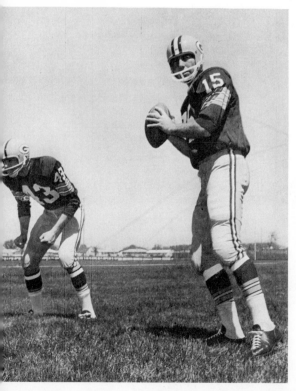

looking at them. The blocker, or the potential ball carrier, has to set up in a position to make the rushing linemen or linebackers believe he is getting ready to lock for a pass.

The way we teach this is to tell the back to have his inside arm raised, just as he would if he were a fullback receiving a hand-off. The inside arm is raised, and he's looking at the rushing linemen or rushing linebackers, not reaching for the ball or moving. With the inside arm up, he forms a pocket that the quarterback places the ball in as he retreats. The quarterback looks downfield as if to simulate a pass, and then by turning and making his hand-off quickly, the ball carrier has the ball and is keying the blocks by the linemen as he moves forward into the hole on the draw play.

Position again of the outside hand on this draw has to be such that, as the quarterback comes out of his pass fake and snaps around to make the hand-off, he must have a stop on the outside to make sure the ball doesn't go all the way through. The hand position for the receiving back is virtually the same as it would be on any other hand-off.

the
art
of
passing

WHY PASS?

Because there are big chunks of yardage to be gained by throwing the ball. You may get 20, 40, 60, 80 yards a play by passing, and it is very difficult to run the ball at such a pace. There are other reasons too. Many times you play defensive linemen who sit back and wait for the run. They will play soft, and frankly this is the most difficult kind of lineman to block on running plays unless you are running straight wedge or power-type stuff at them. To root them back, it is difficult to gain more than three yards or so. But if they sit back and wait for you to run, they cannot mount a good pass rush. (We're speaking now of throwing in a situation where either run or pass is feasible, not pass alone.) This split second gives you another advantage in throwing. They cannot have as good a pass rush as if they were charging in all the time on you, in an effort to get to the passer.

Of course, I don't think we should overlook the fact that you've got to throw the ball a bit in order to make your running game go. You cannot go with one phase of the game and not complement it with the other. In other words, if you have a strong running attack, you should have a good passing attack. If your passing attack is powerful, you should try to develop a strong running attack. One without the other will not win for you.

Why has passing progressed to its present popularity? I think there are many reasons. First, it is exciting. Any time you watch the ball being thrown downfield, a receiver catching it and starting to elude tackles, everyone in the stands senses that something exciting is taking place.

When the pass receiver catches the ball downfield, as we mentioned before, few defenders still have a shot at him. If they miss him, chalk up six points. He catches the ball out in the open usually where everybody can see him and is off to the races like a jackrabbit.

This is the exciting aspect of the passing game—the home run phase of the game. Throwing the long pass, making a long gain, is probably the biggest reason that passing has become popular. It's not only exciting for the fans—it's a real pleasure for the players too. The long pass is fun to pull off, is fun to calculate, in trying to exploit the defense. As a result, you work a great deal at it, refine it, get it to where you can make it work effectively. You have a lot of fun playing pitch and catch with your receiver, working against the linebackers and the defensive backs in an effort to complete the pass. I think the coaches down through the years have done an outstanding job of building the passing game.

There is also the beauty in the timing of the passing game. The quarterback retreats into the pocket, under heavy pressure with linemen bearing down all around him, throws the ball on a dime to a receiver who, on his way out of bounds, stops, plants both feet in, and then literally falls out of bounds.

PHYSICAL ATTRIBUTES

Quarterbacks should have good height. In years past if you were 6' 1" or 6' 2", this was more than adequate, for many quarterbacks such as Eddie LeBaron were shorter and still did a fantastic job. How I'll never know, because I find it extremely difficult to see over some of these big guys at my height and I am almost 6' 2". However, today, with the increased height of the defensive personnel in this league, it is becoming even more important that the quarterback be 6' 3", 6' 4", maybe even 6' 5" in some cases. I know I wish I had an extra couple of inches on my height.

Johnny Unitas said it best when talking about the front four of the Rams. He said that when they got any sort of penetration at all and put their hands up in the air, it was like trying to throw out of the bottom of a barrel. They can actually shut off your view of the downfield receivers.

THE GRIP

I grip the football to take advantage of the laces by placing my fingers about one-third of the way down the ball. I don't squeeze the ball, but I do hold it firmly. As for a rule of thumb on quarterbacks, the smaller the hand the closer to the end of the ball the hand should be placed in order to take advantage of the shape of the ball.

Your left hand should serve as a "helping hand" by giving added control and support to gripping the ball when retreating to pass. Since the left hand is on the ball from the moment of the center's pass, it can be kept there throughout your retreat as a normal aid. This is particularly helpful if a quarterback's hands are small. Actually, mine are about average size.

A

The Grip. Though few passers grip a ball exactly alike, most grips would probably fall into, or resemble closely, the following: **A.** This is a very common grip, with all four fingers placed across the strings. Fingers are comfortably spread and relaxed. This is the grip I use. **B.** Here you see almost the same grip as in **A** except the hand is slightly turned so the little finger is on the opposite side of the laces from the other three fingers. **C.** In this grip, the index finger is closer to the end of the ball than in the other two, resembling a sort of "dart throwing" grip. Remember, grip the ball firmly, but never squeeze it, as this restricts a good, smooth throwing motion. Let your own physical makeup and comfort determine exactly the best way for you to hold it. **D.** The underneath view of the grip clearly shows that pressure on the ball is toward the finger tips, never in the palm of the hand. Note the air space between the ball and the palm.

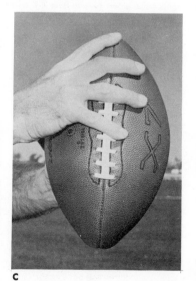

B

C

D

THE FEET

While the arms and hands actually throw the football, the feet and body play an important part as well since the feet provide the base and the power for the body to deliver the passing effort.

STEPS IN PASSING

In getting back and setting up on the pass, the quarterback should get away from the center as quickly as possible with short, quick, jabbing steps—not long, loping, gangling ones. You should practice lining up with the center and pushing away with either foot. It really doesn't make too much difference which foot you push away with, but you should strive to eliminate any false step or jabbing forward before you are able to push away from the center. Many times the center has to back out on pass plays to block and you will not be able to break away as freely and as quickly as you like. So, get in the habit of grabbing the ball and sprinting away from the center.

This sequence of pictures illustrates the different steps I take when retreating to pass. I prefer short, quick steps and attempt to set up as quickly as possible. By this means, I am ready to deliver the ball as soon as the receiver breaks open. In our league, the receivers are not open very long because the defenders are skilled and possess excellent reactions. Note how the quarterback's eyes remain on the defense throughout the entire retreat from the center.

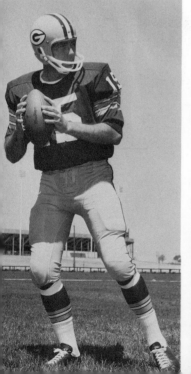

In taking the ball and retreating for a pass, you do much the same thing as you do on a hand-off. The ball is quickly brought into your midsection. As you retreat on the pass, you can raise it to passing height. Here again, the thing to keep in mind is to get back as quickly as possible, for the sooner you get back and set up, ready to throw, the sooner you will be able to pick out your receivers.

Left: The beginning of the end of the retreat. Note how the right foot is starting to brake against the rear movement. *Center:* The "stopping" position of the drop back. The right foot is now braced firmly against the ground. This stopping motion transforms almost instantly into the "forward push" stage of launching the pass. Baseball pitchers begin their delivery with a tremendous push off the ground. As a result, it is imperative to have your feet properly set or "gathered" before attempting to pass. *Right:* I am completely "gathered" here, surveying the defense. The ball is held comfortably high for quick, easy release. I am about to stride forward and begin the passing motion. Weight is evenly distributed over both feet. Try to be completely under control prior to throwing. Hurrying usually results in incompletions or interceptions.

Left: These two shots illustrate a front view of "back pedaling," another method of retreating from the center with the ball, in which the quarterback just backs straight up. *Below:* John Unitas retreats from the line of scrimmage—note how he is looking at the defense, not retreating with his back to the play.

It is most important, in retreating into the pocket, not to turn your back completely on the defense. You should retreat in a ¾ turn position, your body mostly turned but your head still looking over the defense so you are able to see the defensive changes which may be taking place on the snap of the ball. Believe me, today's defenses are so well conceived and disguised that they actually change when the ball is snapped, and not before. They don't show you a thing until that ball is snapped, so you have to be alert to be able to pick these defenses up quickly. It is almost impossible to turn completely, run back, and then start to pick them up.

Frank Ryan of Cleveland operating behind good pass protection. Observe how Frank has his eyes fixed on the defense as he retreats to pass. Note Frank's grip on the ball.

Top: Here is an excellent illustration of the quarterback in the second or third retreating step from center on his drop back to pass. Note that his eyes are still on the defense, so that he can see any changes. Also note that the fullback (31) and center (57) are intently looking for any defensive players who might break through. *Bottom:* This is the final stage on the drop back from center. The quarterback is set comfortably, has the defense well surveyed, and is about to start striding in the direction of the receiver. Note that the right foot is dug in, ready to push off for the start of the throw. It is also interesting to note how excellent protection makes a quarterback appear to be all alone.

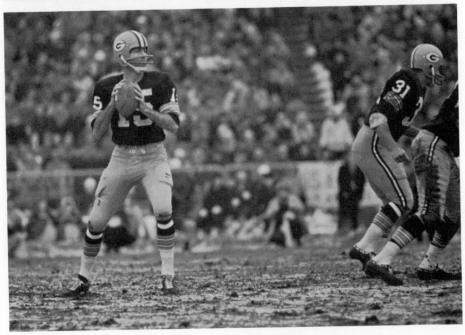

In the actual throwing motion, the left hand performs a different function. After acting as a support for the ball while setting up, it becomes a stabilizer when you begin to throw. It gives you that necessary ingredient of balance, much as a tight-rope walker obtains balance with both hands and arms.

Left: Stride toward the target, side view. The left hand is coming away from the ball and is now a balancing aid. The ball is raised, or cocked, ready. *Center:* Stride toward the target, front view. Observe how the right foot has pushed the body toward the target and the weight is being shifted to the left side. The left foot is positioned straight at the target. *Right:* Here is what I would term a "loose arm" throwing motion, which whips the ball toward its target.

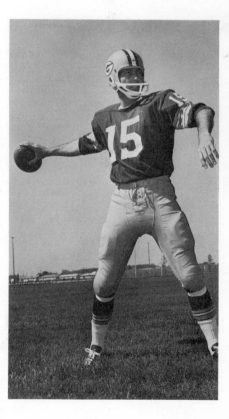

Frank Ryan of the Browns has a strong arm and can "flip" the ball to the receiver.

PASSING MOTION

The actual delivery is a smooth overhand motion with a good follow-through essential to obtain the necessary accuracy and distance. Once the feet are properly positioned, the left foot steps in the direction of the intended receiver and the weight shifts smoothly from the right side to the left. The actual releasing of the ball usually requires moving forward a step or two from your normal set-up position within the pocket. Note how clearly the above points are shown in the accompanying photos.

Left: A good, crisp, overhead motion should be developed by young passers. Right: Here, the ball is just being released. The right foot has already finished its job of pushing and has become a part of the body follow-through. Below: Just as a good pitcher has a fine follow-through, so does a good quarterback.

Top left: A proper follow-through is essential for better direction, accuracy, distance, and "zip" on the ball. *Top right:* Earlier photos showed how the right foot became a "stop" for the retreating action by bracing the body in the final stages of retreating. Once this has been completed, it is imperative that the quarterback be light on his feet so that he can move around and reposition himself for a throw if defenders make such a move necessary. When repositioning yourself, there is a tendency sometimes not to step right at the target, feeling that you can get the ball there otherwise. Whenever you try to throw "across your body," as this photo illustrates, more than likely you will "sail" the ball too high in an effort to compensate for the awkward position. *Bottom:* This is the next step in delivering the ball to the receiver. The left foot steps in the direction of the target as the ball is cocked for release. Though I am completely relaxed when passing, I have a peculiar habit of spreading the fingers on my left hand just before the release. Note excellent pass protection.

Top: Here you see the quarterback in the last stage of releasing the ball. Observe: (1) the stride and push of the legs, and (2) the excellent protection being afforded the passer. *Bottom:* This is another example of how easy it is to make the mistake of not striding in the *exact* direction of the intended target. This forces the passer into the error of throwing off balance, with little leg and body action, because he failed to "gather" himself before throwing. Note how the passer's eyes are downfield and yet the left foot is stepping in the direction of the offensive left tackle. Almost all of the passer's power is lost when throwing form this flatfooted position.

Top: Though he is throwing from behind his own goal line, note the unhurried, smooth, deliberate follow-through of Johnny Unitas. See how his left foot stepped "into" the intended receiver. *Left:* Zeke Bratkowski shows excellent passing form in this photo. Note how he has stepped with his left foot in the direction of the target, and the ball is being released in a line parallel to his left foot. The right foot is already off the ground, beginning a firm follow-through.

Charlie Johnson of the St. Louis Cardinals readies a long heave. Note how his right foot has acted as a pushing lever to give him thrust for his pass.

PASS PROTECTION

All pass protection with the Packers consists of one phrase—big man on big man. On the offensive team the big men are the two tackles and two guards. When we say big man on big man, we mean these offensive big men must block the defensive big men.

We never have a small man on a big one, so consequently we have a guard or a tackle always on a defensive tackle or defensive end, who are the big men of the defense. The center and the two backs are strictly in the pocket protection mostly to pick up the linebackers. There usually are three linebackers in our modern defenses. The two offensive backs and the center are responsible for these three defensive linebackers.

121

Forrest Gregg is regarded by many as the finest offensive lineman in the game today. He's an outstanding pass protector and a terrific blocker and hustler on running plays.

PASS PROTECTION

In the diagrams below, note how big offensive linemen are always pitted against big defensive linemen, and the offensive backs are responsible for linebackers.

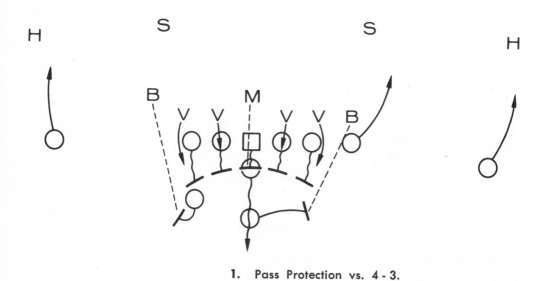

1. Pass Protection vs. 4 - 3.

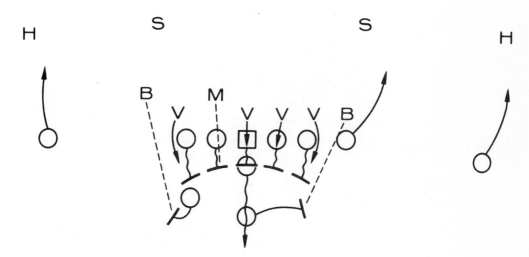

1. Pass Protection vs. 4 - 3 Over.

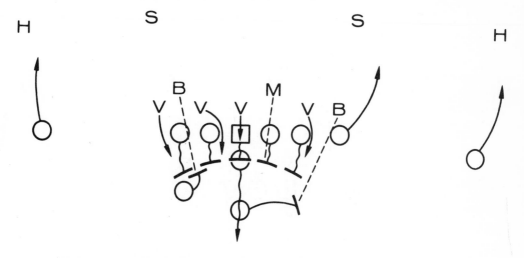

1. Pass Protection vs. 4 - 3 Under.

PASSING POCKET

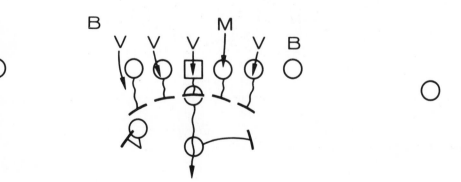

1.   We always use the method of blocking offensive linemen on defensive linemen, regardless of defensive alignment,
so that smaller backs are never pitted against larger linemen.

2.   If everyone does his job, you see a well-formed cup
or pocket which the quarterback can step up into and deliver
the ball.

3.   Linemen are blocking linemen. The remaining backs
have the outside linebackers, and the center is responsible for
the middle linebacker, wherever he goes.

1. In this set-up, the center and right guard have just changed assignments, maintaining the blocking strength of linemen on linemen.

STEPPING UP INTO POCKET

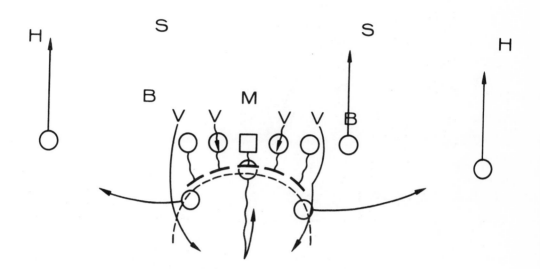

1. Quarterback must step up into pocket after retreating, as the angle taken by the defensive ends forces him to do so.

2. It becomes apparent that offensive guards must do an excellent job of preventing penetration by defensive tackles.

3. When offensive tackles miss a block or do not sustain it long enough, the quarterback may sometimes elude the defensive end, but if an offensive guard misses his block or allows too much penetration, the quarterback is faced with a real problem.

No matter what type of defense shows up, all protection is arranged so that a backfield man—a halfback or a fullback, whom we classify as little men—will never pick up anyone but a linebacker. We'll never have a halfback picking up a 260-pound defensive tackle or end.

In our system we have what we call a pocket type protection. The two guards are responsible for the two defensive tackles and the two tackles are responsible for the two defensive ends. The two guards block the defensive tackles and keep them from penetrating. They are allowed three feet of penetra-

Despite all sorts of accidents and injuries, Jerry Kramer became one on the game's great guards.

tion, and if the guards are doing their job, that is as far as their defensive tackles will get.

The defensive ends are more or less out on the flank, being blocked by our two big offensive tackles. The tackles' job is to let the ends run outside and around the quarterback. The quarterback gets back 7 or 8 yards and then steps forward. These two offensive tackles are charged with keeping the defensive ends to the outside of this perimeter so that the quarterback can step up. Consequently, the two guards must maintain the three-foot maximum penetration by the tackles or else the quarterback will have trouble finding his receivers and also will be unable to step up prior to releasing the ball.

The center is responsible for one of the linebackers. If this linebacker doesn't show, the center is there to help stop immediate penetration from the middle by helping the two guards. His job is to wait there and pick off one of the defensive tackles who may slip through one of our offensive guards.

The offensive backs—the little men on our team—are responsible for the two outside linebackers. No matter where these linebackers are, the backs' job is to pick these people up. If the linebackers don't come in, the backs generally get into the pattern as a delayed receiver or safety valve type target.

This picture gives an excellent view of pass protection about to begin. Observe how the linemen's hands have come up off the ground as they step back to receive the blow of the rush.

DEFENSIVE MANEUVERS AND HOW TO STOP THEM

Some teams will stunt a defensive end and tackle. In other words, they will bring the defensive end way to the inside and stunt the tackle out around him, hoping to confuse the blocking somewhat. With proper training and preparation, stunting can be overcome by the offensive blockers. But the defense must be given some credit. If they are proficient, they can really give the offense some headaches with certain types of stunts.

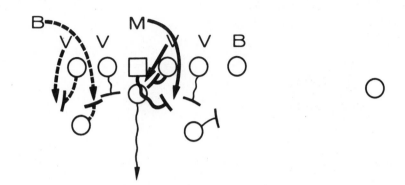

1. The above illustrates a simple yet effective maneuver the defense can pull to upset offensive pass protection.

2. The broken-line action is nothing more than a simple red dog action by the weak side linebacker and is easily picked up.

3. The bold-line stunt, however, can cause problems if not properly handled. The idea here is to have the defensive tackle charge hard into the center, trying to knock him off stride, thus preventing the center from getting out to pick up the red dog of the MLB who has shot right off the rear of his tackle in hopes of beating the center's block. The center must get out quickly; the offensive guard can help by driving his man hard in the direction of his charge so as to prevent as much penetration as possible.

POCKET PASSING

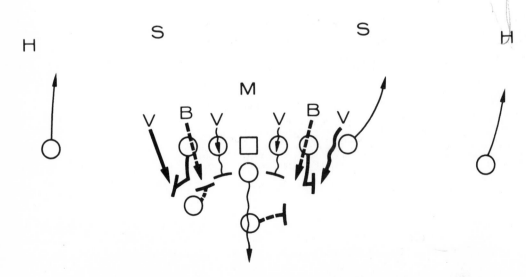

1. This diagram illustrates how easily an offensive pass protection theory could be challenged if the offensive linemen went to sleep. With linebackers (B) over the offensive tackles and blitzing (broken lines), the tackles have to be alert and NOT block them, but turn and block their designated men (bold lines), the defensive ends. The backs pick up the linebackers, thus not having to be matched against the huge defensive ends. Maneuvers such as these can confuse the blockers if they are not alert.

PASS PROTECTION

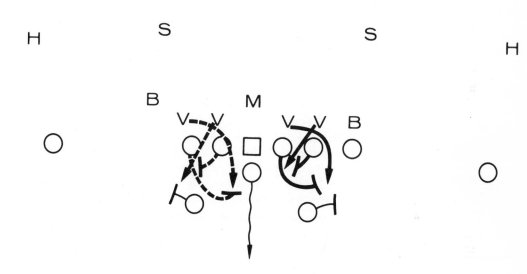

1. The stunts illustrated above by the defensive linemen demonstrate just a small reason why pass protection breaks down on occasion.

2. In the bold-line side, you see the defensive end close hard to the inside and the tackle follow behind to the outside (just switching assignments). This defensive maneuver can be blocked two ways: (a) Have the offensive men stay with their defenders all the way, or (b) switch assignments and block areas.

3. The broken-line side illustrates just the opposite type stunt where the tackle goes first and the end follows.

4. When you add the linebackers to these "twists" of the defensive linemen, you really have people going in all directions.

The fundamentals of pass blocking, whether they be for linemen or for backs, are basically the same. You must usually get yourself in a position to receive the shock of the onrush of the defensive rusher. Your feet should be pretty much parallel, about shoulder width apart in a slightly crouching stance, your head up. Your arms must be in toward your body—they cannot be extended so you can grab or hold a defender. The big thing an offensive lineman must remember is not to overcommit himself and let the defensive rusher pull him out of position so he cannot recover. He must be in a position where, as the defensive man approaches him and tries to maneuver around him, he can hit him, push away, and get back to block him again. So the basic stance for offensive pass blocking is much like that of a boxer; the body is crouched forward with the feet parallel where they can unleash power and yet come back to the same position and not be pulled, pushed, or knocked offstride by the onrushing defender.

We mentioned earlier some pocket patterns with three receivers out. You can have a varied number of receivers downfield, depending on the type of coverage the defense is employing against you and how you can best counter what they are doing. This will be discussed more in detail later.

In addition to the pocket type of pass, there are other variations such as the roll-out, play action, bootleg, etc.

The roll-out pass is nothing more than what the word implies—a type of pass in which the passer rolls out to the same side as the intended receiver so as to put pressure on the defense, forcing them either to drop back and cover the receiver or move up to rush the passer. In either case, one or the other should be open.

ROLL-OUT PASS

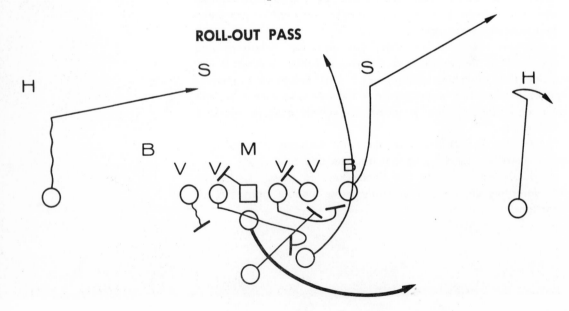

There are occasions where roll-out passes can be thrown very effectively. They are a great change of pace to help offset a strong pass rush from the inside. (With this idea in mind, you can see why defensive ends are coached to keep the passer inside so he can't run around loose outside.)

In running a roll-out pass, the quarterback should remember to try to set himself as he releases the ball. Try to avoid throwing it when off balance. Even though you may be moving, you need to find a solid base for throwing.

Another thing to remember is that if your receiver is running somewhat parallel to you, the lead does not have to be as great as when you are standing still as the receiver runs his pattern. If you are moving approximately parallel to the receiver, you can throw the ball more directly at him. I lead him just about the length of his arm—about 2½ feet. Harry Gilmer, formerly a great pro passer and coach, showed me this tactic when I was in college, and I have never forgotten it.

A roll-out pass by the quarterback. He is focusing immediately on his defensive keys. The roll-out is fundamentally a sprint by the quarterback to the outside in order to get away from the inside pass rush or to put extreme pressure on the secondary.

LEAD ON ROLL-OUT PASS

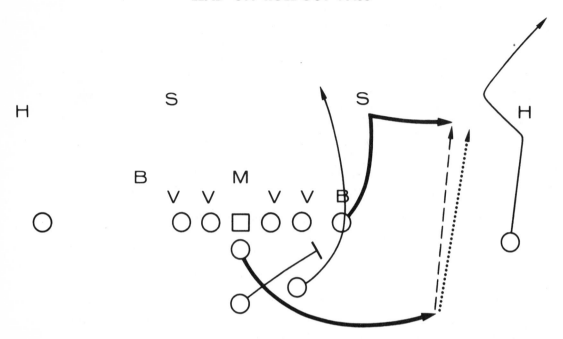

1. When running approximately parallel to a receiver, the amount of lead is reduced because passer is moving also (dash-line pass). Dotted line indicates lead if passer was not moving.

How often the quarterback should carry the ball depends a great deal on the individual; how strong he is, how well he can take punishment, and a lot of other factors too. Much depends on how many good runners you've got on your ball club. The quarterback obviously doesn't have to run it very much if he has other good runners in his backfield. I don't even attempt to run the ball on our club, because we are noted as a running team. We have had outstanding runners for several years, such as Paul Hornung, Jim Taylor, Tom Moore, Earl Gros, Elijah Pitts, and others. Jim Grabowski and Donnie Anderson look pretty good too.

Many times a quarterback will run with the ball as a way of eluding the defense. You may have to end up eating it, but you may pick up some yardage too. Fran Tarkenton is a fine runner, and when his receivers are covered, he often turns the play into a gain. He is a gifted runner with a keen sense of feeling when the defenders are near him.

SURPRISE SNEAK

Among the other types of runs which a quarterback might use is the surprise sneak, the quarterback sneak. If you have a good, strong quarterback who has a lot of power, the sneak is one of the surest ways of picking up a foot or so in short yardage, because the offensive line can just wedge in toward the center. There is hardly any chance of fumbling because the quarterback can go straight ahead behind this wedge. As a big, strong, durable back, Bill Wade of the Chicago Bears has done a fine job through the years of wedging the ball in short yardage.

SURPRISE SNEAK

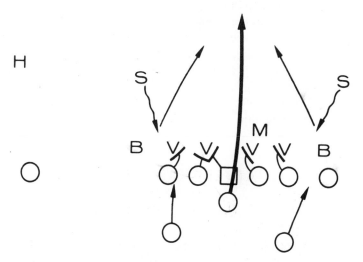

This play took place on about the Colt 35-yard line in the following situation:

1. The defensive line of the Colts was tight in the middle with their middle linebacker moved over opposite our fullback. (This alignment is very common on very short yardage.)

2. The defense must have been looking for the halfback to carry since no one ever saw McHan until he was ten yards downfield.

I think if you were to check with quarterbacks down through the years, you would probably find that somewhere along the line each one of them had pulled off an impromptu sneak on his own. The quarterback goes to the line of scrimmage with a play called. Then he sees a gaping hole right over the center. It's almost always a short yardage situation, but for some reason they are not in tight over the center. This doesn't happen very often, but it has come up on occasion. I have seen many quarterbacks take the ball, step right through this opening, and often go a long way with it.

A classic example of this situation came in 1960 in Green Bay against the Baltimore Colts. It was late in the game and we had short yardage to make. At that time we had a favorite power play—running off tackle for short yardage with one of our backs, a halfback. The Colts were very loose in the middle, though they were crowding the center. There was no linebacker anywhere near the center; he was moved way over to the right, anticipating the off-tackle smash. We were in a right formation, and Lamar McHan was the quarterback at the time. He actually called a sneak in this case, but they were looking for the off-tackle play, and he just stepped through. Even the defensive secondary was up close, ready to make the tackle, and when he burst into the secondary, he was almost parallel with them before they could see him. Mac had good speed for a quarterback, and he ran the ball right into the end zone from 35 yards out, splitting the secondary down the middle before anyone could get to him.

QUARTERBACK DRAW

Another play in which the quarterback carries the ball is the quarterback draw. This is nothing more than a draw play in which the quarterback does the running. There have been several fine passers who could pull this off. I think the best I ever saw was Tobin Rote, who played with the Packers and later with the Lions. Here again, Tobin was a strong, durable quarterback. He was as big—or bigger—than some of the halfbacks or fullbacks and had a real knack for finding a hole, hitting it with a lot of authority. He also had good balance, which is essential to a good runner. Tobin was so good that even today he ranks as the fifth leading rusher in the history of the Green Bay Packers.

QUARTERBACK DRAW PLAY

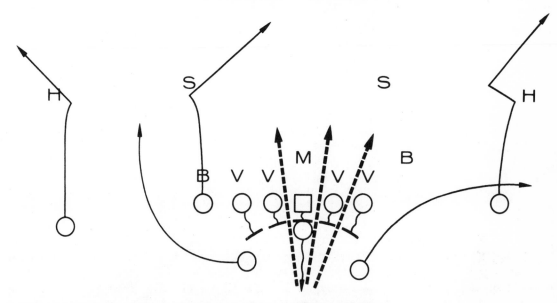

1. The quarterback retreats as if to pass but instead runs the ball into any lane that is created by the designed blocking of his line.

I have never been a good draw runner. I am not big or strong enough to break an arm tackle when starting out to run from the pocket. If I get a running start, I might be able to break a good arm tackle. But I don't have as much power to pick up yardage as a back would have if he were given the ball. The quarterback in this particular play does nothing more than retreat hard into the pocket just as on a pass. But, instead of throwing it (he may even take the time to make a pump) he starts forward, keying his blockers and runs the ball, as does a fullback or a halfback on a draw play.

MORE ON FAKING

The art of faking is so very important that I can't emphasize it too much. Every quarterback must be able to fake well, with his eyes and arms, with little feints of his body. A quarterback should develop ways of deceiving the defense— of being able to make them move in the wrong direction.

EYE FAKING

One method of doing this is through eye faking. Some defenders tend to look at the quarterback out of the corner of one eye and watch the receiver with the other. As soon as the quarterback starts to look in the direction of the receiver, the defender usually reacts almost as quickly as the receiver. With

Notice how Bill George (61), formerly of the Bears, has his eyes glued on the quarterback, in an attempt to anticipate where he'll throw. This illustrates the importance of eye faking.

this in mind, if you can fake the defender with your eyes and make him think you are going to do something counter to what you actually are going to do, you can sometimes pull him out of position.

Eye faking is very important in defeating linebackers. Most linebackers may not have a specific man to cover, but rather are covering an area. As they go back to that area, they are watching you. They know your frequencies; they know your likes and dislikes; they know what you prefer to throw in a certain situation, so they are looking for certain plays. If you can fake them and move them around a bit, it is amazing how you can help free one of your receivers.

It's also amazing how well the linebackers play your eyes when you are not aware of it. (One of the best was Joe Schmidt, formerly of the Lions and now their head coach.) They are in the right spot almost by the time the ball is, if they are able to read your eyes. They sense the direction you're going to throw, so it is very important for you to be able to fake with the eyes—to look them off one way or look opposite the way you are going to throw for just a second. Move your head just slightly—or your eyes—hoping to deceive the linebacker. This will take a little practice, but through experience and time you should be able to fake pretty well.

ARM FAKING

Arm faking is another important area in deceiving the defense. I think the finest arm faker in the business today is Johnny Unitas. He pumps extremely well (by *pumps* I mean he simulates a throw). He steps in the direction of his intended receiver, plants his foot, and starts the forward motion of his arm and the body. Then he just pumps the ball and brings it to a stop quickly about half way through his motion so as to freeze the defender out of position. In so doing, he allows his receiver to gain an extra step or so or make an extra move on the defender. For the defender, seeing this pump, feels the ball has been thrown or is about to be thrown and starts to commit himself. This costs a vital second or fraction of a second for the defender, and every split second is of utmost importance in football. If you can freeze a defender with an arm pump or make him move into a wrong position while one of your receivers goes to an area that is open, your chances of completing the pass are greatly increased.

"Z"-OUT ROUTE (VALUE OF PUMP)

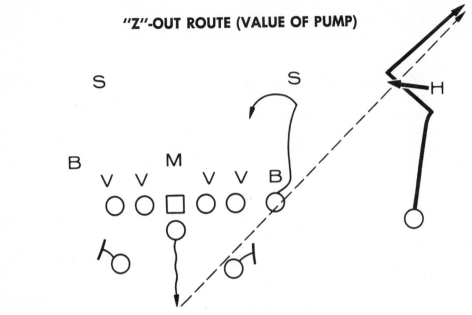

1. By "pumping" or arm faking on a "Z"-out route, for example, you make the defender close in quickly on the post or inside portion of the route, enabling the receiver to break back to the outside and get open.

Let's suppose you are throwing a "Z"-out route. As your receiver runs down the field and makes his break to the inside and the defender starts to go with him, you make the pump. The defender will come up in a hurry, even closer to the receiver, thinking you are going to run the inside or the post route on him. As you make the pump and the defender charges closely to defend, your man breaks on the out part of the "Z" pattern and has a good step or so on the defender.

BOOTLEG

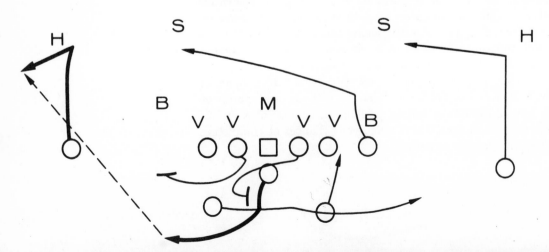

1. Bootleg action showing simple weak side "out" route by split end.

Another method used to fool the defense is a type of fake commonly known as the bootleg play. By this we mean starting action in the backfield one way with the quarterback faking a hand-off and then bootlegging, or keeping the ball himself, slipping out into the flat, many times with no blocking. Or sometimes one or two guards will reverse pull and slip out in front of him.

BOOTLEG ROUTES

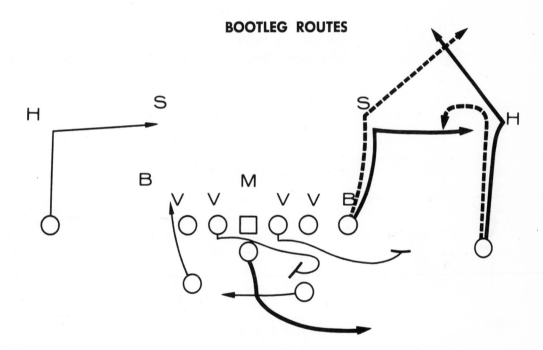

1. The above diagram shows two excellent side routes off bootleg.

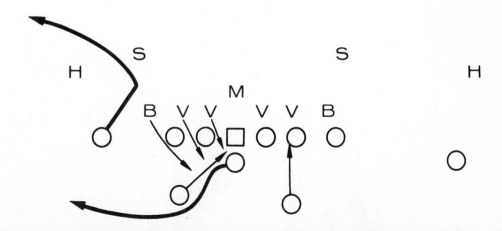

1. The diagram at the bottom of p. 139 shows another form of bootleg play used very effectively by Y. A. Tittle for years.

2. This is used on short yardage when sharp angle of charge by linebacker will allow quarterback to get outside and either run or pass.

3. Play can be used on either strong or weak side.

We've been very effective in the last few years in running bootleg plays. Since Coach Lombardi came to the Packers, we have run a lot of wide end sweeps with our backs. Every time this action would start, of course, the defense was alerted that this was one of our better plays. So they would overplay it to the side where the back had started. The linemen would almost ignore the quarterback, as would the linebacker, and the quarterback had very little trouble getting outside on a bootleg type play. There are some fine pass routes that you can design off bootleg action, and it can be very, very effective if the defense is careless and lets you get outside.

PLAY ACTION PASS

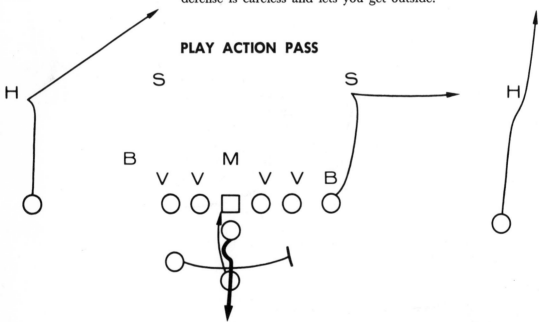

1. This diagram shows the action when our fullback dives into the line and the halfback fakes the off-tackle run.

2. By faking to both backs, the linebackers are "held" and the rush is momentarily halted.

3. Any number of routes can be run off this.

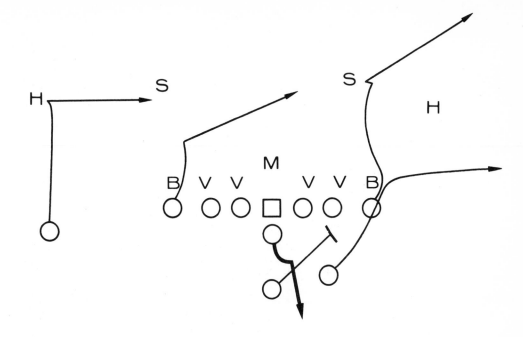

1. Another example of play action passing is diagramed here, off the fake of a favorite maneuver—the fullback slant off tackle.

2. As you can see, the quarterback has a number of excellent choices.

Other forms of pass faking include play fakes or play action passes. By this we mean simulating run fakes and passing off of this. For example, we have a fine play where we dive Jimmy Taylor straight ahead and bring our halfback across on a cross-buck type action. This is one of our lead plays. We can give the ball to Taylor, we can give it to the halfback, or we can fake it to both of them and throw it. This is another excellent type of pass faking that freezes the defense momentarily because, here again, they think a running play is coming. Therefore, you don't get the deep drop back of the linebackers, but you still get your receivers off the line of scrimmage in a hurry and down into their designated areas.

DEVELOPING VISION

A passer needs to develop the sharpest vision possible. It is very much in a quarterback's favor to be able to see surrounding action quickly and clearly. A split second's delay in picking out his receiver can prove fatal. There are many drills that can be performed to develop this vision.

You can have your receivers breaking between linebackers, running to open spots, and then make the quarterback decide on the spur of the moment if he should throw the ball into the pack. One means of accomplishing this is not to tell the quarterback where you are going to place the defenders, in order to sharpen up his reactions. By this we mean allowing the defense to react as it wishes, rather than the way they should to your offensive action. With linebackers ending up where they aren't supposed to be, your reactions quicken considerably.

Many coaches have their own methods of developing good eyesight and the quick pick-up of potential pass receivers, but every quarterback should go through a certain amount of training in this function.

Up to now we've covered only one phase of the passing game—the fundamentals or mechanics associated with the passer. You may possess all the qualities we've been talking about and be willing to put in the time to improve your shortcomings, but if you can't pick out the receivers and deliver the ball to them, you haven't accomplished anything as yet.

Being able to pick out the receivers in a crowd of defensive people and deliver the ball effectively to them is, in essence, the most important part of the passing game. A lot of people can stand and throw rocks at trees and hit squirrels and tin cans, or even throw footballs great distances, but they still would not make topnotch quarterbacks. They couldn't be top quarterbacks because they couldn't hit receivers with the football under pressure. This ability is absolutely necessary for a quarterback.

You've heard of peripheral vision. I suppose you are born with it. I don't really know any way to develop it. I have seen certain passers who seemed to possess better peripheral vision than others and, as a result, could see their receivers breaking maybe an instant sooner. They have a better feel and picture for the entire defense in relation to the receivers. I think this is something you subconsciously develop by knowing the defense, knowing what you're trying to accomplish, and knowing how your offensive people will move the defense to enable you to create a hole in which to put your receiver and thereby get him open.

Most passes are designed to be thrown in front of the deep secondary; thus, you're working against linebackers. So if you, as an offensive quarterback, realize how your offensive backs are used to move the defensive linebackers, you know about where the hole is going to be before you even walk to the line of scrimmage. You have a mental picture of where this area is going to be, and if you come away from the line of scrimmage with your head turned back toward the defense so you can see them react to your offensive people firing out of the backfield, you will have better peripheral vision because you begin to see the whole picture developing before you.

As for throwing to alternate receivers, many teams use a timing pattern. Let's say you're throwing a long pass to the split end, and your split end in this case is to your left. For timing purposes, you may be running the flanker and the tight end on a shorter pattern, so that as you come back and take a look at the tight end or the flanker, you may prefer to throw the ball to them if they're open. Or you can pump to them, make a good arm fake which might freeze the defense for just a second, and allow the split end to run his maneuver.

In another case, you might be throwing a short pass to the split end. As you come back and get ready to throw, you see that he's covered. In this case your left end and flanker are on deeper patterns, so that as you look to the right for the split end—and he's covered—you just pan back to the left, picking up the tight end next who has run a little deeper pattern. If he's covered, then you go to the flanker. If they're all covered, then we get into the area of either eating the ball or throwing it away.

You can see from this that many passing games are designed to set up your receivers in such a manner that you have time to come back to another one if your primary target is covered. Some quarterbacks (Y. A. Tittle was one) are great

Y. A. Tittle is one of the finest quarterbacks of all time. A great student of the game, this dedicated performer is caught in a pensive mood while on the sideline.

believers in having a specific reason for calling a pass play and going almost entirely with the primary receiver. Tittle supposedly seldom came off of it, feeling that he could make it go. If he didn't, he just threw the ball away, believing that time doesn't permit you to come back and pick up alternate receivers. (Sometimes you don't have time to attempt this.)

BASIC RULES

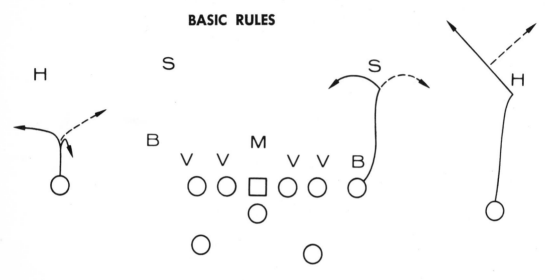

    1. Here is still another look at the basic philosophy behind pattern or complementary route passes.

    2. The short pattern on the left (three short ones are shown) is complemented by the deeper routes on the right.

    3. The basic passing game is begun this way each year during training camp.

I think much depends on how you've been trained. Frankly, we set up our pass patterns so we can come back to alternate receivers. By training and working with this type of action for a number of months and years, you can learn to do it.

When we start our practice each year in July, one of our first practice procedures is tied in with this primary and alternate choice of receivers. It is developed in our initial contact with the passing game on the blackboard sessions and on the field. We begin with certain basic rules (i.e., short and long receivers in a pattern).

Let's say the weak end or the split end runs a five to seven yard quick-out or hitch, or a slant-in. Then the tight end and the flanker will run corresponding deeper patterns. Let's say the tight end might run a deep hook, either to the inside or the outside, depending on what the split end is doing. And the flanker will run a corner or a post or a deep-out also. We have the freedom to make this particular call ourselves.

So you see how the quarterback, in coming away from the line of scrimmage, takes a quick look to the left for the short receiver. If this man is covered, then the quarterback continues to retreat and pans to the right, picking up next his tight end and then finally his flanker, hitting the player who is most open. If he's called it to the split end and he's open first, he gives him the ball. He forgets about everything else. He hits the man that's open.

Sometimes the defense covers your primary receiver, so it's good to be able to come back and to locate an alternate. This is another mark, I think, of a good quarterback—not only the ability to locate this alternate receiver, but also to move around in the pocket. He's come back, prepared to throw the ball, planted his feet, started to step forward, and his receiver is covered. He then has to collect himself, shuffle his feet around in a hurry, and get ready to throw to some other position in some other direction.

You don't have your feet planted in clay or cement. You must be able to move around and shuffle, not becoming frustrated or panicky, but able to move and to locate these alternate receivers.

SHUFFLING YOUR FEET

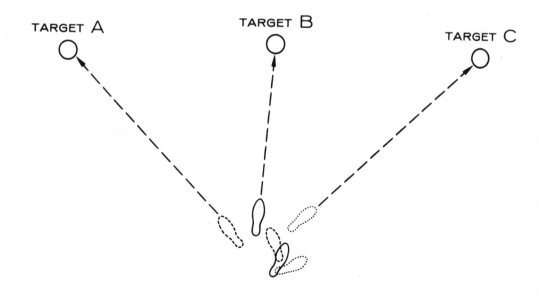

1. Earlier, we discussed the importance of "gathering yourself," having good control and balance before attempting to pass. The lead foot (left foot for right-handed passers) must point in the direction of your target to insure accuracy, control, and "zip" on the ball.

2. If your primary receiver were located in target **B**'s area but, just as you started to throw to him, became covered, you could not allow your feet to remain in the same position while going to targets **A** or **C**.

3. If you didn't readjust your feet and tried to hit **A**, you would be throwing across your body, causing the throw to "sail" or rise. If you tried to hit **C**, you would be throwing flat-footed, with no impetus to the throw, the result of which would probably be a low, weak, poorly thrown pass.

4. There are times when you must throw off balance (being tackled, etc.), but if at all possible, always attempt to follow the passing procedure and motion discussed earlier. Strive to be light, nimble, and nifty on your feet. It'll really pay off.

BACKS MOVING LINEBACKERS

1. Sometimes, when the defensive coverage by the line-backers calls for them to remain at "home" while the remaining backs block, it is unnecessary to call a back out into the action when throwing outside to the left or right (as shown above).

2. However, with a different coverage called under the

same conditions (bold lines) the linebackers may be out "underneath" to help.

3. When this happens—and let's suppose you are trying to hit your split end—then it sometimes becomes necessary to swing your halfback out to hold the linebacker (broken line); should the linebacker ignore the back, then your halfback becomes your first choice to receive the pass.

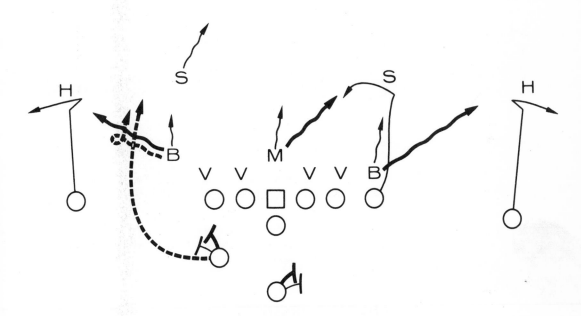

1. Using just the split end and halfback to that side, let's suppose you're trying to hit the split end on a hook to the inside, but the drop of the linebacker gets in the area you're throwing to. (This happens when the halfback blocks.)

2. By swinging your halfback outside, you force the linebacker to move with him, creating a nice hole for the split end to work into. (See bold lines.)

3. On the other side, suppose you're trying to hit your tight end on an out break, but the linebacker on that side is in the way.

4. By putting the fullback in the pattern, you force the linebacker to cover, freeing the tight end. (See bold line.)

Of course, these offensive tactics are defeated by other defensive coverages which, in turn, leave still other areas for exploitation by the offense.

ALTERNATE RECEIVERS

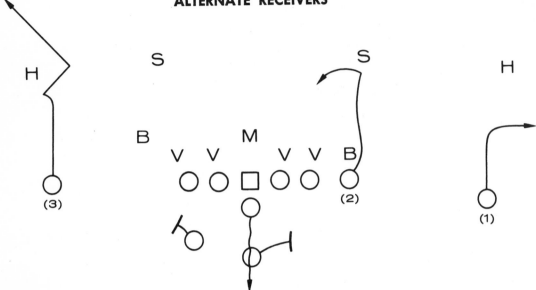

1. The quarterback can look right for the very quick pattern to the flanker and, if necessary, can pan in to his tight end who is doing a deeper turn in.

2. If both these receivers are covered, the quarterback still has time to come all the way back to his split end who is running a still deeper pattern.

CHOOSING RECEIVERS

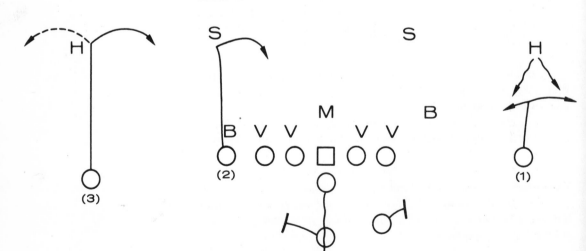

1. The diagram at the bottom of p. 148 clearly shows how an overall pass pattern can be designed to give the passer an instant choice yet a chance to go elsewhere with the ball should his first choice be covered.

2. You will notice the first choice receiver is running either a hitch or quick out (both are short routes). The quarterback looks to this receiver first, and if the latter is open, the ball is thrown to him.

3. Should the first receiver be covered (defensive halfback comes up fast) the quarterback can continue to retreat, turn to pick up receiver No. 2, and be ready to fire the ball.

4. Receiver No. 3 is running a slightly deeper complementary route to allow the quarterback to continue to pan left for an open receiver.

In a crucial situation recently, I fully wanted to throw to No. 1 receiver but ended up hitting receiver No. 3 from this pattern.

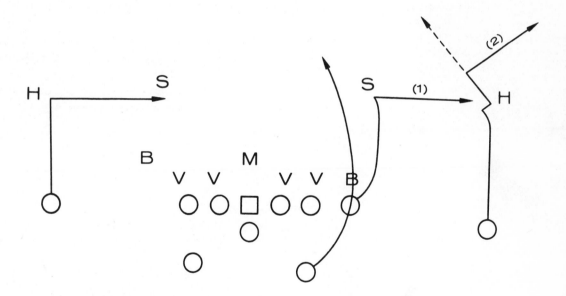

1. Here's another example of an advanced pass pattern giving the quarterback a built-in choice of receivers.

2. The tight end (1) should show first, and if he's open, the ball should be given to him.

3. After the tight end has had time to show, the wing will then break into focus (wing's route is a takeoff of a post route he may have been running to set up route shown).

4. If both receivers are covered, quarterback has legitimate throw away out of bounds as receivers are headed that way.

5. Never pass up an open receiver in hopes that another will get loose (unless you are going for broke on a long one).

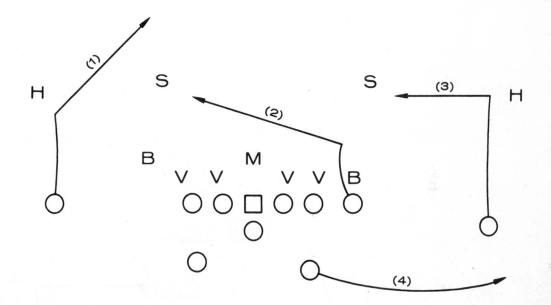

1. Here's an advanced example of a pattern designed to give the passer a chance to go to several choices.

2. Beginning on the left, he can look to choice number one, then if covered, pan to his right and begin to pick up his second, third, and even fourth choice (this one very late as a last ditch relief valve) with confident regularity.

3. By seeing the defensive reaction all the way, the quarterback will have little trouble in finding his receivers.

Left: Here is Carroll Dale catching a pass in the open. Carroll took the ball slanting over the middle about 10 yards past the line of scrimmage and carried it 77 yards for a TD against Detroit.

offensive formations and pass patterns

7

Every football team must have a number of basic offensive formations from which to operate. Just how many formations, and which ones are selected, are strictly a matter of choice by the coaches.

While some coaches lean heavily on favorite formations year in and year out, most good high school and college coaches select their formations to fit the talent available. True, they may go several years straight without changing their fundamental formations. Then there usually comes a time when they have a key player or two, or possibly a different type of personnel such as a faster or slower squad, and they choose to change to a different style of attack.

Following are the basic offensive formations used in football today. Of course, any of these may be varied in one of numerous fashions to fit a specific defense or some other deviation in plan.

OFFENSIVE FORMATIONS

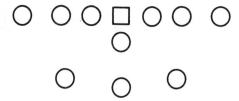

STANDARD "T"

1. After years of the Notre Dame Box and single wing formations, this new alignment became an immediate hit.

153

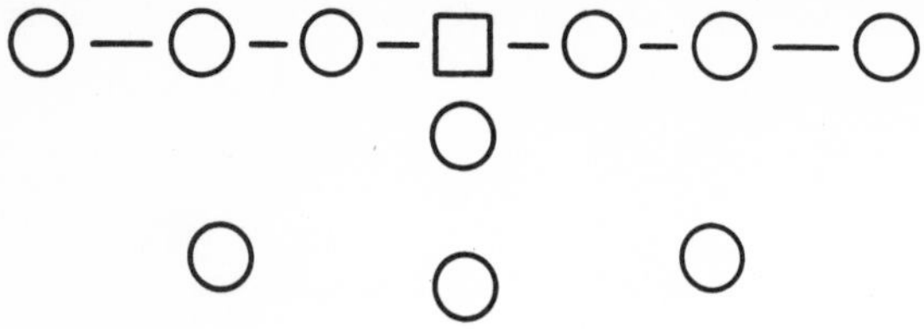

SPLIT "T"

    1. The offensive line has wider splits than the standard "T" formation.

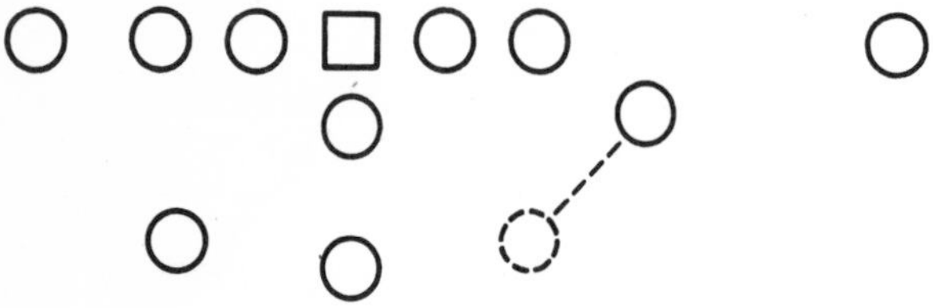

SLOT BACK

    1. In an effort to get another pass receiver out quickly and to promote good blocking in the area, the halfbacks could be shifted quickly into the position shown above.

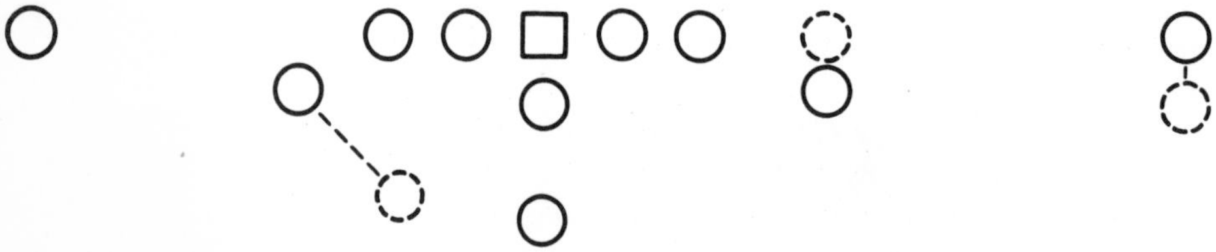

DOUBLE WING

    1. Though this is primarily a passing formation (you have four receivers in position to hit immediately on passes), some effective runs, draws, or screen passes may also be used successfully from this formation.

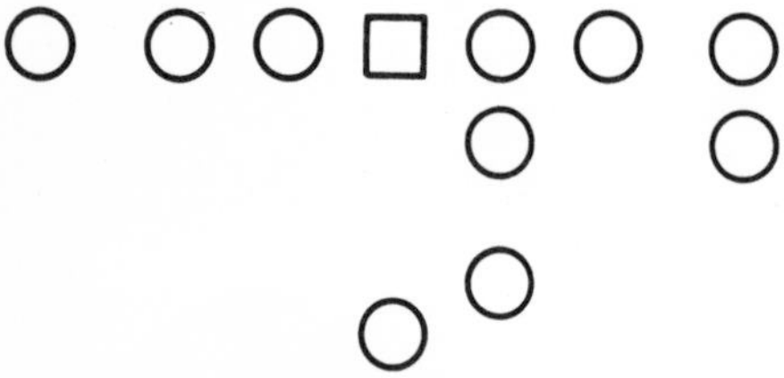

SINGLE WING

    1. The University of Tennessee still used this as late as a few years ago.

NOTRE DAME BOX

1. Many teams shifted from "T" into this when this formation was still popular.

2. Even though the "T" became popular, some teams liked to combine both formations.

STANDARD PRO FORMATION

1. Dotted lines merely show how simple "T" formation was changed to give the above look.

SPLIT BACKFIELD

1. Same alignment as above, except that the fullback is moved over to a position behind the tackle.

LH

QB   FB

SHOTGUN OR SPREAD

1. Quarterback may either line up as shown or shift back from his normal position.

2. Though this is primarily a desperation passing type formation, some running plays can be used.

3. Fullback can also be moved up closer near tight end for quick release into pass pattern.

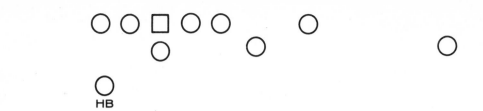

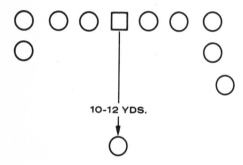

HB

TRIPLE WING

1.   This formation is likewise primarily a passing formation, but when you have a halfback like Gale Sayers of the Chicago Bears, you can run to the strong side, run to the weak side, or throw the ball.

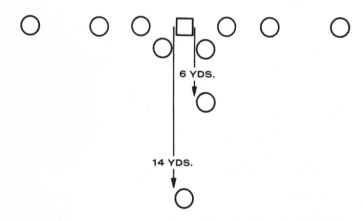

10-12 YDS.

REGULAR PUNT FORMATION

1.   This type of punt protection is still necessary at times when backed up on your goal line.

6 YDS.

14 YDS.

SPREAD PUNT FORMATION

1.   This lineup for punts permits fast coverage and limits runbacks of fielded kicks, if used properly.

PASS PATTERNS

You don't need very many pass patterns to be effective; you just need a few good basic ones and also a couple of counterpasses off of them where the receiver starts one way, lures the defender in, and then breaks out in a counter-type motion.

Occasionally, however, you need something a bit out of the ordinary—something designed to take advantage of situations which require a close coordination between the quarterback and receiver. It requires a great deal of practice to get these maneuvers down pat. On third down and eight, for example, if you figure the defender is going to be playing you tight and tough, knowing that you are going to try to pick up the first down, this is an excellent time to run a pattern like a hook and go. This is a pass where the receiver runs down and fakes a hook at about eight or nine yards. The defender will come flying up to try to make the tackle to prevent you from getting the first down. So the receiver spins hard to the outside and runs right by him.

On a somewhat similar pattern, the receiver comes off the line really hard, as if he's going to try to drive the defender back. Then he starts to slow up, as if to turn to receive the ball on a break of about nine or ten yards, therefore picking up the first down. Suddenly he puts it in second gear and runs right by the defensive back.

HOOK AND GO

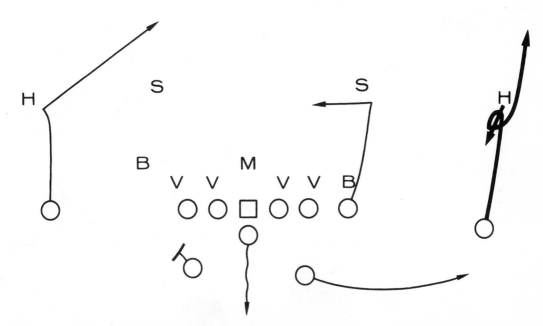

"LULL"

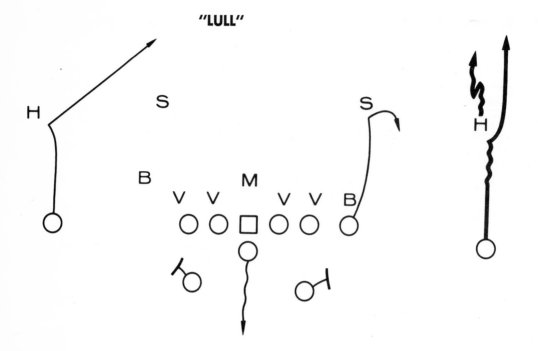

TWO-MINUTE DRILL

I think right now we should discuss the category I like to think of as two-minute passing—that is, the two minutes preceding the half and the final two minutes of the game. As a quarterback, I feel these are the most important minutes of the game because so many are won or lost just prior to the half and just prior to the end of the game.

A team that is poised and well disciplined, thoroughly coached, can handle a crisis in a tough situation like this. Such a team often comes on to win. Most teams spend a lot of time practicing running off a maximum number of plays in a two-minute period or less.

I can recall a situation in a 1965 game against the Colts which we won by a narrow score. Late in the game Unitas and the Colts had the ball and were moving. They started on their own 20-yard line, and he had moved them down to about our 20, with more than a minute to play. Finally a fumble by one of their backs gave us the ball. Had it not been for this, we would have really been in trouble, because he was able to move his team a long way in a short time with a minimum number of plays.

We work a great deal on our two-minute offense. We line up at the line of scrimmage without huddling and run our plays from there. We're disciplined to know exactly what we want to do in a given situation. Here again, from previous scouting reports and game films, we usually know how a team prefers to play us in a situation like this.

There are times when the defense will fool you and thwart you momentarily, but for the most part I think the advantage in a situation like this is with the offense. You know what you are trying to do, and the defense doesn't have a chance to compose itself, take a time out, get together, or discuss things. You're lining up right at the line of scrimmage every time without huddling. You are forcing them to hurry their defensive calls and to readjust themselves very quickly. As a result, many times you have them somewhat shaken up and can do a good job of exploiting their confusion.

The quarterback here was forced to run, was tackled, but then bounced up to call "time out" quickly to conserve time. (Packers went in to score from here.)

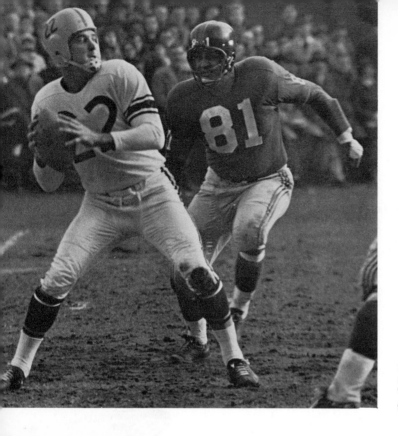

Bobby Layne was a great quarterback, especially on the two-minute pass. Doak Walker once said, "Bobby never lost a game—time just ran out."

Bobby Layne was a master at moving his team many yards in a short time. He did this for years with Detroit and with Pittsburgh. Johnny Unitas is another one who does a fine job of moving his team. You must have skilled, poised quarterbacks who can do a good job under pressure.

BASIC PASS PATTERNS FOR SPECIFIC DEFENSES

There are plays, however, that require specific strategy, prior thinking, the results of scouting reports, and game plans. You have a feeling how the corner back will tend to play you under certain situations. Here again, I want to emphasize that the end can probably help the quarterback call the play which he thinks is best at that time. After two or three series, the end knows what will work against that defender in certain situations from certain formations.

The category of basic pass patterns to fit specific defenses is one of my favorite topics. This subject also helps explain why we have the utmost respect for Coach Lombardi. One of the first things he did to our passing game when he joined the Packers was to give it mobility, make it pliable, make it work against any defense we would encounter.

As an example, if we were to call a fly or a streak pattern to our wingman, and on the snap of the ball we were confronted with a zone defense in which a deep outside man would shut off the fly route, then what's the use of continuing through with the play? You stand a good chance of having the ball intercepted if you throw it out there, for there is a defender right in the area, thus you probably are not even going to be successful with the route.

Coach Lombardi's theory was that when you encounter a defense that defeats the play you have called, if it's a basic route, then you change it slightly.

What we do in our passing game is to alter the route to meet the change of the defense. For every strong point a defense has, it must somewhere have a weak point—if you can find it. So we try to change our routes just slightly by possibly cutting down a bit on the distance we are going to run or some other slight change to fit this defensive change. The reason I am impressed with this thinking is that I have talked to some of our ends who have gone to other clubs, and they have told me how they will continue through with a route even when the defense has defeated it. We used to do this with the Packers before Coach Lombardi came here. Having seen his system work for us many times to fit a specific change in defense, I am thoroughly impressed with it and know it's the best way to do it.

Now, let's get the ball to the receiver. Some quarterbacks never develop the ability to throw the ball crisply. By that I mean a pass that zips to the receiver and finds its target immediately as the receiver turns and is ready to catch the ball. To a degree, you have to throw the ball hard on occasions. But I think the big thing is that the timing be perfect between the quarterback and the receiver. If the ball is thrown crisply and sharply, you don't have to worry about overpowering it or obviously trying to knock the receiver down. If you have worked and conditioned yourself properly, you should have a normal amount of strength and be able to get the ball there in plenty of time.

John Brodie of the 49'ers has an excellent sense of timing, and his shots to such receivers as Dave Parks and Bernie Casey are tough to defend against.

I want to play down the idea of throwing hard, for I feel that too many kids try to overpower the ball, try to throw it too hard, and this can hurt. If you strain to throw hard, you tend to be a little more erratic. Many times, too, when you are growing up and developing through high school and college, perhaps

ADJUSTING ROUTE TO CHANGE TO ZONE DEFENSE

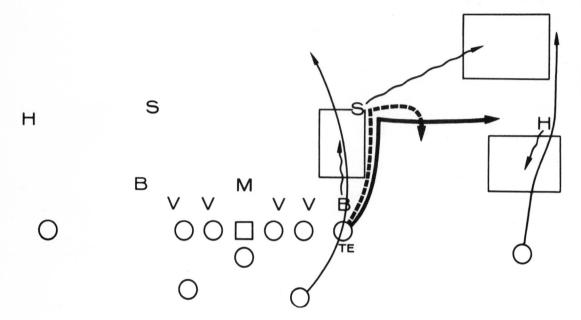

1. Bold line shows simple drag-out pattern to tight end.
2. Broken line shows adjustment tight end must make (he simply turns out) against zone lest he run into zone covered by halfback on his side. Tight end merely stops between two zones (shown by rectangles).

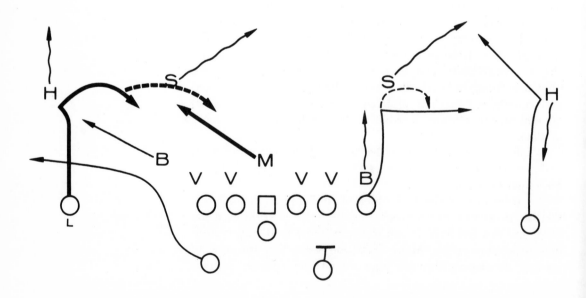

1. In this drawing the split end (L) should be open in the alley shown in a zone, but should the middle linebacker come hard to his outside, then the split may have to adjust by continuing beyond the middle linebacker (broken line). This adjustment requires some work between quarterback and receiver.

CHANGING ROUTE AS ZONE DEFENSE

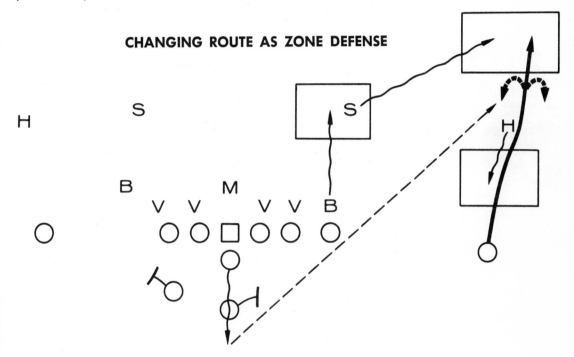

1. Here's another example of altering a route slightly as a change in defense.

2. If receiver who is running his fly route continues in a zone, he will run right into the deep zone covered by safety.

3. By having him pull up deep between the two zones, you may be able to complete the pass (broken lines).

4. Some people will try to hit the flanker between the two zones on the run after he clears first zone.

you're stronger than your receiver, and you can throw the ball too hard for him to catch it. You won't have this problem if you reach the professional ranks, because almost every receiver can catch the hardest ball thrown by the strongest quarterback. But as you are growing and developing, why throw hard if your receivers can't catch it? So let's speak in terms of throwing it crisply and with good timing, rather than throwing it hard.

Basically, the pass should be thrown crisply on any route, but especially on routes run underneath the deep secondary. By this we mean a crossing route, a hook route, an outside break

ROUTES IN WHICH BALL MUST BE THROWN CRISPLY

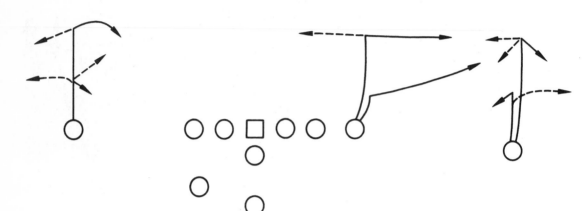

1. Any routes similar to the ones shown above where the receiver is catching the ball in front of the deep secondary defender (and in between or behind a linebacker). The ball must be delivered sharply and crisply with a flat trajectory.

2. There are some occasions when the ball is "drilled" at the receiver on longer passes, but these are the exceptions rather than the rule.

route, a sideline, or a square-out route—something that is thrown 10 to 20 yards or less—where a deep defender is between your receiver and the goal line.

In other words, the defender is behind your receiver. If you are throwing in front of a deep defender, the ball must be thrown crisply because the defender will come up in a hurry. He will knock it down if you float the ball out on an outside break or to an end running a crossing route. If you float the ball into the middle, it's really up for grabs. You've got to throw the ball crisply when you're throwing the medium distance routes.

When you are throwing the ball a longer distance such as on the streak or the fly pass going down the sideline, then the ball has to have a higher trajectory and be a somewhat softer

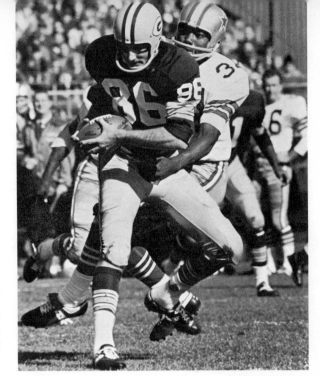

This photo gives an excellent idea of the swift reaction of defensive backs. Dallas Cowboy's Cornell Green is right on top of Boyd Dowler on an "out" break. The ball has just arrived, as Dowler's head is still turned "looking" the throw in, yet Green is right there too. Had Dowler not come "back" for the ball, Green might have broken up the pass.

type throw, for you are trying actually to throw over the defender. Your man has beaten the defender and you want to try to keep the ball in front of your receiver so the defender can't get it. This pass lets your man continue to pace himself, run down under the ball, catch it, and continue on his way to score. This is the situation when you throw the long, looping pass.

Remember, when you throw the long fly pass downfield, you should keep it as much to the outside as possible so your receiver has a better chance of catching the ball than the defender. If you throw the ball to the inside, this is usually where the defender is located. He can reach up at the last minute and flick it away or even intercept the pass.

On a long fly or streak route, if you overthrow your man, you should overthrow him slightly to the inside. This permits him to adjust to the ball if he clearly has his man beaten. If you were to overthrow your receiver to the outside, leading him out of bounds, this would be a rather difficult catch for him, because he must turn his head and catch the ball coming in blindly over his outside shoulder.

As a right-handed quarterback throws the ball downfield, the ball spins in a clockwise motion. So if you are throwing to a receiver on the right side, who is breaking in toward the goal post, remember the ball is going to drift slightly into the receiver. Be aware, then, that you should lead your receiver slightly more in breaking "in" routes from the right as opposed to the left. If you are throwing an "in" route to a receiver breaking in from the left, remember that the ball will have a tendency to drift just slightly away from the receiver. If you were to overlead him, he might just miss the ball. Give less than proper lead to a receiver running a post route on the right side, and you've crossed him.

LEADING THE RECEIVER ON LONG PASSES

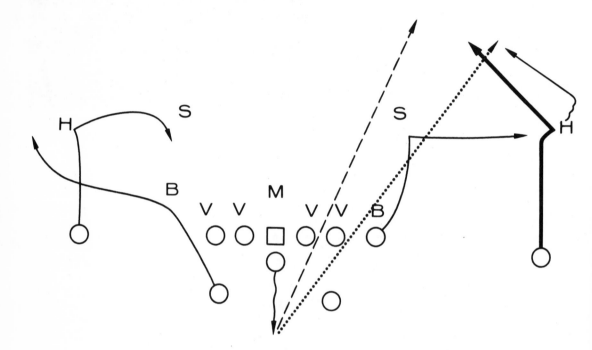

1. When a receiver is running a deep route (in this case, a post or middle) it is very important to get the ball to him quickly as he breaks open and in a manner so that the receiver does not have to break stride. (Dash-line pass)

2. Many times you've seen a receiver get open only to have the ball be underthrown, the defender recover and knock it down or even intercept it. (Dotted-line pass)

3. Remember, the receiver has speed, he can cover a lot of ground, so let him run under the ball. (I've had trouble through the years of not giving the receiver some credit and thus just firing the ball up there for him to go get it.)

4. The ball should also be delivered so as not to "cross" the line the receiver is running. (Dashed line shows good throw, dotted line poor throw—crossing receiver.) Even if ball thrown along dashed line is underthrown, receiver can adjust. He can't if ball crosses behind him.

5. On a pass of this type, it's better to loft the ball and allow the receiver to run under it (a ball thrown on a flat trajectory would have to be near perfect) so that if the passer is a little off his mark, the receiver can adjust.

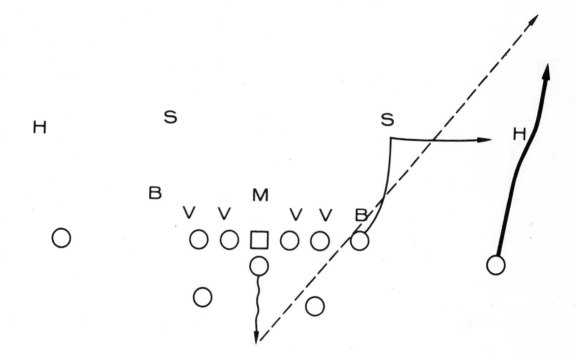

1. In the above drawing, you see another type of lead pass in which the ball must be "hung" in the air allowing the receiver to run under it.

2. Under no circumstances should the ball be underthrown on this type of pass.

3. This pass requires a lot of work between passer and receiver, for ball must be kept outside, but not too far, lest it go out of bounds; ball must be delivered on rhythm and yet be thrown in high floating trajectory so that receiver can catch it in full stride.

SPIN OF THE BALL

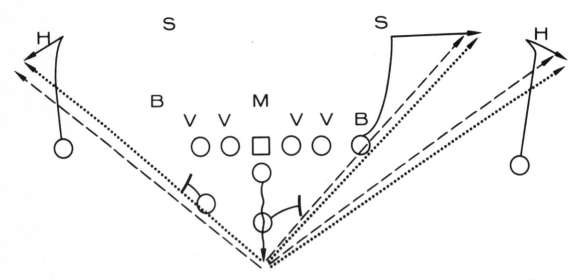

1. Dash lines indicate actual intended flight of ball.
2. Dotted lines show how spin action of ball causes it to be drawn into and away from receiver.

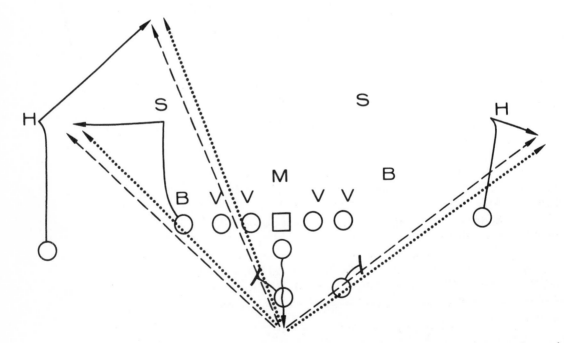

1. Note how on left side the "out" break by tight end will result in ball coming "into" him whereas "in" break by flanker results in just the opposite.

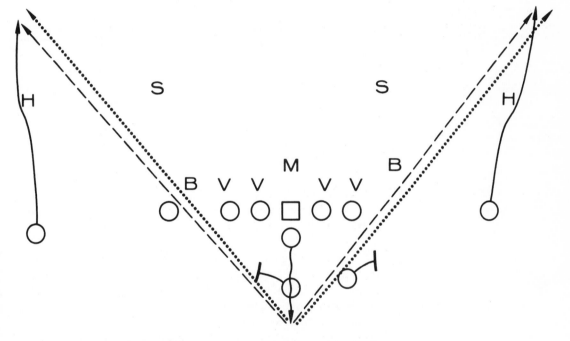

1. When throwing the deep pass straight downfield to a receiver, remember that the spin of the ball on the right side will tend to carry it across the receiver and out of bounds (dotted lines) whereas on the left side the ball will tend to drift down and away from the receiver.

2. These facts should be remembered when leading a receiver with a pass so that misfires can be turned into completions.

BASIC ROUTES

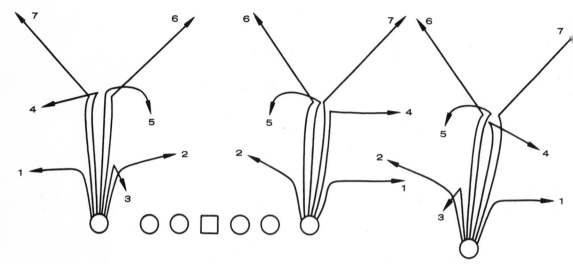

1. Quick Out
2. Quick
3. Hitch
4. Out (tight end's route is called a drag)
5. In
6. Post
7. Corner (move is just the opposite from 6, with each running to the outside)

This same general principle holds on even shorter passes. If your split end on the left side runs an "out," you must learn to keep the ball well out in front because it will drift back to him. On the other hand, if your split end is on the right side running an "out" you must remember the ball is spinning away from him, so don't overlead him—he'll never get it!

We have diagramed the three principal receivers and their basic routes. These are the routes that we throw most of the time.

There is no secret to attaining so-called perfection in the passing game. It is just a matter of timing and practice—working on it, working on it, working on it. There is no substitute for hard work and practice, and there is no way to build timing and perfection other than through practice. You can't do it simply on a blackboard. You can talk about it and iron out some things on a blackboard. The more you discuss it, the more ideas are offered and the more familiar you become with all aspects of what you are trying to accomplish; but you must go out on the field and work against live people in a training situation to perfect your skill so it will stand up in a game.

These diagrams show a few of the routes we work with our split end, our tight end, and our flanker. These are the chief routes we work on continuously to attain the highest degree of perfection.

DRAWS AND SCREENS

Draws and screens are two of the best "change-of-pace" weapons a quarterback has at his disposal to combat pressure from the defense.

A draw play begins as a simulated pass, with everyone blocking as on a pass. The quarterback retreats, inviting the pass rush, and hands the ball to a waiting halfback or fullback, who then slips into a lane or hole created by specific blocking techniques in which the offensive linemen shield or turn the rushers as the latter press toward the passer.

A few simple examples follow:

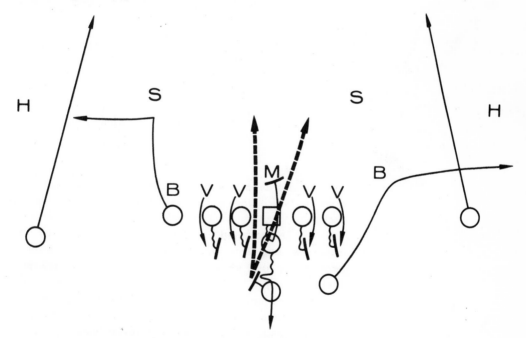

1. Looking at the rush above, you can see that a wide alley is created right up the middle if both guards turn the defensive tackles out. Hard charging linemen almost overrun the ball carrier on occasions.

2. It's not too difficult to see how a very deliberate defensive tackle is tough to draw on. He simply does not penetrate (allowing himself to be easily turned) and is in position to move quickly to the ball carrier.

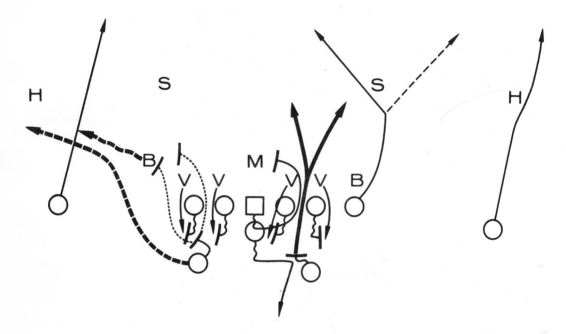

1. Here's a look at the same draw play (opposite formation) in which the defensive left tackle closed hard on his
charge.

2. This created a hole or lane between the defensive
tackle and end. The center, who is the lead blocker for the fullback in this case, leads around his guard's block for the middle
linebacker.

3. The halfback is responsible for the linebacker on his
side. Sometimes merely running out of the backfield is sufficient
to hold or occupy this linebacker (broken line).

4. Simple draws such as these can also be executed by
the halfback or quarterback. In addition, any back can run
draws as far outside as around the defensive end, should an
end be notoriously bad about "giving up" to the inside and
close hard inside on a pass rush.

QUARTERBACK DRAW PLAY

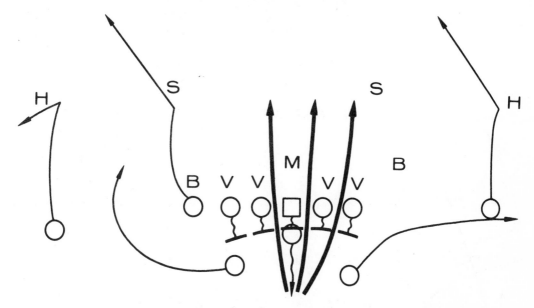

1. Some teams which possess good running quarterbacks have draw plays designed for them also.

2. Quarterback retreats as to pass, then runs with ball to whatever lane develops as a result of the blocking designed.

Screen passes are effective countermoves by the offense when the defense is applying heated pressure on the passer. These plays require a lot of practice and timing but, when perfected, can be a real stimulant to a sputtering offense.

The offensive linemen must work precisely and efficiently and must be good "con" men on screens. They must first sustain the block and then allow their man to think he has defeated the pass block and is about to gobble up the quarterback, only to discover he's been fooled.

Many times outstanding pass blockers do not make good "screen men" because when they ease up, the defensive man immediately senses something. On the other hand, an average group of offensive players may execute screens very well because they are legitimately beaten enough to make it difficult for the pass rusher to distinguish between a good and poor effort.

There are basically two kinds of screens: (1) regular, in which a normal retreat is begun by the quarterback and after about a "three" count, the offensive linemen "lose" their blocks and slip into the designated area to form a wall or screen for a back, and (2) quick screens, which are thrown on a much faster rhythm, with less finesse necessary on the part of the offensive linemen.

Some simple screens are diagramed as follows:

REGULAR SCREEN

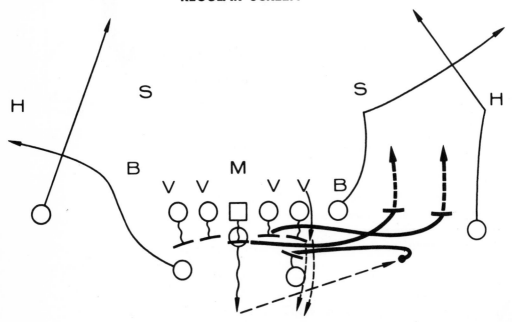

1. This diagram shows a simple two-man screen forming in front of the fullback, who delayed and slipped out to his right. Sometimes more offensive linemen are involved in the screen.

2. The receiving back may catch the ball on the run or sprint to a spot, come under control, turn toward the quarterback and receive the ball. (We prefer the latter method if time permits.)

3. Just prior to actually receiving the ball, the back should yell "go" or something similar to alert his blockers to take off.

4. This type of screen can be run just as effectively to the weak side or split end side with the halfback receiving the ball.

5. These are only a couple of examples of regular screens, since you can conceivably run screen passes off any pass or run fake you have in your repertoire.

QUICK SCREEN

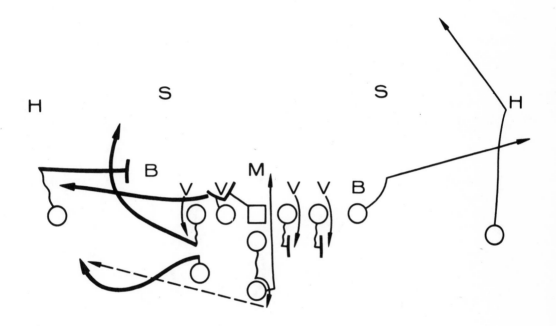

1. This diagram shows a quick screen pass underway. The quarterback retreats quickly, fakes a draw to the fullback to help hold the defense, then flips the ball to the halfback out in the flat, who just paused momentarily before sprinting outside. (Note good "belly" halfback took to give the quarterback a good target.)

2. The split end cracks back on the linebacker. The tackle sets, brushes his man, and sprints for the safety on his side. The guard slams his man (along with the center) and then sprints into the flat for the defensive halfback.

(Some teams run an effective regular screen to the fullback by faking this quick screen maneuver—this draws a lot of attention away from the fullback—and then throwing the pass back to the opposite side.)

DELAYS

Sometimes during the course of a game, you may find the defensive linebackers getting so much depth that they actually clog up your short to medium distance passing game. Combine this with a strong pass rush by the four defensive linemen, and your passing game could suffer considerably.

Along with draws and screens, delayed action route running by the offensive backs can many times be very successful.

For example:

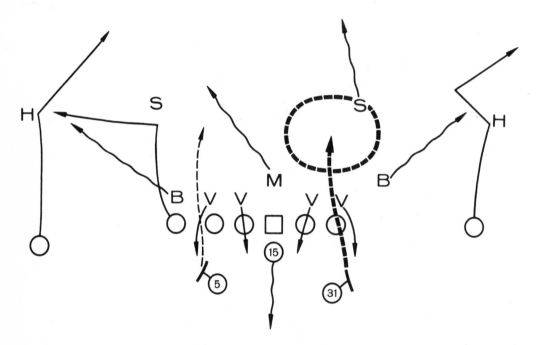

1. You can easily see how open the offensive halfback is after the linebackers employ a very deep drop. After simulating a block for a couple of counts, he slips into the large hole which has been created by the coverage. Once the back has the ball, he can run quite a way with it.

2. In like manner, the fullback could be just as open had the middle linebacker dropped straight back on to his left.

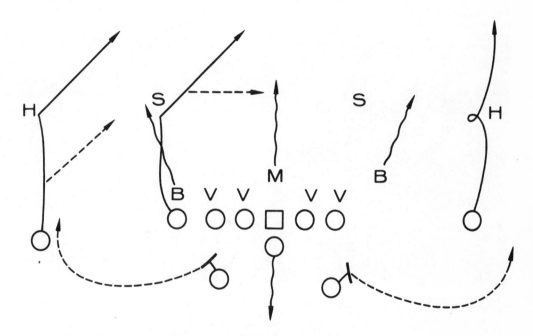

1. Delays can be worked effectively to the outside as well sometimes, and though they don't look like much, if a good back can catch a ball outside, he seldom has greater odds than "one on one" (he is challenging the linebacker on that side). If he breaks that tackle, he again can gain substantial yardage.

Here, in action sequence, is a classic example of the delay pass to the halfback. The halfback (5) simulates regular pass blocking.

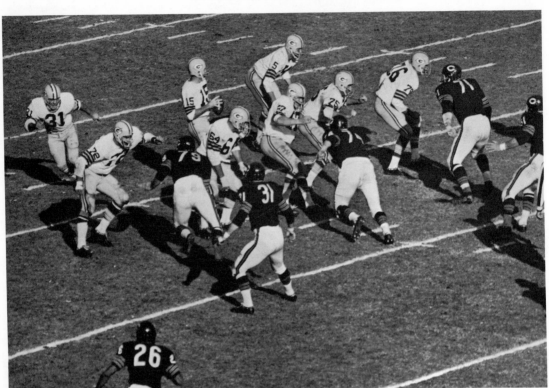

He begins to slip through the line. Note that (81) in dark is only three or four yards from the quarterback.

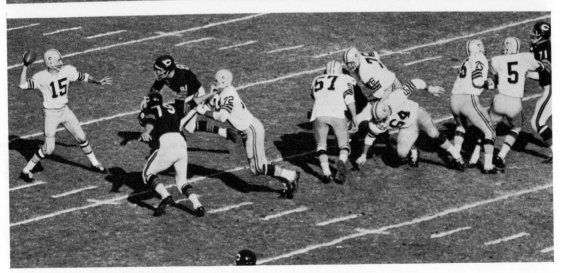

The halfback is breaking through the line and the quarterback is releasing the ball for a short flip over the line.

The quarterback releases the ball and takes a tackle from (81).

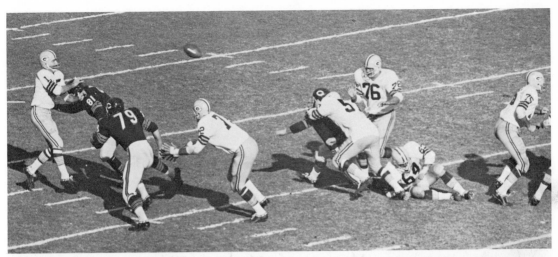

The ball is on its way to halfback (5). Number 75 in white completed the block on
(71) in dark, enabling the halfback (5) to break up the middle for a long gain.

BACKS' OUT PATTERNS

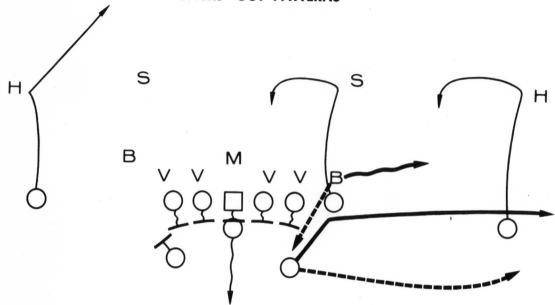

1. Here is a diagram of a pass in which only one back is sent in the pass route. (Backs are sent into the pass route for two chief reasons: (a) to act as a decoy and force linebackers to make some movement, thus opening up some other receiver, and (b) to be a primary receiver—working against a linebacker on a "one on one" situation in which the speed of the back should allow him to get open.)

2. With these thoughts in mind, whenever you send a back out, there must be some method of handling the linebacker on the side to which the offensive back is called out.

3. This is usually done by two methods: (a) The offensive back merely calls out "red dog," should the LB red dog and the back be in a flare action (shown above, broken lines)—and the quarterback just lobs the ball out to the back. (b) The back can run a "pick-up" route whereby he takes the linebacker if he's blitzing, and if not, the back continues in the pass (bold lines). Offensive back is doing his job either way, for he is occupying his linebacker.

FLOOD PASS

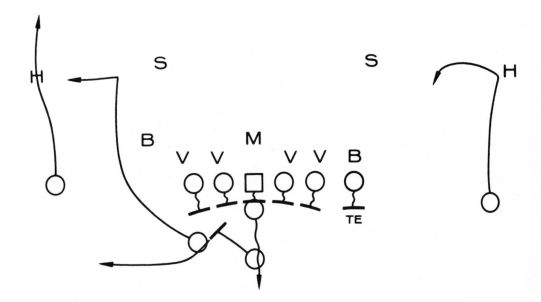

1. The above diagram illustrates sending both backs in the pass pattern.

2. When this is done, there are compensations to be made. The center is still on the middle linebacker (M). The fullback checks the weak side linebacker (picks him up if the latter red dogs) before going into pass action. The tight end (TE) takes the strong side linebacker if he comes. Once again, all are blocked.

interceptions
and
rules
of
passing

In order to win football games, you must keep your own mistakes to a minimum and try to avoid beating yourself. Many times a football game is won by one team's capitalizing on the other team's mistakes, not by superior effort on the part of the winning team. And interceptions, of course, are mistakes.

A quarterback must be a realist. He should realize he is going to have certain passes intercepted. Over the course of a season he can't avoid interceptions either from tip-ups, miscalculations on his part, a receiver falling down and the ball going over his head into a defender's hands. All sorts of things can happen in the course of a year, so he is going to have interceptions.

The big thing he must remember is not to let the interception discourage him. He cannot belittle himself or his own efforts. This is almost tragic, and though I hate to admit it, I was guilty of this for a number of years. It wasn't until Coach Lombardi came to the Packers that he convinced me to be mentally tough enough to overcome this feeling. He taught me that if I make a mistake, profit by it, but then come back free-wheeling the next time. By free-wheeling, I mean you are loose. You cannot play the game of football cautiously, carefully. Many times you may plot methods by which to accomplish something. Yet when you actually start to employ that method, you should be free-wheeling and "reckless," so to speak.

There's a great deal of difference between carelessness and recklessness. You can throw caution to the wind and still not be careless. Once you start to be careful, you tend to tense up, to tighten up and to limit your own ability, your own coordination, and your effectiveness.

185

Learning when to throw has to come with practice, but remember one thing: you never, never throw the ball into a crowd. Your receiver has to be in a position so that if the ball is thrown to him, no one is going to get the ball but him. And if there is any doubt in your mind that there might be someone who can get a hand on it, or get between your receiver and the ball before it gets there, then you don't throw it. You throw it into the ground toward the feet of your receiver, so that no one can get it, you run with it, or you eat it, but you never throw the ball up for grabs.

Throwing the ball away is an important subject for passers. A quarterback should strive to throw the ball away very close to his receiver so it looks as if he is making a legitimate effort to throw the ball to him. I might mention here that the NFL officials do a great job in their calls on throwing the ball away illegally, grounding it illegally, or trying to throw the ball to one of your receivers. They do a fine job of making this call because it is a judgment call and one that is a little touchy sometimes.

Sometimes there just isn't anyone to throw to !

One of the finest quarterbacks I have ever seen in throwing the ball away to avoid a huge loss was Charlie Conerley of the New York Giants. Charlie had a tremendous knack of getting rid of the ball under heavy rush or if his receivers were covered. He would throw it down into the dirt in such a way that his receiver would be coming back and appear to be making a vain attempt to get it. It looked like it was just barely missed, and yet I am sure if it had not been for an extra effort on the part of the receiver, it might have been assumed that the ball was thrown away. This is another mark of a fine quarterback—throwing the ball away in a legal manner.

A passer should always remember that he must never throw the ball away when there is a man between him and his receiver in such a way that the defender has a chance to intercept the ball. If it's crowded around your receiver, you throw the ball down hard toward the ground in front of him. You throw the ball down so low that it doesn't have a chance to get flicked or batted up into the air, where the defense has a chance at it.

Charlie Conerley of the New York Giants under heavy pressure.

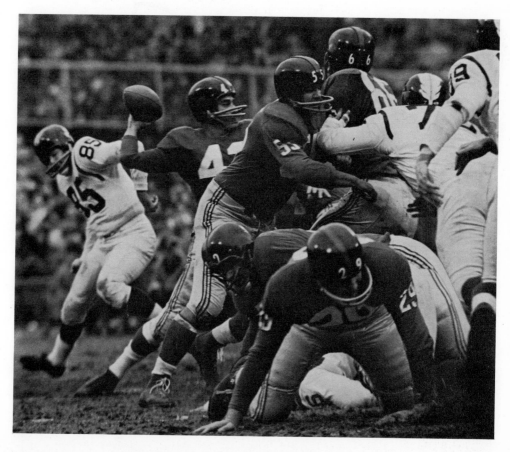

It takes a bit of experience to learn to do this effectively and yet throw it close enough to your receiver to make it look like a legitimate effort to complete the pass. But it is very important not to get caught for big losses. If you can throw the ball away legitimately, it's a lot easier to pick up six than it is to pick up 15. With third and 15, the burden is on you and not on the defense. They can play you a little more loosely.

However, there are times when a quarterback must run with the ball or eat it (and by that, of course, we mean not throw it). Any time you cannot legally, safely, effectively throw the ball away, you should keep it yourself, take the tackle, absorb the charge, and eat the ball regardless of the yards involved in the loss. You should protect the ball when you are tackled. Just pull it in close to your side as a runner does when he is running with it so that if you are jarred from one direction, someone coming along from the other side doesn't have a free shot at the ball. If you pull it in next to you, you'll very seldom lose it when you are being tackled.

GUARDING AGAINST INTERCEPTIONS

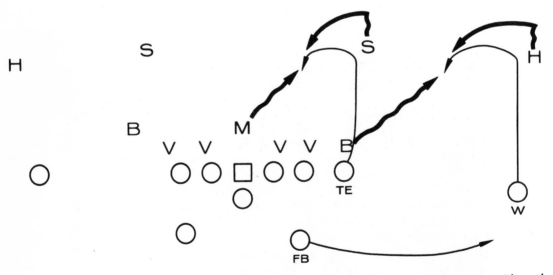

1. Let's suppose you are trying to throw to either the tight end (TE) or the wingback (W) and each is covered well by their defenders with help from the linebackers (bold lines).

2. Rather than risk the chance of an interception, the ball can easily be "dumped" off to the fullback out in the flat whom the outside linebacker has ignored.

3. Though the receivers can usually work free around linebackers and get open, if there is any doubt in the passer's mind, he should not throw the ball.

4. Another good axiom to remember is NEVER FORCE THE BALL; that is, don't throw it if the opening isn't there.

I had an interception in this year's Pro Bowl because I forced a throw to our tight end, the linebacker deflected the ball, and Larry Wilson, a great defender, alertly picked it off.

JUDGING WHEN TO THROW

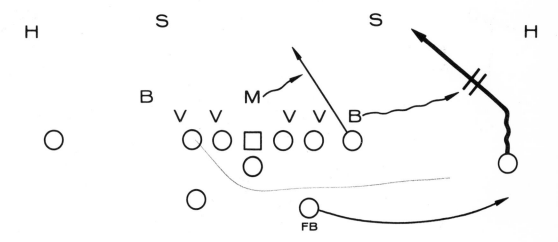

1. Let's take a look at a simple, quick, inside route to the wingback or flanker.

2. The outside linebacker on the fullback's side is drawn to the outside to cover.

3. The quarterback can actually release the ball when the receiver is still in front of the linebacker (note two lines) because each is going in opposite directions and the linebacker can't recover to knock the ball down. Lead the receiver; don't throw the ball behind him.

4. Also, by releasing the ball before the receiver is actually "open," you give the defender on the wingback less time to react. (The longer a receiver runs without the ball, the longer a defender has to react and make up lost ground.)

5. Never throw the ball into a crowd. This should be the quarterback's first axiom when passing.

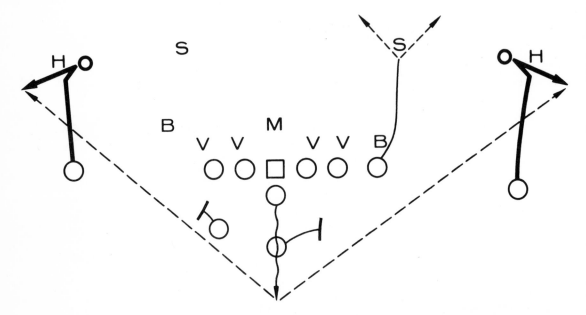

1. Here's a case of timing personified. On all "out" breaks by receivers, the quarterback should release the ball before the receiver begins his outward move. (Ball should be released when receiver has faked or paused inside or at least driven the defender well off before making his break. See bold circles.)

2. Ball is thrown sharply and crisply on a flat trajectory in a manner that allows the receiver to actually come back away from the defender. (Note line of pattern.)

3. It's better to underthrow short routes (outside or inside) as receiver is usually coming back for the ball and has a better chance to get it than if you "cross" him by throwing a high one over him.

The matter of proper leading of a receiver is an interesting one because I don't have any measures or standards by which to tell you how much to lead receivers. (See diagram on "Spin of Ball," p. 168.) All receivers are different. They have different speeds, paces, quicknesses. Many times in All-Star games, quarterbacks have difficulty for a while in getting accustomed to the moves of receivers and leading them properly because they are all different. Learning this comes with practice, with experience—getting to know how fast a man is, how well he comes out of a break on a double fake, and so on. These are things that come with time. I think this is a matter of feel rather than any set standards.

The big point to remember is to lead him. Don't underthrow him. Seldom will you have a pass intercepted if you overthrow the receiver. But many times, when the receiver has the defender beaten, if you underthrow him the defender steps in and intercepts. Let your inner guidance system take over for you. There is something inside you that will do this for you. Just relax, be loose, and throw the ball.

The receiver is like a baseball player catching a line drive or a long, looping fly in center field. His brain takes into consideration the speed the ball is traveling, where he has to move in order to get to it, and the wind and direction as he is running to catch the ball. In an instant this information reaches him, enabling him to get into a position to catch it.

Any time you throw a pass, the passer should be the safety man. If he is throwing to his left or to his right out into the flat, he should cover after he throws the ball. He becomes the safety man in case of an interception. I was hurt prior to our 1965 championship game in a situation similar to this. We opened the game against the Baltimore Colts in Green Bay for the 1965 Western Division title with a fake draw. We ran a short pass, a little square-out maneuver to our tight end. Bill Anderson caught the ball and turned up field. As I threw it, I saw him catch it, and then I became screened off from him and didn't see what was happening until I was running into the flat to cover.

The next thing I knew, Don Shinnick of the Colts had the ball, running down the sideline with it. I did not see Shinnick come up with it. I didn't see what happened until later, in the movies, when I found out that Anderson, when tackled by their corner man, Lenny Lyles, bobbled the ball and Shinnick came along and picked it off. I just instinctively moved over to cover and in so doing was blocked by Jim Welch, one of their safety men. He threw a fine block, I might mention, in my rib section, and I was laid low for the rest of the day.

The point I am making is that after you throw the ball, you should cover. I went to the left as a safety man in case there was

PASS AGAINST COLTS RESULTING IN INJURY

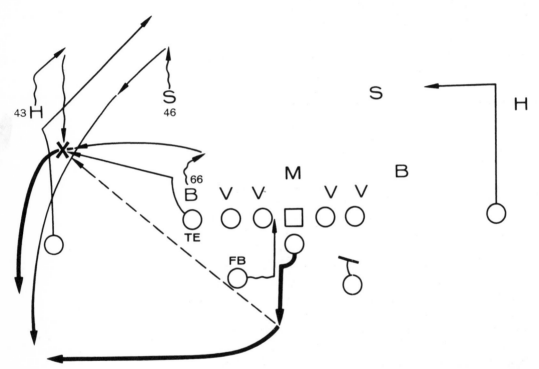

1. In 1965 we opened the game against the Colts for the Western Division Championship with the above play.

2. We faked a draw to Taylor (FB) and then threw the ball to our tight end, who was running a short outside route.

3. The end caught the ball but was tackled quickly by Lenny Lyles (43), the result being a fumble which was grabbed off in midair by Don Shinnick (66), the right linebacker for the Colts. Welch (46), the right safety for the Colts, led Shinnick down the sideline, and in covering on the pass, I was blocked so well by Welch that I had to leave the game with some bruised ribs.

4. Alert play by the Colts gave them a score on the first play of the game, though they were on defense.

an interception. Sometimes you can turn the runner back to the inside where help can arrive. It is important for the quarterback to be the safety man in case of an interception or a fumble.

Let me emphasize, however—throw the ball with all the correct form and technique first, and then cover second. I've actually seen quarterbacks start to cover before they have finished throwing the ball. In other words, they're almost running out to cover before they release the ball. They're more concerned with covering than they are with hitting their receivers. This is a fault, a bad fault. Throw the ball first. You've got plenty of time to cover.

Many coaches will teach their quarterbacks to call "left" or "right" as they throw the ball, to alert the offensive linemen where the ball has been thrown. In case there is an interception, they can get a few people over to help out.

Sometimes the strategy behind calling a certain pass play might be hidden. For instance, in Detroit in 1962 we were being beaten pretty badly by the Lions after having won ten straight games. We had third and 10 in the third quarter. I turned to Tommy Moore, our left halfback who was filling in for Paul Hornung that day, and said, "Tom, how about a sweep around right end?" He said, "Bart, I'd really like to help you out of this jam, but old Darus McCord, the Lion defensive end, has really been roughing me up on these end runs today. Give it to Taylor."

I went back to Jimmy Taylor, but he was black and blue and shaking his head, indicating he didn't want to run it either. I said, "Jimmy, how about a run up the middle?"

"Are you kidding?" he answered. "Roger Brown has me so sore, I can hardly walk. Why don't you throw it?"

Actually, I didn't have the heart to tell him I didn't want to throw it because I had been dumped all day long. So I thought, well, I'll try one more time. Then I looked at Boyd Dowler, our flanker, and said, "Boyd, how about running me a 12-yard hook? Let's stop this foolishness and pick up a first down."

He looked at me and said, "You know, you're in a jam. And I'd really like to help you out, but old Dick Lane over there has been crushing my ribs every time I run a hook pass today. Why don't you throw it to McGee?"

I looked at McGee, and he was running off the field. He didn't want any part of it either.

But Fuzzy Thurston, our left guard, who was having a rather uncomfortable day with Roger Brown also, had not lost his poise or his sense of humor. He pushed me away from the huddle a bit and whispered in my ear, "Say, Bart, I've got a great idea. Why don't you throw a long incomplete pass, and that way nobody will get hurt."

Well, everybody in the huddle heard it—Fuzzy didn't realize he was talking as loud as he was—and we just about broke up. We almost got a five-yard penalty for standing there laughing. I am sure the Lions thought, "What in the world is that idiot group over there doing? We're beating the daylights out of them, and they are standing there laughing about it." It so broke us up that I think we made it through the rest of the game in a little better shape than we would have if Fuzzy had not come through with that comment.

Thank goodness we haven't had to call on too many stories like that in the huddle to save our face and our bodies too. But I think it points up how a fellow can call on his sense of humor in a situation like that even though we were getting thumped pretty badly.

RULES PERTAINING TO PASSING GAME

Since we have attempted to include all the elements of passing in this book, we would like to include a discussion on the various rules of the game that affect some phases of passing.

LATERAL PASS

We'll start with a lateral. The rules state that an offensive man carrying the ball may, at any time, hand or pass it backwards or to the side to a teammate.

INTENTIONAL GROUNDING OF THE BALL

An official must make a "touchy" ruling when a passer is hit just as he releases the ball. The passer may have legitimately tried to hit a receiver, but the impact of the tackle took all forward momentum off the ball. Or the quarterback could have been throwing in the direction of a receiver with no thought of trying to hit him, but rather to avoid a loss on the play. If the official rules the pass was intentionally grounded, the loss might be more than ever.

ILLEGAL PASS

If the passer steps beyond the "neutral zone"—the area between the offensive and defensive lines—and throws a pass, it is considered incomplete.

RECEIVER STEPPING OUT OF BOUNDS

An eligible pass receiver cannot step out of bounds on the sidelines and then return to the playing field to catch a pass unless that pass was touched by a defensive player.

LATERAL PASS

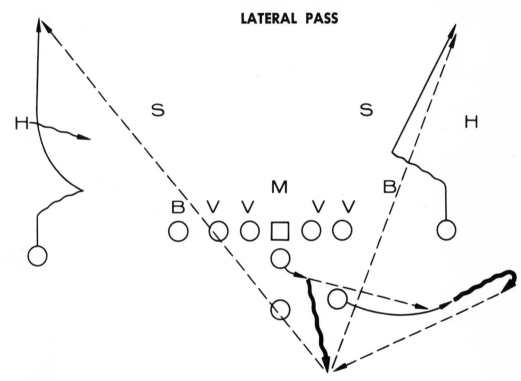

1. If the quarterback pitches a ball out to a halfback and then receives a pass from that running back, the flight of the ball, from the beginning of the snap from center, must be backward.

2. The play diagramed above is called a "flea flicker" and is designed to lull the defensive secondary to sleep so that the quarterback may uncork a long bomb.

ILLEGAL PASS

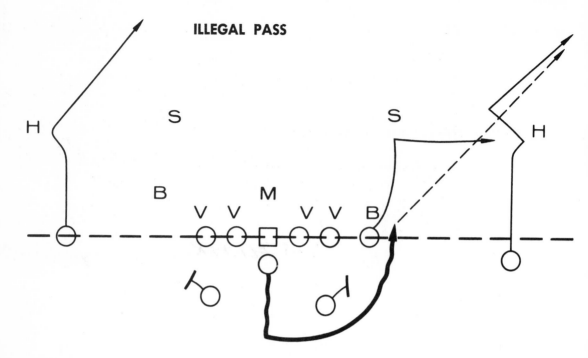

1. If the passer ever gets beyond the neutral zone and throws a pass, it is illegal and considered incomplete.

RECEIVER STEPPING OUT OF BOUNDS

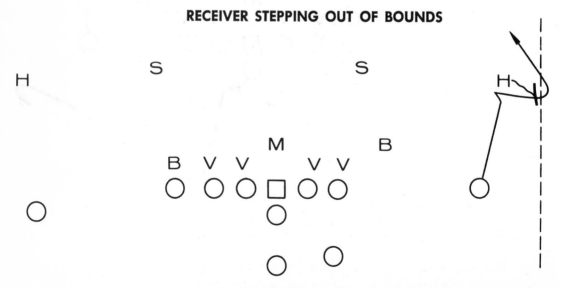

1. If a defender bumps a receiver out of bounds before the ball is thrown, the receiver cannot return to the playing field and catch a pass unless the defender touched the ball first.

Ray Berry of the Baltimore Colts exhibits his specialty of catching the ball barely within the playing field, just prior to stepping out of bounds.

RECEIVER LANDING OUT OF BOUNDS

When a pass receiver catches a ball near the sidelines, you will see him go into a "toe-dancing act." This comes from the training and practice of getting both feet down inside the sideline after a catch. Both feet must contact the ground before he goes out of bounds, or the pass is ruled incomplete. However, if the pass receiver is hit by a defensive man and knocked out of bounds, the pass is complete.

SIMULTANEOUS CATCH

If an offensive and defensive player appear to have caught a pass simultaneously, the offensive player will be awarded the catch. The ball is dead at the spot and may not be advanced.

PLAYING THE BALL

Players on both teams have equal rights to a passed ball, provided they both make an honest effort to catch it. Often this play appears to be "pass interference," but it is merely "playing the ball." The officials watch this play very closely.

FACE GUARDING

This is pass interference. The defender is waving his arms and facing the intended receiver. This constitutes distraction or face guarding. In such cases the ball is given to the offense on the spot where the infraction occurred.

PASS INTERFERENCE

If the defender is guilty of interfering with the intended pass receiver from the moment the pass is thrown, his team will be penalized and the offensive team awarded a first down at the point of infraction. The passed ball does not have to pass the scrimmage line, as many fans believe.

Left: Whenever a *simultaneous catch* occurs on the field, the offensive player is awarded possession. *Above:* This is another foul by the defensive back—*face guarding.* A player is not permitted to interfere with the vision of a receiver by such practices. *Right:* This is flagrant pass interference. The defender is all over the receiver before the ball has arrived.

INELIGIBLE RECEIVERS

If any linemen other than an end crosses the scrimmage line before a pass is thrown, the offensive team is penalized for having ineligible receivers downfield. The penalty is 15 yards.

ELIGIBLE PASS RECEIVERS

All the backs and ends, except the quarterback, are eligible pass receivers and may receive passes at any time. Any player wearing a number other than that of an end or back, but desiring to play one of these positions, must notify the official who, in turn, relays this information to the defensive team. This procedure will make him an eligible pass receiver.

the
art
of
pass
reception

Much has been written and preached about the necessity for passers to spend countless hours working with their receivers so that both understand each other precisely. This mutual understanding between passer and receiver goes far in making a successful passing attack. In fact, no passing attack can be successful without it.

As a result, it behooves a good passer to learn and comprehend the various maneuvers of each of his receivers. We have asked Packer End Coach Bob Schnelker to give us a hand in describing to you the basic fundamentals of pass receiving.

RECEIVING

(1)   (2)

1. Receiver is shown here making sharp sideline cut at least parallel to the line of scrimmage (thin line) or, better yet, coming back toward line of scrimmage (bold line). *Receiver should never round off the route* (broken line).

2. Receiver should run directly at the defender (bold line) so as to drive the defender straight back; otherwise, he can give you only one way to go.

Here is a list of maneuvers to teach receivers how to get open.

One, make sharp sideline or inside breaks parallel to the line of scrimmage. Either cut or drive off the outside foot by just crossing over to make the break quick and sharp, parallel to the line of scrimmage or even back toward it. By all means, avoid rolling, looping, or making a circle out of the maneuver. Make the break sharp and distinct.

Two, get the defensive man directly in front of you. Drive him back with a burst of speed and then just run away from him in the particular pattern that is called.

Three, use the type of running fake where you drive hard in one direction, then cut back in another direction without breaking stride, in a smooth motion. Run at top speed through the entire pattern.

Four, find an open area between two defenders who are in a zone type of defense. The receiver is taught to recognize the defense and to adjust to it, as a quarterback adjusts to a defense.

Five, find the open area between two linebackers who are covering the short areas in most pass defenses.

Six, step up into the ball as it comes from the quarterback. This pulls you away from the defensive back and gives you a greater advantage in catching the ball. It is a tough maneuver to teach, and most receivers have a tendency to wait for the ball to come to them.

This sequence of photos demonstrates one of the pass receiving techniques discussed by Coach Bob Schnelker. In this particular sequence the receiver is driving the defender off until the latter is out of position. At this point the receiver makes his break to take the ball.

RECEIVING THE BALL

As for receiving the ball, there are several things to keep in mind.

One, always look the ball into your hands. Never take your eyes off it until you have complete control of it.

Two, practice catching a ball thrown through several pairs of arms or hands. This develops concentration on the ball and not on the obstacles it is passing through or around.

Three, relax—learn to relax the arms and hands while accepting the ball. Don't snatch it or grab at it. You are receiving the ball; accepting it, not fighting it.

Four, always catch the ball in the hands, if at all possible. About the only time it should be caught against the body, cradling the ball, is when you are closely covered by a defender or two.

Five, you must learn to turn or snap the head around quickly as you make the final break on a pass pattern, so you can locate the ball as quickly as possible and still remain relaxed enough in the hands and arms to handle the ball immediately. On short and medium passes, the ball should be there just about the time you turn around, or as quickly as the pattern is run, if the ball is thrown on time.

MANEUVERING ON PASSES

On short and medium passes, the receiver must drive the defender back by taking off at full speed as he starts the pattern. Or he can start at a good rate of speed and then turn on full speed to make the defender believe he is going deep. Thus, he can run by the defender. After he has driven the defender back, he can make the break in the direction the pattern calls for.

When maneuvering on long passes, keep these things in mind.

One, the receiver must get the defender head up again and started in the direction away from the final pattern that the receiver wants to run. Make the pattern similar to a medium or short pattern you have run previously, then break away from the original pattern the defender has seen you run before. Turn on all the speed you have in the final break and beat him deep.

Two, on some long patterns it is just a simple case of outrunning a defender with sheer speed, or perhaps getting as

Boyd Dowler of the Packers displays an example of "keeping your eyes on the ball" when receiving a pass, despite close coverage by the defender.

close as possible to the defender with good speed and then changing speeds and simply outrunning him to get behind or beyond him. It involves no faking. This is a pure percentage pass, but it does accomplish one thing in that it loosens up the defense and makes it depth conscious.

STAYING IN BOUNDS

Another receiving fundamental that needs a lot of work and attention is teaching the receiver to know where the sidelines are at all times and to keep both feet in bounds when he catches the ball. You have to teach the receiver that as he catches the ball near the sideline, he should come down with the forward striding foot or leg in bounds and drag the other foot or slap it to the ground as quickly as possible as he goes out of bounds to insure having caught a legal pass.

In college, of course, receivers need have only one foot in bounds. They have to be taught to keep their eyes on the ball and to catch it first before worrying about keeping their feet in bounds. The receivers have to learn to feel where the sidelines are by repetition of this maneuver. This is a difficult thing for a young college prospect to accomplish in the professional ranks, because he's never been concerned about having to put both feet down at once inside in order to make it a legal catch.

In professional football, both feet of the player must touch the ground before going out of bounds for a pass to be ruled complete. Observe the receiver in these two photos executing this maneuver perfectly as he comes down in bounds after the catch.

OVERHEAD PASSES

Another area to discuss is catching the ball that comes directly overhead. This is one of the toughest passes in football to catch, and it happens quite frequently. It's rough because as the receiver looks back to locate the ball directly overhead, he has a tendency to lose his balance and lose the relaxation in his arms and hands. He tends to pull his arms into his body and the ball invariably goes beyond his finger tips. He "short-arms" it, as Coach Lombardi likes to say, because he doesn't look the ball all the way into his hands.

This is one pass where the ball definitely must be looked into the hands. Receivers need practice in catching this type of pass and concentrating on staying relaxed in the hands and arms while watching the ball.

These two photos are excellent illustrations of the position of the receiver's hands on a pass to be caught over the shoulder on the run. Note that the little fingers are close together. In an earlier illustration the hands are observed with the thumbs close together when catching "head on" throws. These pictures are also fine examples of a receiver "beating" a defender.

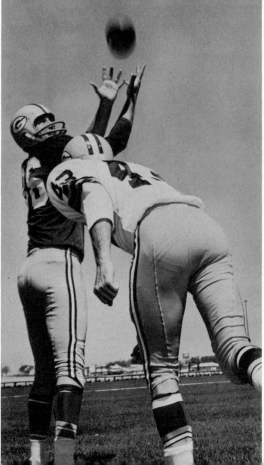

CATCHING BADLY THROWN PASSES

If the pass is thrown short, or behind a receiver, he must pivot back toward the ball so that he continuously keeps his eyes on the ball. He should not continue running and reach back one-handed to try and make the catch.

PASSES THROWN LOW

Passes that are low and in front of the receiver should be caught by diving for them. It's important to remember here again to keep the hands relaxed. When you are diving for a ball, the natural tendency is to become stiff or tense about it, but as you extend your arms, try to keep the hands as relaxed as possible. Attempt to get them underneath the ball, so they cradle the ball off the ground—thus making it a legal catch.

To field a low throw, a good receiver often has to drop to one knee, or dive for the ball, in an effort to keep the hands underneath the ball. Despite close coverage, note how the receiver keeps his eyes on the ball.

STEPPING INTO THE BALL

Another topic of importance is stepping into the ball as it comes from the quarterback. This is another drill that must be constantly worked on and emphasized. The receiver must develop a knack of coming back toward the quarterback as the ball heads toward its target. The receiver should never stand and wait for the ball to come to him.

He has gained an advantage over his defender by running a good pattern, so he must maintain this advantage, or even increase it, by coming back with the ball as it approaches him in flight. He should not drift upfield and wait for the ball to come to him or the defender will recover and make up the ground he has lost. This maneuver prevents a lot of interceptions or batted-down passes that the defender might reach at the last minute.

AFTER THE RECEPTION

Finally, let's discuss the receiver after he receives the ball. First, he must be taught to put the ball away quickly, so as not to fumble it if he is hit immediately. He should tuck the ball under one arm or the other, with one end of the ball in the crook of the elbow and his hand covering the other end.

Next, the receiver must be taught to turn and drive directly upfield as quickly as possible. The direction he pivots depends on his natural feel of knowing where the defenders are. He should turn upfield as quickly as possible so he can survey the situation and run accordingly. It is hard to teach a receiver to be a good runner after the catch, as this is generally a natural ability. At this point he uses what speed or agility he does possess to gain more yardage.

Here the receiver executes another important fundamental—*putting the ball away as he turns to run from the defender.*

pass
defense

During the 1966 season, the Packers gave up the fewest points in the NFL. In 1965 and 1966, the Packers' pass defense was rated the best in football. Our defense is very proud of its reputation. While other teams may have an outstanding front four, or some other outstanding defensive feature, no team has· the overall defensive balance the Packers have.

Many times our defense has won games for us or protected a slim lead by coming up with a great play to stop the other team just when it seemed they would score. I remember Herb Adderley's great block of a Viking field goal attempt, which saved a game for us. And who will ever forget the interception by Tom Brown in the NFL title game against Dallas? There are many, many more instances I could list. Let's just say the Packer defense is pro football's best.

In talking about defense, we now come to a category very dear to the heart of my roommate, Henry Jordan—defenses against passing. I mention this because during training camp, Henry really tries to get in and flatten me in scrimmages, claiming this is the only chance he gets during the year, and he wants me to think that he is still the best tackle in the National Football League. He really makes an effort to get in there, and he's pretty difficult to keep out when he wants to get to the passer.

Probably the best defense against passing is a strong pass rush. One of the best rushes I've ever faced is that of the Los Angeles Rams. They may not have won any titles in the last few years, but their pass rush has created havoc among some of the more outstanding teams in the league. The Rams' defense has almost completely thwarted many passing attacks. If you are going to put pressure on the passer, you must have at least

A true champion rises to the occasion and pulls off the big play. Herb Adderley is shown here blocking a field goal against the Vikings, which preserved a close win for the Packers. Hank Gremminger picked up the blocked kick and converted it into a touchdown for the Packers, changing the course of the game.

a few of your front four who can get in there and create some
pressure.

The passing game is built around timing and perfection,
and the best way to throw off timing is to force the quarterback
to move around or force him out of his normal routine of being
able to get back, get set, and deliver the ball. If you force him
to scramble around, you upset his timing (although some
scramblers do a mighty fine job of passing). Fran Tarkenton

The best pass defense is a good pass rush. Here, Henry Jordan chases the Rams' Roman Gabriel.

of the Vikings makes a living by scrambling and converting broken pass routes into gainers. He will elude a rusher, turn outside his own end, and will ad lib, so to speak, on the rest of the play. Still, one of the best ways to defeat the passing game is to develop a strong pass rush.

Earlier I mentioned that when you encounter defensive tackles who play off the ball and fail to charge, you can throw the ball almost at will unless they get exceptional coverage in the secondary. You cannot play soft off the line of scrimmage and have a good pass rush too, so most teams with a soft playing tackle usually have a strong charging one on the other side. They complement one another.

I am thinking specifically now of the Dallas Cowboys, who have Bob Lilly, a slashing type tackle, on one side and Stevens on the other. Although Stevens comes hard on occasion, he tends to be one who will read the play a little more before he makes his move. They complement one another very well. On occasion Lilly will stay off the ball and read, depending on the defense called and the offensive formation facing it.

I already mentioned the Rams and their outstanding pass rush. They have two big, strong ends in Dave Jones and Lamar Lundy who do a fine job of getting deep penetration into the backfield. Jones, particularly in the last couple of years, has started to mix up his defensive play. He'll jump way inside the offensive tackle on occasion and really come boring in on the passer. If he does this effectively, and the quarterback is not able to get outside, Jones can get quite a bit of deep penetration and force the quarterback into some mistakes.

The Ram tackles, Rosie Grier and Merlin Olsen, are a nice study in contrast. Grier is usually the waiting type tackle, though he still comes hard on occasion. But Olsen is more the slashing type, the hard charging tackle who will come boring in. Here again, you have a fine complement.

When Dave Hanner was with the Packers, we had this same complement. Henry Jordan was a slashing, daring type tackle, and Hanner was the reader, the conservative type who sat and covered for Henry.

These examples point up how a good, strong pass rush by the defense is one of the more effective methods of defeating the passing game. But there are other methods, such as blocking the offensive ends. Certain defenses afford you the opportunity to knock down the receivers. (The zone defense diagram later

One of the toughest tackles to execute a draw or screen pass against, because of his deliberate style of play, was the former "Grandaddy" of the Packers, Dave "Hawg" Hanner.

in the chapter shows where the defender can block the receiver as the latter starts to run. The accompanying photo illustrates this point very well.)

Usually the best method of knocking down an end is to surprise him—catch him completely by surprise as he comes off the line of scrimmage. If you have a defensive man coming at him really hard, this will often catch him by surprise. This tends to unnerve him momentarily and may even throw his whole route out of timing. That is the idea—to knock the timing out of the pass route.

The defensive back coming up to try to knock the pass receiver down as a way of defending takes a big gamble if he doesn't have someone to cover for him. If the receiver is experienced and has been alerted to this sort of thing, he may completely dodge the block and be off and running for a score. I have seen this happen on occasion. A receiver would slip the block of the defensive man, cut cleanly by him and have the quarterback lay the ball in his hands on the run, and it was a quick score. I think defenses today are quite careful about letting one of their defensive men come up to knock someone down unless they have someone deeper to cover in case the defensive man misses and the offensive receiver is still running free.

The Chicago Bears are notorious for knocking down receivers. I don't know if they were taught this system through the years because of the element of surprise or the change of pace, but they are very good at it. Their linebackers, particularly, are good at knocking down receivers. Many times they will be

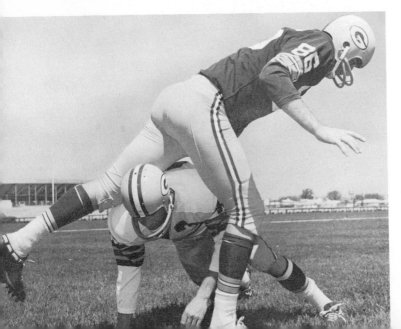

This is a maneuver that many defensive cornerbacks employ when in a zone defense. Since the defender is responsible for the short zone, he can come up fast and throw a block at the receiver just as the latter is starting off the line. The Chicago Bears employ this tactic on numerous occasions.

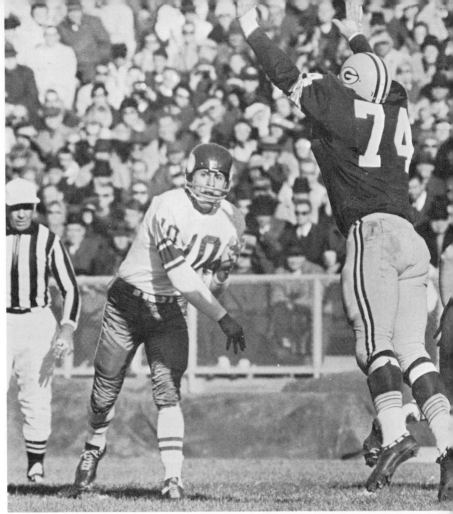

This photo clearly shows what damage can be done by a penetrating tackle (Henry Jordan of the Packers) on a pass play. Fran Tarkenton had to throw more to his right and threw behind his receiver.

playing off the tight end or a wide receiver and as he starts out on a pass, they'll cut him down. This again is an effective way of fouling up the timing of the offensive pass game, but keep in mind that if you miss, you leave yourself open to a huge gain or six points.

I mention the Bears because when I was a rookie, Tobin Rote hit Billy Howton with a long pass for a score after Howton neatly sidestepped a Bear halfback who was trying to block him. I have not seen that happen many times in recent years. Most of the time when they try to knock down a receiver, they have some type of zone coverage, either with the halfback or the safety man lying back to protect.

Getting back to the defensive line and rushing the passer, the defensive tackles try to get as much penetration as they can into the pocket. This is what causes a quarterback more trouble than the wide, deep outside rush of the ends. If you can get good penetration from the defensive tackles, you give the quarterback the problem of being unable to see his receivers.

Secondly, a tackle can actually penetrate an area to the point where there is no more pocket. He has crushed in the front side of the pocket. And if the pocket breaks down, the passing game breaks down. A good defensive line rush will try to get as much penetration as possible from the tackles and have the wide rush of the ends contain the quarterback. If he has to retreat from these onrushing tackles and backs up, the ends then have a shot at him.

Many times today you see an excellent pass rush plus blitzing linebackers. In fact, you even see teams blitzing their safety man. Here the idea is to overload or outnumber the offensive blockers (should you have too many receivers out, or if you have all the defensive men accounted for) in an attempt to force the passer, if he does get the pass away, to hurry his throw. And if he takes his normal time, because the defense outnumbers the blockers, one of the defensive men can slip in and throw the passer for a loss. It's a very exciting type of play, defensively speaking, because all these men are charging at the passer, trying to break down the coverage assigned to block the defense and hoping to slip someone through. It's a very good defensive technique if it's used well.

In order to make your passing offense function at its maximum, it is necessary to possess a thorough knowledge of the defenses you will be facing every time you step on the field. Most teams and every coach will have their own favorite adaptations of how to shoot down your passing efforts most effectively. Your best chances of beating them are in your knowledge of how they probably will defense you.

Undoubtedly one of the most astute defensive coaches in the National Football League is Packer assistant Phil Bengtson, who has helped us in preparing this chapter.

Defense against passing is our big concern in the National Football League, and we spend a lot of time on it. It has evolved into what is pretty much a standard defense: namely, the four-three. In that four-three defense, the linebackers are lined up near the line of scrimmage with one of them usually opposite a tight end. They try to give underneath coverage to flanking patterns, so it's a combination actually of the linebackers in the short areas, the two halfbacks and two safeties in the deep areas. This, of course, is combined with rushing the passer, which we consider one of the most important phases of pass defense. Briefly, this is an overall pass defense.

DEFENSIVE ALIGNMENT NOTING POSITIONS OF LINEMEN

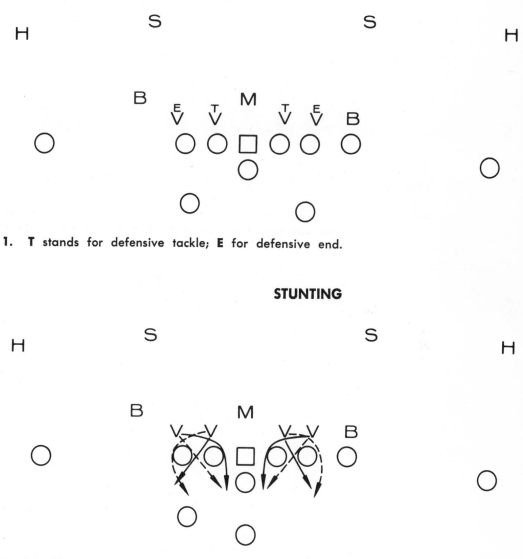

1. **T** stands for defensive tackle; **E** for defensive end.

STUNTING

1. In addition to the simple stunts diagramed above, line-backers or even safeties can become involved in a stunting-blitzing action.

RED DOG

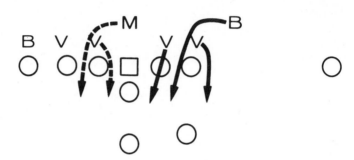

1. A very common red dog maneuver is the one in bold lines with occasional combined effort through the one in broken lines.

BLITZ

1. When more than one linebacker (and sometimes a safety) takes part in a blitzing action, you can observe several techniques.

Ray Nitschke (66) of the Packers shows a good example of the blitz. Willie Davis (87) is also putting on pressure. The quarterback running for his life is Rudy Bukich of the Bears.

The conventional formation that we face has a tight end, and we normally will have a linebacker facing this player. He will key this end, of course, as to run or pass. One of his assignments for pass defense is to make it difficult for the end to get off the line of scrimmage. We refer to this as chucking, and the more we can do of this, the easier the job of the deep defenders in covering deep passes.

On the spread side, normally our linebacker will be close in to his own defensive end, but we do have certain defenses where the linebacker will line up out near the split offensive end. His assignment out there is to slow the split end as he comes down the field. We very seldom actually block the end or attempt to knock him down, although some teams do. The linebacker then helps the deep defender underneath on shorter patterns, enabling the deep man to defend against the long one.

The third linebacker, whom we call the middle linebacker, is concerned primarily with running defense. However, he plays an important part in our pass coverage, as he is back in what

This shot dramatically illustrates the quick reaction of the defensive backs in professional football. The Packers' Herb Adderley has his left hand on the ball almost as quickly as the Lions' Pat Studstill. This is why a pass just barely off course can be easily intercepted or broken up.

we call a hook area and is in a position to stop delayed passes, react to screen passes, and furnish underneath coverage on any pass pattern going across the middle.

Our defensive halfbacks and safeties are really highly specialized football players. We think that certain physical requirements must be there in order to meet all of the challenging assignments that we face from week to week. This is particularly true of the defensive halfbacks, who are required almost by themselves to cover those speedy split ends or flankers. These halfbacks are selected mostly for their speed and physical reactions. As they study their position and gain experience, they develop the techniques and the other requirements so necessary for these key defensive spots.

Although they are often isolated on short passes, the safeties are more apt to have help underneath by a linebacker or by combining in their coverage with a halfback. On other occasions they perform as a free safety in a zone type of defense or a defense where all the offensive receivers are not employed in the pass pattern.

Although the individual requirements are absolutely necessary, we think that coordinating these four men—the two halfbacks and the two safeties—into a unit, and combining this with the linebackers, is of greatest importance. The Packers think that the coordination of the coverage promotes a better type of defense against passes and prompts interceptions, which is the big item we are striving for. An interception is as encouraging a move as a defensive team can make and probably is as discouraging a development as the offensive team can suffer. As a result, we are always concentrating on picking off as many interceptions as possible.

In order to accomplish this, our defense must develop quick reaction to the ball. The purpose of four-deep pass defense is to stay between the receiver and the goal line in order to prevent the long pass and/or the touchdown. The requirement of staying in position makes it necessary for the safeties and halfbacks, or anyone else covering a deep receiver, to see the ball leave the passer's hand. Then they must be able to react to the ball in the air and thus improve their chances of either knocking it down or making an interception.

A well-timed move by a defensive back can "strip" the receiver from the ball. Here the defender's hands are coming down hard and pulling sharply against the arms of the receiver.

Playing the ball is a big and necessary fundamental of pass defense. We feel that when the ball is in the air, it belongs as much to us as it does to the offensive team. Once the ball is in flight, we feel that an aggressive move in playing it is absolutely essential for a sound defense.

Basically, the organization of the defense comes under two categories—a zone defense or a man-to-man defense. Most of the teams in our league combine both, using a zone part of the time, man-to-man part of the time, and then move into certain defensive patterns that result in a combination of man-to-man and zone.

A zone defense is exactly what the name implies—each player in the coverage is assigned to a certain area of the field. Any receiver coming into that area must be covered by that player.

Each one of the eligible offensive receivers is covered man-to-man in our four-deep pass defense. The two halfbacks will cover the split end and the flanker, or the receivers on the extremities of the line. One safety will cover the tight end, and the other will take the remaining halfback, leaving the fullback

DEFENSES

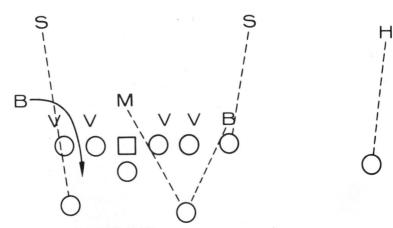

MAN-TO-MAN

1.   Except when there is a red dog or blitz, or a short yardage situation, you seldom see very much man-for-man defense today.

2.   If there is man-for-man coverage, the defensive players are responsible for the offensive player noted. (The middle linebacker and outside linebacker would be responsible for the fullback, depending on what his action was.)

to be covered by the linebacker in the area where the fullback runs his pattern.

As mentioned before, most of our defenses are restricted to four linemen, so we usually have a four-three defense. That doesn't mean that the four front men are always in the same position or that the three linebackers are always in the same position. There are wide varieties of four-three defenses. Some of the men play in front of the center, some of the men line up in front of either guard, thus making what we refer to as an odd-man line or an even-man line.

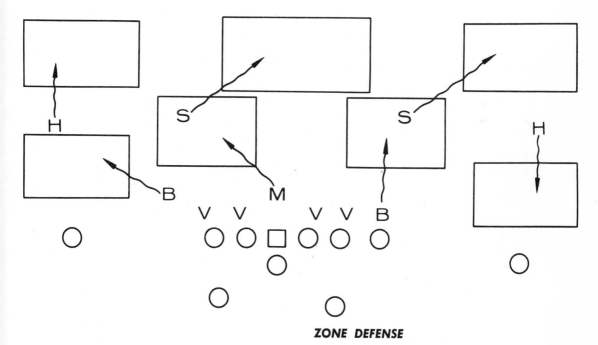

ZONE DEFENSE

1. The zone defense against passes simply means that defenders are responsible for areas or zones rather than for individuals.

2. This is an excellent defense to prevent the long gainer, but though the areas shown appear to cover most routes pretty well, a good passing team with intelligent pass route execution and quick recognition can eat it up.

3. For this reason, no one plays strictly zone in professional football.

4. There are all types of pass defense used today. We have talked about only three common ones. You, can readily see how combining zone and key coverage, or using a weak side zone, with these defenses we've discussed makes it hard for you to figure out what the defense is trying to do.

Linebackers are employed as linemen in a wide variety of blitzes. We may blitz one man, we may blitz two line-backers, or we may blitz all three of them, thus giving quite a variety of play and a fancy assortment of problems for the offensive pass protection.

The six-man line, as referred to in our league, usually describes the two outside linebackers lining up in a three-point stance on the line of scrimmage and penetrating at the snap of the ball.

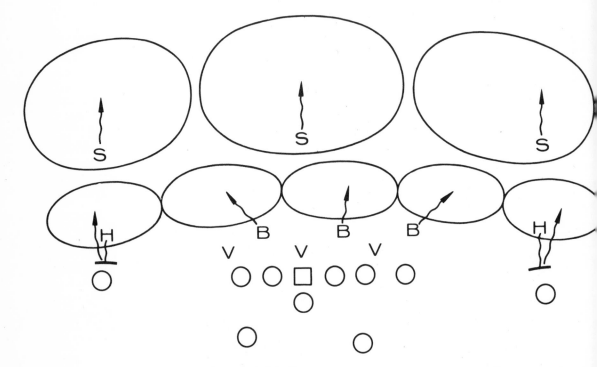

PREVENT DEFENSE

1. The prevent defense is designed to prevent the long strike by the offensive team.

2. The three deep defenders are very deep, with the responsibility of letting no one behind them.

3. The linebackers and halfbacks on the outside are responsible for the "underneath" areas. (The halfbacks may come up quickly and try to "chop down" the receivers also.)

4. As you can see, if executed properly, this defense covers a lot of area.

5. There is practically no pass rush, however, unless you have three good rushers.

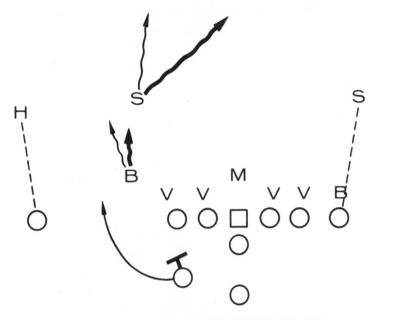

FREE SAFETY OR KEY

1. This defense is based on "keying" into the offensive backfield and is probably the most widely used pass coverage defense today. It's tough to throw deep down the middle against this.

2. Defensive linebackers today have such outstanding speed that they are capable of doing a good job of covering most halfbacks. Thus, the weak side safety can afford to play center field and prevent any deep passes in that area.

3. The key usually used is the halfback. If he blocks, the safety is "freed" immediately to play the ball. Even if the halfback swings out of the backfield, the safety still would not cover him until he got very deep down the field, since the linebacker can cover the halfback almost anywhere else.

4. If the other defensive backs are alert on this defense, they will play tougher to the outside because they know they have help to the deep inside by the "free safety."

5. Obviously, if you are going to throw effectively down deep in the middle, you must hold the weak side safety at home.

the
kicking
game

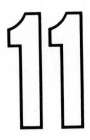

One of the greatest means a quarterback has of increasing his effectiveness is to combine his talents with punting. The fact that a passing quarterback can also punt not only increases his value to his team, but also creates a doubt in the minds of the defense in critical instances on whether he is going to kick or cross them up and throw in a gambling situation.

There is no single element that makes a punter great. Most quarterbacks have excellent timing and coordination, or they wouldn't be playing the position. As a result, it would be my recommendation that you make an earnest effort to become a punter. The chances are that you will be successful.

By the time you reach the professional ranks there may be a specialist on the roster who does nothing but punting and/or place kicking, but even then there may be instances where your ability to punt in a specific situation may prove of great value to your team.

There is no single physical requirement needed to become a great punter, although the taller player with longer legs does have the advantage of that extra leg snap required to deliver long, booming punts. Still, one of the greatest kickers of all times was Yale Lary of the Detroit Lions, who stood only 5 feet 11 inches and weighed 190 pounds. Much the same can be said for Bobby Joe Green of the Bears, who may not weigh even that much. Both were capable of delivering high, spiraling kicks that gave their teammates plenty of time to get down under the ball and stop the return before it got started.

Yale Lary once told me that each year at training camp he had to start over almost from scratch. His muscles had become stiff over the long winter layoff, and his routine for getting

229

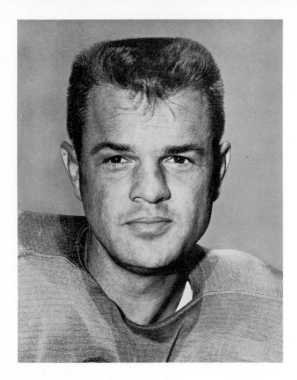

Yale Lary of the Detroit Lions.

back into shape was a deliberate and sometimes painful one. He spread his legs far apart and locked his hands around the right knee. Then he pulled his forehead down to the knee to loosen the hamstring muscles of his kicking leg. He loosened up the groin muscles by rotating on his hips. In addition, he did sit-ups and ran a lot to get his legs into overall condition.

Early in the year, Yale started his kicking without a ball and merely went through the motions. When he got around to using the ball, he kicked only lightly and worked on his form rather than distance. In fact, it was about the third week in practice before he ever really kicked at all. Yale confirms our feeling that almost any quarterback can become an acceptable kicker. Just what heights he reaches will depend a great deal on how hard and how long he practices.

THE SNAP

As for the fundamentals included in punting, they start with getting ready for the snap. First, it becomes necessary for you to keep your eye on the ball from the moment you take your position, some 12 to 14 yards behind the center. The body should be bent slightly at the waist with the weight evenly distributed, the knees flexed and the left foot about six inches forward. However, make sure that the left foot is not anchored. If you touch your little fingers together, the hands can be spread to form a cup to receive the ball and, at the same time, offer a target for the center. From that point on, it becomes a matter of concentrating on receiving and kicking the ball. At no time should the kicker be concerned with the rushers.

Once the ball is received from center, it should be quickly brought into position in front of and across the body at about the level of the right hip. The heel of the ball should be covered with the palm of the right hand, with the thumb at the mid-seam. The nose should be cradled in the left hand. This must be done quickly, as no more than two seconds can be allowed to get the kick on its way.

If the punt is executed correctly, a good long, spiraling kick can be heard as well as seen. It will sound like a thud more than a big boom. In order to obtain this spiral for better distance, the ball should be dropped with the laces pointed up and to the outside. If the laces should end straight up, the ball will travel end over end, rather than in the preferred spiral.

Many kickers attempt to drop the ball low on the instep at a 20-degree angle. However, some outstanding kickers strike the ball unusually high on the instep and almost at right angles with the line of the shoe.

Dropping the ball becomes one of the most important phases of the punt. A good drop will go far in resulting in a good kick, and a bad drop will end most times in a bad result. The right hand always controls the ball and acts as a guide for the release. The left hand performs the function of a soft guide.

Punters vary on the number of steps they take, but most of the better ones are three-step kickers. The first stride is pretty much of a half step with the left foot moving in the direction of the intended flight of the ball. The second step brings the right foot into action, the hands moving up simultaneously to get the ball into position for the drop. The third step involves a cocking of the kicking leg and ankle with the toes pointed inward and downward.

On a normal kick, the ball should be released just below waist level. The contact of the foot takes place just above knee height. If an especially high kick is desired to gain the advantage of a strong tail wind, the nose of the ball should be placed upward and it should be released above the waist with the contact taking place at about thigh level. For a low kick into the wind, the ball should be dropped at about the thigh, and contact should take place just below the knee.

A

B

C

When you take the basic position for the snap, focus your eyes on the ball and never lose your concentration on it. Take your stance some twelve to fourteen yards behind the center and bend slightly at the waist, weight evenly distributed and knees flexed. The left foot should be about six inches forward, but not anchored. The hand is spread to form a cup, as Boyd Dowler illustrates in this punting sequence. Concentration should be maintained on receiving and kicking the ball—without concern for the rushers (A). B. First, the ball must be "looked" into the kicker's hands. Once the ball is received, it must be brought quickly into position in front of and across the body, at the level of the right hip (C & D). E. The heel of the ball should be pretty well covered by the palm of the right hand, with the thumb at the midseam. The nose is steadied by the left hand. F. At the point of contact, the laces should be facing up and to the outside center to obtain a spiral and produce maximum distance. Most punters try to kick low on the instep, the ball at a 20-degree angle to the shoe. With no more than a couple of seconds to get the kick away, the stride must be begun and the ball dropped in almost a single motion. Most bad kicks are the result of a poor drop from the hands to the foot. The right hand controls the ball and is the guide for the release. The left hand serves as a rather soft guide (G & H). I. As the kick is begun, the right leg is extended and the ankle locked, with the toes turned down and in.

G

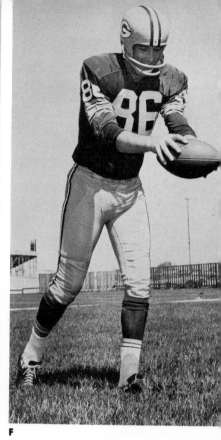

D   E   F

H   I

A good follow-through must be practiced for the best results. Shown here are two vital stages of the follow-through.

FOLLOW-THROUGH

Once the ball has been contacted, it must receive proper follow-through to attain maximum distance. The follow-through must be accomplished with stability and balance, which is not always easy, with a strong whipping leg action. The right foot ends up near the kicker's head.

The arms must serve as a balancing factor and allow the kicker to come down approximately on the spot where the punt began. This strong follow-through is a must for all punters, the same as the proper follow-through is necessary in swinging a baseball bat, a golf club, or a tennis racket.

FAKE KICK AND PASS

Earlier we mentioned that a good punter also enhances his value by keeping the defense alert to the possibility of his passing in a punting situation. Many times this fake kick and pass can take your team out of a real hole. Pulling off a fake punt and pass becomes a matter of assuming a normal punting position and going on from there. A punter-passer must take his initial jab step with his left foot as if starting a normal punting stride. Then he must be able to rise up quickly and pass without hesitation. Of course, the short span of time involved will necessitate a rather short pass. These normally are directed into the flat zone or to the split end on a down-and-out maneuver.

When faking a kicking position, the key to success is starting the motion exactly as though the play is to become a punt. Receive the ball and position it exactly as though beginning a punt, as shown in the first four pictures. Then take a jab step with your left foot, turn quickly, and throw. Since most kickers are not necessarily great passers, we recommend shooting either for the halfback in the flat zone or the split end about ten yards from the line of scrimmage.

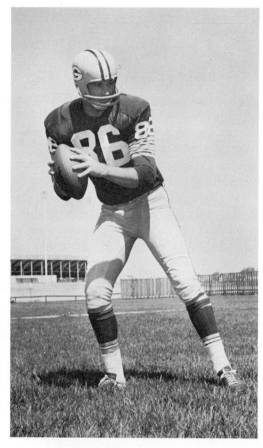

FAKE KICK AND RUN

One other variance of the fake punt and pass play is that of the fake kick and run. This is performed in much the same style at the beginning, with the quarterback taking the normal position as if to receive a ball for punting. Once the push-off is made on the left foot, it then becomes necessary to change directions immediately. Pivot on the left foot and run to the right, tucking the ball under the arm immediately. Normally, the best avenue of escape is toward the sidelines and then downfield as soon as possible, since the shortest distance between any two points is a straight line.

Since you are basically a passer in the defense's eyes, it will be difficult for you to pull off this fake, but it is worth a gamble under the right circumstances, and you should learn the fundamentals on how to perform it in the most effective fashion.

On a fake punt and run, follow the same style as in the fake and pass. Start off on the left foot and then change direction quickly. Normally, it is easier to run to the right. Swing wide, if possible, to get outside the charging linemen and cut downfield as soon as you can.

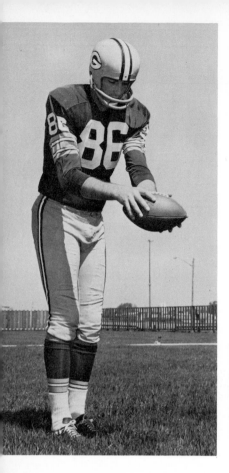

QUICK KICK

Another advantage in being a combination passer-punter involves your ability to quick kick when the occasion is right. While this play seldom occurs in professional football, it is used quite often in collegiate and high school football. Such outstanding college coaches as Frank Broyles of Arkansas employs it often. Since high school secondaries are much less sophisticated than either professional or collegiate defenses, they are often susceptible to quick kicking. A good quick kick practically nullifies any possibility of a return.

As for the mechanics on a quick kick, it normally is performed from only about six yards behind the line of scrimmage. There is little time to get the kick off, so you must be well schooled in your fundamentals.

Of several quick kick methods, Yale Lary recommends the one referred to as the rocker. In this particular technique, the kicker lines up in a normal running position with the single wingback or similar offenses. Upon receipt of the ball, the kicker quickly rocks back on his left foot and swings forward on the same foot. The ball is released at about thigh level. The right foot strikes the ball just below knee height, and the laces are almost on a line with the laces on the kicker's right shoe. This kick normally will be one of low trajectory with a great deal of roll and quite often an unorthodox bounce that makes it exceedingly difficult for the defense to handle.

BAD PASSES FROM CENTER

With as many passes as a punter takes from his center in the course of a normal season, some erratic ones must be expected. When this happens to a punter, he has one basic maneuver—to shift his body and get in front of the ball first. This is a principle that is applied by baseball catchers to wild pitches.

It is absolutely wrong for a punter to attempt to reach out and grab a wide pass or stoop down from his hips to catch a low one. Instead, he should shift his feet so that the body is directly in the line of the flight of the ball and facing downfield at all times. In the case of the low punt, the punter should kneel down, rather than stoop over, to first make sure he has blocked the flight of the ball.

Once the ball has been fielded, his kicking motion then becomes the same as in any normal punt except that he must hurry it in order to make sure that he does get the kick away.

When a bad snap comes from the center, drop to one knee and be sure to have your body serve as a backstop for the ball in case you do not field it cleanly. If you are going to bail out of a bad situation, first you must catch the ball, and be sure it does not go past you for added loss of yardage. A baseball outfielder is taught to field ground balls in much the same manner.

PUNTING PERSONALITIES

Over the years, several of the real quarterbacking greats have also been excellent punters. Names that come to mind quickly are Sammy Baugh, Bob Waterfield, and Norm Van Brocklin. They were outstanding kickers. Of course, there are some today who punt on occasions. Earl Morrall punted in some instances when he was with the Lions. In addition, King Hill has performed some punting with the Eagles. Ed Brown did practically all of the punting when he was with the Bears, prior to joining the Steelers and later the Colts. My good friend, Zeke Bratkowski, punted for the Bears when he was playing in Chicago. There undoubtedly are many other good quarterbacks who doubled as punters. Young players should work at this aspect of the game in order to round out their capabilities.

SPECIALTIES IN KICKING

The quarterback can, of course, increase his value to the team by specializing, if nothing more than in the art of holding the ball for field goals and extra points. There is an interesting story about how I became a holder with the Packers. I had never held much prior to that. I held only a few times in college, the reason being that I was on the other end of the play and kicked the ball.

When I came to the Packers, Tobin Rote was the holder for Fred Cone, the kicker at the time. One day I was standing around watching them after practice, and Tobin said, "I don't know why I am doing all this work all the time. You could relieve me of some of this. Get in here and hold a few." So I did. I had observed Tobin on occasion—how he received the ball from center, moved it so the strings were to the front, and so on.

Fred Cone was a very patient person and had a tremendous sense of humor. We had a lot of fun as I was learning, for he was very dedicated and took a lot of time to work with me and make a holder out of me. He and Tobin soon did the trick, and I have been holding the ball for field goals and extra points on our team ever since.

The only time I have ever missed was when I suffered a broken hand in 1963. Jesse Whittenton held the ball then, or we had someone as a back-up holder who, late in the game, wanted a chance to hold a couple.

You'll find a lot of quarterbacks in the league who are extra point holders and/or field goal holders because most of them have good hands. This is a requisite for being a good quarterback, so they can take the snap with ease. They can catch it well coming back from the center and, since they are sure fingered, are able to place it down quickly.

You should keep in mind, if you are going to try to become a holder, that after you have spaced yourself 6½ or 7 yards back from the center (depending on how far your kicker likes to kick from) you must learn to take the snap very quickly and get it down onto the ground so that the kicker can continue the kick as quickly as possible. Approximately 1.3 seconds is the period we allow, so you see there is not much time to get the ball and put it down. That 1.3 seconds is the total time we feel we have to kick the ball, from the time it is snapped from center until it is placed and on its way.

I line up with my left knee on the ground, opposite the spot from which the kicker is going to boot the ball, and place the tips of my left hand on the spot where the ball will be placed. Then I extend my right hand about two feet off the ground out toward the center to give him a target at which to shoot, much as a baseball catcher gives his pitcher a target with his mitt.

The center then snaps the ball to this right hand. I never really take my left hand, the marking hand, off the ground. Some holders do. Some will mark the spot with their hand for a second so that the kicker sees it well, then point both hands for receiving the ball.

There also are a number of holders in the league who are defensive backs. Here again, these are players who must have good hands. If they didn't have sure hands and were playing on defense, they'd be out of luck, because they must be able to intercept passes. As a result, many times these men also make outstanding extra point and field goal holders.

I like the snap to come back as low to the ground as possible. It should be just about knee height. My right leg is extended and bent slightly with the foot on the ground. My right hand is extended just about knee height, and that's where the ball should arrive.

If the ball comes back much higher than this, it throws the whole timing off. Then the holder must raise up, grab the ball, pull it down, get it into position, and hope that the kicker hasn't taken his eye off it and been upset by following the flight

A

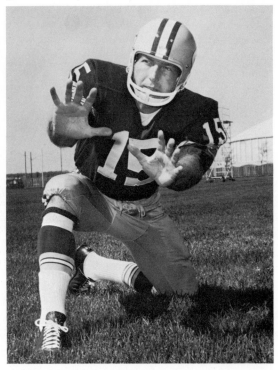

B

C

A. Marking spot for the kicker. **B.** Ready to receive snap from center on a field goal attempt. **C.** The holder is in the motion of moving the ball onto the spot for the kick, getting the ball down as quickly as possible. Give your kicker a consistent hold every time. With a lot of practice, you can learn to "spin" the ball after it's down in order to have the laces in front of the ball, away from the kicker. (On long kicks in windy weather, laces to one side or the other can cause the ball to drift well off the target.)

Right: I'm just completing the "turn" of the ball (laces forward) before Paul Hornung kicks it.

of the ball coming up. A high pass upsets the kicker more than it does the holder.

Place the ball practically straight up and down. Most of the kickers I have held for prefer it this way—Jerry Kramer being the one exception. Line it up so the laces are away from the kicker, so he has a smooth surface to kick at. Hold it straight —don't tilt it from side to side—with the laces pointing toward the goal post.

I hold only with my index finger on top of the ball and apply just enough pressure to keep the ball upright. Make sure never to push the ball down into the ground and create a vise-like effect. The finger just rests firmly on it so that the ball can be kicked out from underneath with ease.

Many kickers have their own little quirks. One of the biggest differences between Fred Cone, when he was kicking with the Packers, and Paul Hornung was that Fred never wanted the strings on the side of the ball. If you could not get the strings in front, he said, get them in back. If the ball came back, the strings had to be either closer to the front or closer to the back—never on the side. If they were on the side, I just rotated them one way or the other, whichever was easiest. He would actually kick the ball with the laces staring him in the face— striking it just underneath the laces. It would go very true to target.

If the laces are on the side of the ball and it has to travel any distance at all in the wind, those laces will actually move the ball several feet off line and can cause you to miss a field goal. That was the reason Fred wanted them either front or rear and would kick either way.

Hornung was just the opposite. He never wanted the laces looking him in the face. He preferred them to the front, of course, and I have always tried to put them in front for any kicker. However, if I couldn't, then I would just let them stay somewhat on the side for Paul, because he would literally panic if he saw those laces staring at him.

Still, on one of the finest field goals he ever kicked, I had no choice. We bobbled the ball from center, it skipped around on the ground, and I finally slapped it down with the laces toward him. He kicked it for about a 35-yard field goal against the Chicago Bears in a tight situation. They put on a good rush, so I didn't even have time to turn the ball, and I don't think he realized he had done it until it was all over.

Among the fine field goal men I have been able to hold for is Jim Martin, who played with the Lions for several years and later with the Baltimore Colts. As I recall, I only held for Jim one time, and this was in a Pro Bowl game, where I held for most of the people who are not on our ball club. Jim had a tremendously strong leg. The ball literally zoomed out as he kicked it, and he had a fine follow-through, an excellent kicking style.

I have also held for Tommy Davis, who plays for the 49'ers. Tommy has one of the smoothest, easiest kicking motions I have ever seen. He is almost nonchalant about it, and yet he's one of the finest kickers around today. He can really boom the ball in from long distances. In addition, Tommy is an outstanding punter.

When he was with the Packers, Fred Cone was a great kicker, though his style wasn't classic. His kicking action was smooth, but he approached the ball in kind of a hoppy, bumpy movement. He didn't flow up to it, in other words. Still, Fred was one of the finest kickers for whom I have ever held. He certainly was one of the most patient, because he had to put up with me when I was just learning how to hold the ball properly for him.

Of course, I have held the ball more for Paul Hornung than for anyone else, and in my book he is as good a kicker as there is. He has suffered through a lot of adversity. He has been hurt a great deal, being the full time performer that he is. This also has hurt his average in field goal kicking. Many times on third down I have called him in a pass pattern because he is a fine pass receiver. If the pass was incomplete, he had to come right back and kick. Paul has a good style and an extra strong leg. When he is in form, he is probably as good as anyone in the business.

Ben Agajanian was with us in 1961, when Hornung was in the service, and did an outstanding job for us. This fellow, for his age, was as fine a kicker as I have ever seen. He was unbelievable. Hornung used to kid him and say, "With that big wedge of a toe you've got up there, how could anybody miss?" Ben did have an awfully wide toe on his kicking shoe, but he could really kick the football. The team would stand around after practice just to watch him kick with such tremendous consistency. I don't know what his age was at that time, but he was just fantastic.

Believe it or not, Jimmy Taylor of the Packers has kicked on occasion, due to injury or someone not being in the lineup. I have held for him in practice on a number of occasions. If Jimmy worked at it, he probably could be a fine kicker. He is good now but could improve with a little practice, as he is a very jerky type kicker.

He gets up to the ball and then almost slaps his foot at it, like he's going to kick it and get his foot back in a hurry. He kicks at it with a kind of a snake action of darting his foot out and back, although his whole body motion produces a definite follow-through.

Jerry Kramer is a study in himself. The best way to describe Jerry's field goal kicking is that he is like the golfer who scuffs the short chip shot to the green, yet knocks a 90-yard wedge shot six inches from the cup. Jerry is uncanny, hitting them sometimes from 30, 35, 40 yards out, and yet we can get 10 or 15 yards in, and he'll kick the ball through sideways. He might hit a spiral and go through. I never can really figure

Don Chandler of the Packers is one of the great punters and field goal kickers. These illustrations show his faultless form, in both punting and place kicking.

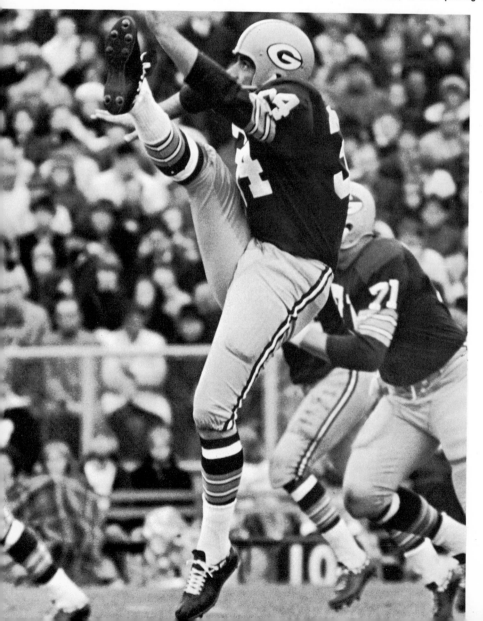

Jerry out. He has the strangest kicking style you have ever seen. As he approaches the ball, he gets a good lick at it, has a very strong leg and good kicking action, but as he kicks, he doesn't swing up and glide on through the ball. He kicks and then plants his right foot down hard. It's quite a style. You have to see it to appreciate it.

I have saved our current kicker, Don Chandler, for last because I feel he is a prime study for youngsters. For years Don was the outstanding punter and place kicker for the New York Giants. He took up field goal kicking late in his career, after

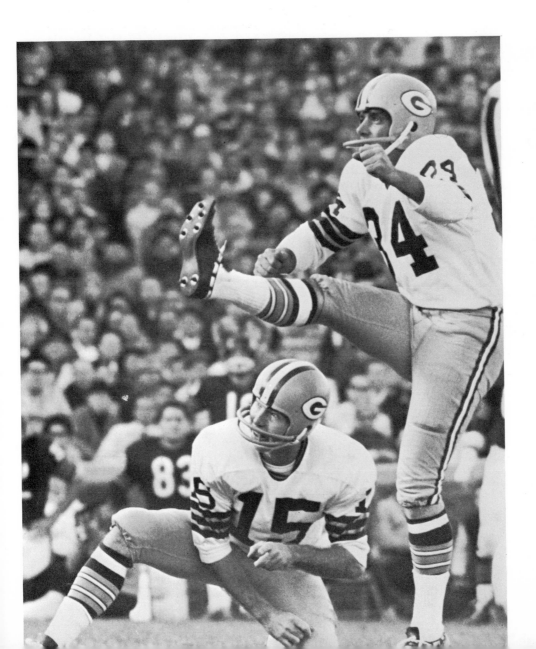

being strictly a punter. Pat Summerall had done the field goal kicking for the Giants, and when Pat retired, Chandler took over.

The reason I point this out is that youngsters who have not given too much thought to it should attempt to develop a knack for punting and place kicking. This can be an asset to your team now, and you may create a position for yourself later on a professional team. All professional teams are looking for good kickers. If you can punt and place kick, you are doubly valuable because this enables a team to carry one less player.

Getting back to Chandler, he has a smooth kicking style, possesses a very strong leg, meets the ball well, and, for a fellow who took up place kicking several years after he had been punting consistently, does an outstanding job. I hope he can keep booting them through the uprights for us for a long time to come and that I will have the pleasure of holding for him.

There will be some rare quarterbacks who also can increase their contributions to their clubs by becoming place kickers. As mentioned earlier, I did a lot of place kicking in high school and in college. Young players certainly would do well to spend some time on this phase of the game.

As for the mechanics of place kicking, the records show that Lou Groza probably stands at the head of the class on all-around place kicking. Lou is a good friend of mine and has talked to me at some length on his technique of booting the ball—both on kicking off and for extra points.

KICKING OFF

One of the great advantages in kicking off is the opportunity to use a tee for the ball. Of course, this helps get the ball airborne quicker, which is especially helpful to young kickers. Normally, the ball is placed on the tee straight up and down so as to assure accuracy in direction. In many parts of the country wind becomes an important factor during the football season, so this straight up and down placement also aids in keeping the ball from being blown off center.

As in placing the ball for extra points, it should be set so the laces face straight toward the goal posts at the opposite end of the field. The problem of the laces causing the ball to fly right or left, if not placed head on, is the same as discussed in the paragraphs on holding the ball for extra points. The wind resistance would be uneven, and the ball would fly toward one side of the field or the other, instead of straight ahead.

Lou Groza told me that he attempted to kick the ball all

the way into the end zone. While length obviously is desirable, the matter of height on the ball also becomes important in order to allow the kicking team to get downfield and drop the ball carrier as soon as possible.

This calls for a note of caution. Never try to swing the leg so that the foot will deliberately kick the ball upward. This will lead to lofting the ball or giving it a motion of squirting directly up in the air instead of down the field.

Always attempt to kick through the ball. If you drive your right foot directly through it—slightly beneath the center—the height will come automatically.

The proper target to shoot for at impact is directly on the seam just slightly below center. The right ankle should lock an instant prior to impact, and the knee should lock at the moment of impact. One of the greatest means of hitting the target with the foot is to follow much the same procedure as that of a receiver looking the ball into his hands. Never take your eyes off the spot on the ball where you are aiming your foot. Attempt to watch your toe actually make contact with the ball.

One of the additional aids a place kicker receives is the privilege of wearing a custom shoe with a square kicking toe. All the pro kick-off men wear this special kicking shoe. Groza even likes his kicking shoe to fit one size smaller than his dress shoe in order to give him the maximum "feel" for the ball.

The starting point for kicking off probably will vary for each player. Groza stands about 10 yards directly behind the ball, with his right foot on the 30-yard line and the left foot slightly back. Push off the left foot and pick the spot on the ball which you wish to strike as soon as you begin your motion. You should reach three-quarter speed in just a couple of steps and maintain that speed until after you have completed the kick. It is the feeling of Groza and other good kickers that the individual has better control by moving at this clip and still will have time to compensate for any miscues that may occur.

Start your actual kick about half a yard from the ball. You should be on your left leg, with the right leg back and just beginning to swing downward in a pendulum-like motion. At this point, you will start locking your right ankle and your toes should be pointed upward. The body should be bent forward to provide maximum balance and the momentum to carry you straight ahead. Kicking through the ball will swing the right leg high and furnish you the necessary follow-through to impart maximum effort to the kick. Once you have kicked, you should land on your right foot and prepare to defend yourself against the blockers, since you will be the prime target at that moment.

FIELD GOAL KICKING

One of the major differences between kicking off and field goal kicking is the fact that we are not permitted to use a kicking tee. The ball must be kicked off the ground, and this, of course, increases our margin of error. In addition, you must be prepared to kick fast, for statistics show that you will have no more than one to one and one-half seconds to get your kick away. Not only does the onrushing defense create this necessity for speed in getting the kick off, but it also necessitates your getting the kick up in the air within about five yards in order to avoid the outstretched arms and hands of the defenders.

Most good place kickers line up about 6½ to 7 yards behind the line of scrimmage for field goal kicking. With the ball coming back from the center to the holder in a low, fast pattern, it is necessary to be ready to react immediately. As the ball hits the holder's hands, the kicker should be taking his first step. All his momentum must be generated within just a couple of yards. He should take a long, lunging step, landing on his left foot. The pendulum action will begin with his right leg as he lands. The ankle locks, the foot swings down and forward, and the kicker should be leaning over the ball as he makes contact.

As in passing or punting, a proper follow-through is necessary in order for the ball to gain good elevation and distance. The target for the ultimate flight of the ball should always be the center of the goal posts.

Sequence of a kick-off showing approach, kick, and follow-through.

ANGLE KICKING

When field goals are attempted from sharp angles, maximum accuracy is required, since the margin of error can be reduced as much as three feet. One of the recommended procedures here is to use your center as a direction finder. Groza always keys on his center and actually lines up on the center's right heel. He then aims his kick to travel directly over the center's head. This gives him a quick target at which to fire.

Place kicking undoubtedly is the most highly specialized phase of football. It is a part of the game in which a player can excel for many years, after other parts of his game have yielded to Father Time.

Unfortunately, the Packers have not been blessed with the great kick-off men in the game. Even in the days of our good ball clubs in 1963 and 1964, we had problems in the kick-off department. One of our players even went so far as to quip that we were the only team in the league that went into a goal line stand immediately after the kick-off. It wasn't quite that bad, but there were all too many occasions on which the opposition ran the ball back way too far or the kicks traveled such a short distance that the competition put the ball into play practically at midfield. A strong man kicking off really can have a great bearing on field position on numerous occasions during the course of a normal game.

the
game
plan

12

There is a great deal of mystique about professional football today. One of the terms bandied about by players, coaches, writers, and broadcasters is "the game plan." It is spoken of in hushed tones, almost as if the plan contained top-secret information. Some writers will tell readers that the team's game plan was so constructed that the opposition didn't have a chance because of the wisdom held in this plan.

Actually, a game plan is no more than the notes put down by the coaching staff and the players about the opposition and plays that they think will work against the opposition. I don't want to downgrade the game plan, but it really isn't as mysterious as some writers would have the fans believe.

When a team enters any football game, it should have a well-conceived game plan. Previous game experiences, scouting reports, and movies provide most of the information necessary in building such a plan.

Using a hypothetical team, let's see how we can design a basic game plan.

Should the average fan pick up a copy of a game plan and read it, he would find a maze of statistics, diagrams, and phrases and a sentence structure that would drive an English teacher wild. What is unintelligible to the fan is clear and concise to the player. In 1963, after the Bears had beaten us, 26–7, Coach George Halas showed his game plan to some writers, saying that this was the reason his Bears had won. I have great respect for Coach Halas, but I think the blocking and tackling of the Bears had much more to do with their victory than the game plan.

SCOUTING REPORT

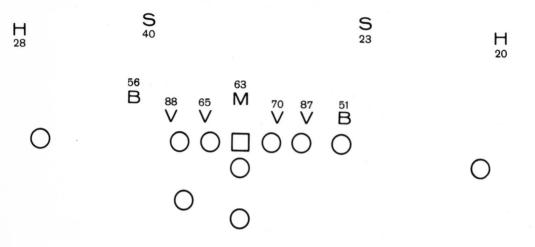

A scouting report which each offensive player would receive might read something like the following.

Left End Hickey (87)	6' 4", 238, second year, quick, active, consistent outside pass rusher, not strong against the run. *Can be double teamed easily.*
Left Tackle Ross (70)	6' 6", 265, very *strong*, particularly against straight plays, "reader," receives block, controls it, then reacts to the play, not good pass rusher. *No draws this side.*
Right Tackle Moore (65)	6' 5", 255, *outstanding player*, great desire, very quick, aggressive, fine pass rusher, excellent pursuit, chases. *Gives on him.*
Right End Lindsey (88)	6' 5", 250, solid performer, dependable, seldom out of position, good recovery. *Likes to stunt with Moore.*
Left Linebacker Jacobs (51)	6' 3", 240, doesn't play sweep well, average strength, pretty quick, good reactions, covers area well on passes.
Middle Linebacker Bowen (63)	6' 3", 245, spirited player, great hustler, always near the ball, punishing tackler, not outstanding pass defender.

Right Linebacker Reese (56)	6' 4", 240, strong, defends well against the run, not real active, average pass defender. *Work on with halfback passes.*
Left Corner Russell (20)	6' 1", 190, experienced back, excellent speed, quickness and reactions, good tackler. *Will gamble on occasion.*
Left Safety Cassidy (23)	6' 2", 200, always strong side safety, good speed, tackles well, aggressive, covers closely, can be faked easily and beaten deep. *Work on this back with tight end routes.*
Right Safety Williams (40)	5' 11", 185, always weak side safety, has tremendous speed and range, hard-nosed tackler, very alert performer.
Right Corner Walls (28)	6' 1", 190, rookie, for 1st year man plays his keys pretty well, conservative, very deep conscious. *Will not let you get behind him but gives you underneath routes all day.*

We'll sketch a few running plays first that should be good.

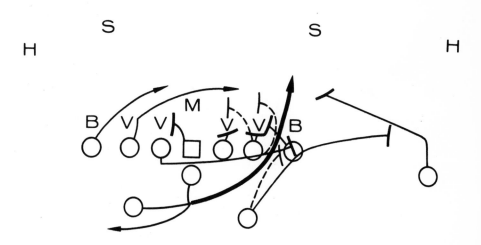

An obvious play we would use in this game would be the off-tackle play, since the scouting report indicated (and the movies verified) that the defensive left end could not stand up to the double team block. In addition, the linebacker on that side is not particularly strong against the run.

The blocking may be done in several different ways.

The method shown in solid lines would seal off the middle linebacker from the action by driving the defensive end so deep to the inside that the middle linebacker could not get around. The off guard pulls and kicks out the linebacker who has been set up by the fullback.

An alternate method of blocking (broken lines) would have the offensive tackle slam the defensive end and release for the middle linebacker as the tight end handled the defensive end by himself.

It's possible at times also for the linebacker on that side to get so much penetration that the fullback has no choice but to take him. When this happens, the pulling guard merely ignores the linebacker (unless he's getting away from the fullback) and turns up in the hole, looking to the inside for the most dangerous man.

Since the linebacker on the left side is weak defensing the sweep, this fact surely would be included in your attack.

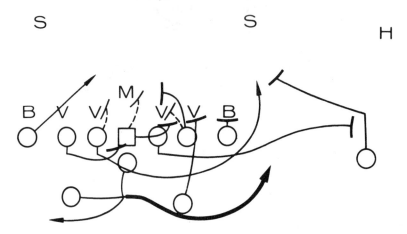

This play requires close coordination blocking by a number of offensive players. For this reason the style of play of the defensive players must be instantly recalled when the play is called in the huddle.

The solid-line blocking is normally used if possible. Since the defensive left tackle is a "reader," close study in the movies determines if the center can make an "onside cutoff." If not, then the tackle must block down and the center through for the middle linebacker (broken lines).

If the offensive left tackle can't cut off the defensive right tackle (remember, he has excellent pursuit) then you may be forced to lead with only one guard, keeping the left guard at home to block their tackle opposite him (dotted line).

This play could be run from a left formation also.

The defensive right tackle is noted for excellent pursuit but also chases plays hard from the rear. The following plays would probably be in your plan of attack.

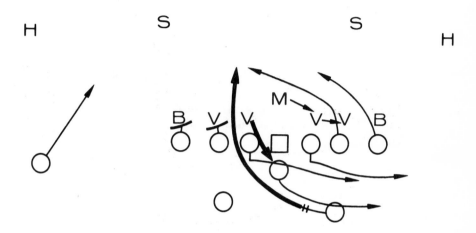

The above play is a *give* or *sucker* play run back into the hole created by an over-zealous defensive man. This type of play can also be run as shown below with the fullback carrying.

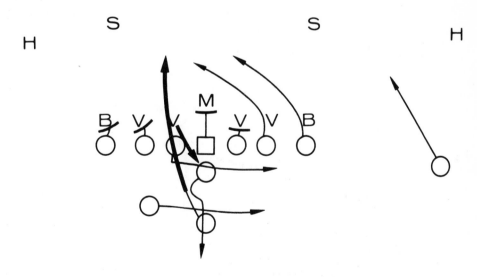

These simple illustrations should give you some idea how a team goes about designing its offense for a coming game. Other plays will be arrived at the same way. These, together with a few basic ones you carry each week, will comprise the running game.

Now let's take a brief look at how we would design some passes.

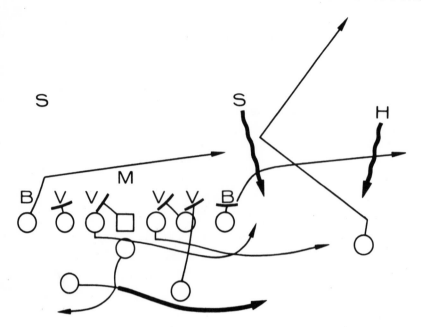

After viewing a few sweeps in the movies, you learn that though the defensive cornerman is forcing, the aggressiveness of the strong side safety is drawing him up rather quickly also.

You install an option pass to be used after you have set it up with some end runs. This play has been a timely weapon through the years for us.

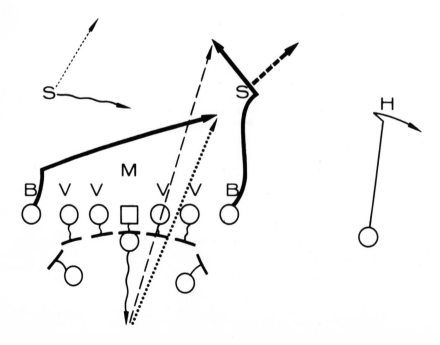

The diagram at the bottom of p. 258 represents one way to take advantage of the strong side safety. Remember, he can be beaten deep, so you run your tight end on a deep inside or outside route. To prevent the weak side safety from interfering with the deep inside route, you run your weak side end on a crossing route.

Since a rookie cornerback is covering your end, you probably will hold the safety by having him help on your crossing end. If the safety covers this way, throw to the tight end.

Should the safety ignore the crossing route and drop back deeply into the middle, your best choice becomes the weak side end crossing over. Only the rookie cornerback will be chasing him.

The rookie cornerback plays very loose and will not permit the deep pass. Several excellent routes can be drawn up to take advantage of this. The quarterback should exploit this position completely.

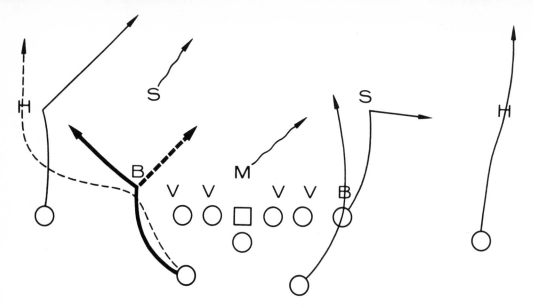

Though there are other valid routes which can be run against a linebacker who has trouble covering a halfback (broken line shows another one), the one drawn in bold lines is basic.

You see that the middle linebacker almost always goes with the fullback, so you pit your halfback one on one against the linebacker. It's almost impossible to cover this situation without some help.

As was the case in setting up the running phase of your attack, you carry certain basic pass patterns which you feel will be effective and can be adapted to the coverage used. Add a couple of screens and draws and the special passes designed to exploit specific weaknesses, and you have your passing attack for the week.

In addition to the scouting report on player personnel, your complete portfolio for the upcoming game will include the various defenses your opponent likes to use and when:

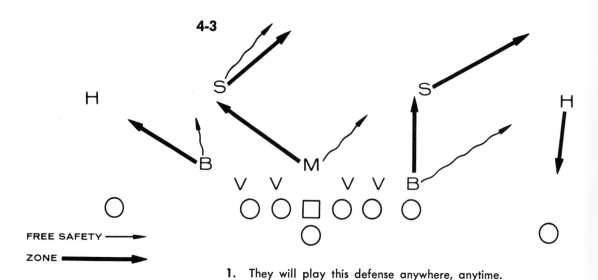

4-3

FREE SAFETY ⟶

ZONE ⟹

1. They will play this defense anywhere, anytime.

2. They like zone on a very long yardage situation, occasionally on 1st down.

4-3 BLITZ

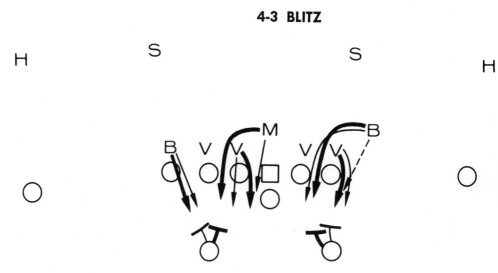

1. *They do not tip blitz.*
2. *They use all the typical blitzes.*
3. *Remember, man-to-man coverage is in effect when blitz is on; if you can sense it, throw the ball.*

4-3 OVER

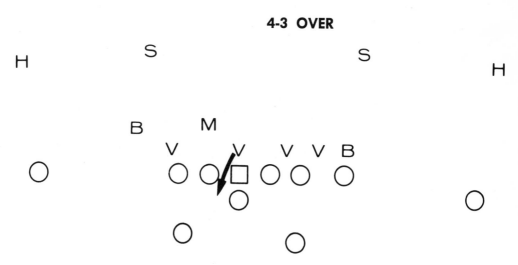

1. Defensive tackle on center's nose *always* charges weakside.
2. Remember, they can blitz from this too, though they haven't to date.
3. *Can play zone or free safety from this.*

4-3 UNDER

1. Remember, our opponent likes this defense.
2. Weakside linebacker may line up in any position noted.
3. Defensive tackle on center's nose *always* charges strongside.
4. They like to blitz off this defense.
5. *They don't like zone coverage when in this.*

This defense should be carefully studied by offensive linemen.

4-3 STUNT

1. Any of the above stunts can be expected anytime, but *they like to stunt on a passing situation.*

6-1

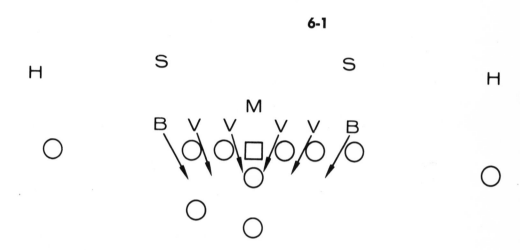

1. They will use this defense out in the field on short yardage. (In actual scouting report and game plan, the specific plays would be noted here for use in short yardage situations.)

GOAL LINE DEFENSE

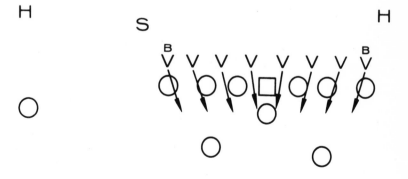

1. Inside two-yard line you will get this defense.
2. *Attack it as usual.*

SUMMARY OF DEFENSES

Defense	Three games times used	Down and distance		Comments
4-3 Free Safety	98	no set pattern		
4-3 Zone	21	1-10	8 times	
		2-long	3 times	
		2-short	1 time	
		3-long	9 times	
4-3 Blitz	15	1-10	10 times	
		2-long	2 times	
		3-long	3 times	
4-3 Over	6	1-10	3 times	
		2-5	1 time	
		3-long	2 times	Zone coverage in secondary
4-3 Under	9	Predominantly 1st down Couple of times on 3rd and short		

One of the most important things to remember about the game plan is that although it is designed to be successful, based on the knowledge available, there is absolutely no guarantee that it will be, because there is still that human element which must execute the ideas. You may also encounter some defense you had not prepared for. When this happens, the ability to adjust is often the difference between winning and losing.

Speaking of adjusting, your own teammates can help you immeasurably. Smart, experienced players contribute more to the success of the game than most fans are ever aware of.

Boyd Dowler and Max McGee are two excellent examples of experienced receivers coming back to the huddle after the first few passes and informing the quarterback if the defender is covering the way you have him scouted or if he is playing noticeably different. Their experience enables them to offer suggestions, preventing wasted plays.

Our interior linemen are capable of giving timely tips too about their opponents. You must remember that the defensive team has an excellent "book" on your offense and may be playing certain formations slightly different than they played their last opponent. Quick analysis by your linemen can provide you with valuable information.

In the beginning of this book, we noted that an analytical mind is one of the requisites for a good quarterback. I think you can now see why this is true. Though you have at your disposal ample information on your opponent, you must be capable of analyzing it and making the best possible use of it under all conditions.

Weather conditions cause changes in your plans and tactics and often limit you considerably. You must *never* allow weather to defeat you before the game begins, regardless of how severe the elements might be. Remember that your opponent must perform under the same handicap, so never let weather conditions "psyche" you, particularly the element of wind, which is encountered more frequently during a season's play than snow, rain, or mud.

It's obvious that if you're facing a strong wind for half a contest, you probably will be forced to make slight adjustments concerning the passing and punting games. From a quarterback's standpoint, some concern for wind is necessary to carrying out a successful attack. However, through experience you learn how much to compensate for such things.

It is important that a quarterback learn how to pace his own players' energies. I am perhaps a little careless about this many times because we have one of the strongest, most dependable runners in the league in Jimmy Taylor. I probably overwork Jimmy. I am probably guilty of not realizing when I have run him two or three times in a row, and I continue to call on him for four or five plays, with maybe only a break or two. Jimmy does a great job. I have a great deal of confidence in him, and I know he is going to do the job for us, and so I like to run him. This may include putting him in a pass pattern too. Then I turn around and ask him to come right back and sweep the end.

You must be aware of your players' energies because you could literally wear them out. Then, when you want to call a pass pattern and hit this particular person, he might not have the extra zip to go out and get the ball and be able to get away from the defender. So, in selecting your plays, you should be aware of your players' energies. Try to conserve them. If you are anticipating running a halfback on a long pass play deep down one side, I think you should be aware of this in your previous call and perhaps use him as a blocker. Don't use him on the end run. Let him do the blocking to conserve as much energy as possible, so he doesn't have to run too far.

Let's talk about plays sent in from the bench. At Green Bay we don't have too many plays sent in because we spend a great deal of time during the week preparing for a game, getting our game plan in order. By spending this extra time in

preparation during practice, we are better prepared when Sunday comes.

I have already talked about listening to my own players' recommendations because I think this is highly important. Often our coaches on the field or in the press box can pick out defensive weaknesses and send in specific calls to exploit them. I feel this strategy should be worked out between the coaches and quarterbacks on each team, independently of outside influences. If you follow your coach's instructions and encounter trouble, he'll back you up.

I remember an incident in 1962 in Green Bay between the Packers and the Lions. Late in the game, with the Lions ahead 7-6, they were trying to run out the clock to preserve the win. The ball was on about their 40-yard line. Milt Plum tried a sideline pass to Terry Barr. Barr slipped, Herb Adderley intercepted, ran it back close enough for a field goal, and we won 9-7.

After the game, George Wilson, then the head coach of the Lions, defended Plum by saying that he, Wilson, called the pass. Whether he did or not is immaterial, since he removed all blame from Plum (and Barr's slip caused the interception anyway) and made it clear that this call was considered necessary to hold on to the ball.

Right: The Lions' Milt Plum tries to elude the grasp of the Packers' Willie Davis.

GOAL LINE AND SHORT YARDAGE

In short yardage situations (3rd and 2, 4th and 1) and down on the goal line, the defensive team usually employs some form of defense which limits your attack.

Actually, this is to your benefit because you can make up a few plays which are perhaps better in these situations than normally. You should remember also that you don't need many short yardage plays, but rather two, three, or four which will get the job done.

Usually, on short yardage, you attack the defense in two ways: (1) In an area where the defense is somewhat weaker, and (2) on a particular individual whose style of play can be exploited.

The following diagrams show how a short yardage defense is vulnerable to certain plays.

6-1 DEFENSE

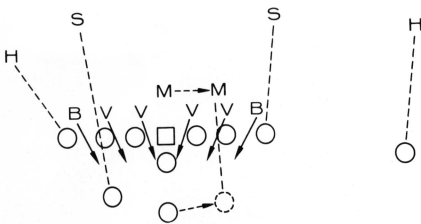

1. The defense drawn above is commonly called a 6-1 defense in our league (the two outside linebacks definitely coming hard across the line of scrimmage, together with the severe closing action of the linemen change a simple 4-3 set up to this —six linemen, one linebacker).

2. The defensive players, for passing purposes, have the men designated. The weakside safety and halfback are responsible for the end and offensive halfback on that side and may switch assignments. The middle linebacker has the fullback and may be opposite him when the latter is in a split backfield position.

3. This is a common defense used out in the field of play on short yardage.

TRAP PLAY

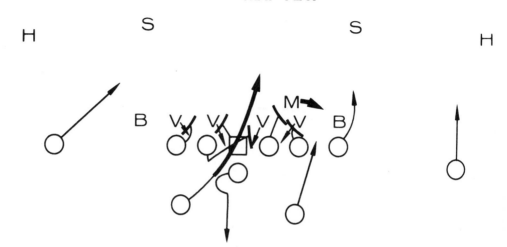

1. One area where many teams attack this defense is in the middle with a trap play.

2. With a split backfield, the middle linebacker will move over opposite the fullback (remember he's responsible for the fullback) and the middle, without the middle linebacker to "plug it," is somewhat vulnerable.

3. It's surprising how effective this simple play can be, despite even the smallest space between the two defensive tackles. All that's needed is a standoff, and the back can slip through.

Elijah Pitts scores on the trap play just diagramed.

FULLBACK SLANT OFF TACKLE

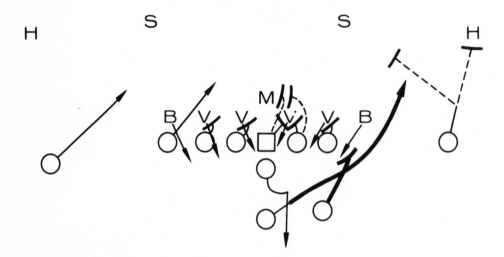

1. This is another example of using a play that takes advantage of what the defense is doing.

2. Since the defenders are closing down to the inside, each key offensive blocker has a man at least ahead of him or to his inside, affording good blocking angles.

3. A key block must be performed by the halfback on the linebacker to his side to insure success of the play.

4. The offensive center and right guard are responsible for the defensive tackle on that side and the middle linebacker.

5. The split end blocks the most dangerous secondary man.

This off-tackle slant by the fullback has been Jim Taylor's favorite play for a number of years, on short yardage and

Right: "Golden Boy" Paul Hornung slumps hard on the bench after scoring 35 points against the Colts a few years ago. He is one of the finest all-around football players in the history of the game.

otherwise. One of the principal reasons for its success was the good blocking on the outside linebacker by Paul Hornung, one of the finest blocking halfbacks who ever played.

The two previous diagrams were simple illustrations of plays which could exploit the defense as a whole. Of course, there are others. This next diagram will show how the particular playing style of a player can be exploited on short yardage.

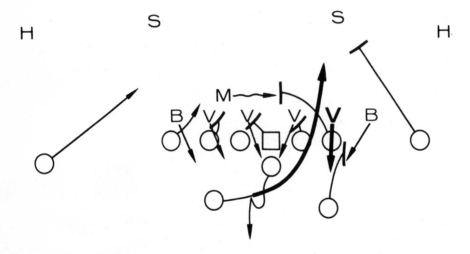

1. The defensive left end here (bold "V") is not closing the way he should on this defense. This creates a big hole which should not go unnoticed.

2. From previous experience or game films, you learn that certain individuals tend to play hunches or revert to their own style when they should be playing the defense as it was designed.

3. When you get a player doing this, you should immediately take advantage of it.

4. In the case above, with the defensive end coming up the field instead of closing, you can trap this player rather easily.

In addition to the 6-1 short yardage defense, here are a few other common ones used by some teams.

GAP DEFENSE

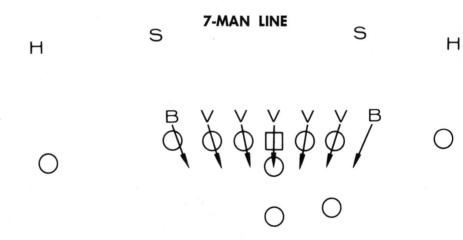

1. This defense places defensive men in all the gaps or spaces between the offensive linemen.

2. Most teams use a defense like this only when you are about to score on them and will many times bring in two extra big linemen to replace a linebacker and a safety.

3. If you want to take the gamble, you can effectively throw against this defense since they can't cover the pass well when aligned this way.

7-MAN LINE

1. The defensive player facing the center may be an extra lineman on the middle linebacker down in a three point stance.

2. This can be a good short defense if played well.

5-1

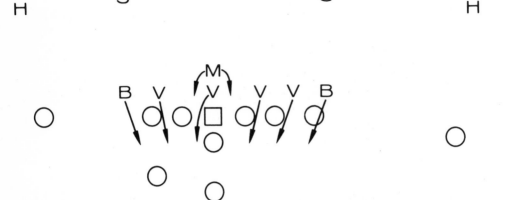

1.   This is a fine defense against the running game and is used today by several teams. It is even more effective against the run out in the field under normal conditions.

REVERSES

A reverse play is a one- or two-shot per game effort to cut down on wild pursuit or chasing tactics by the defense.

One of the greatest "chasers" in the game today is David "Deacon" Jones of the Los Angeles Rams. He has such outstanding speed that he can actually catch an end run going away from him in his normal pursuit action.

To combat this, you must run a reverse to at least make a player like Jones aware that you have one. (What most fans don't realize, however, is that Jones or any player who chases in such manner is usually not responsible for reverses and, therefore, is never concerned about being fooled.)

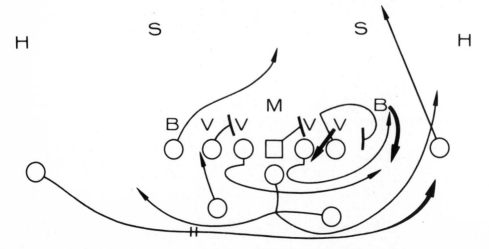

1. Whenever a defensive end disregards the consequence of a reverse play being run on him, you can bet the linebacker on that side is the "contain" man and is responsible for turning in such plays (bold lines).

2. The diagram at the bottom of p. 274 shows a reverse being run using the flanker as the ball carrier. Reverses may also run with only the two running backs involved such as:

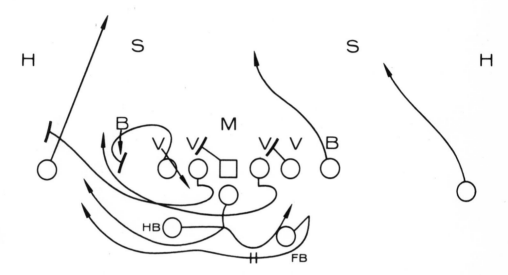

1. The fullback starts to his right, turns and comes back behind the halfback to receive the handoff. (Halfback has received it from the quarterback.)

(For still another type of reverse, look at the diagram under laterals.)

championship games

13

The first championship game that I played in was the 1960 game that we lost—the only championship game since Coach Lombardi came to the Packers in which we ended up on the wrong end of the score.

The lead-up to this game started a year earlier, in 1959, when Coach Lombardi first came to the Packers and we won the final four games of the season. This was the move that we really needed, in order to start believing that we were a winning football team. When Coach Lombardi arrived, he told us that if we would do two things, he would assure us that we could start winning football games.

One was to have a great deal of faith in his system and to realize that it was designed with simple execution in mind and built around the premise that you must block and tackle better than the other team to get the job done. He stressed that the system was basic and fundamental, not built around any frills that would vary from time to time. By contrast, a system constructed of solid football would seldom vary. Regardless of the defense we encountered, we would always have the proper answers to cope with it.

Second, he told us that we must be willing to pay the price, to be totally dedicated, to practice and work harder than ever before. We must keep our mistakes to a minimum. Then we could begin to win. This was his first effort at drumming his philosophy into us. Once it began to take hold, we knew we could win, and we did.

By the end of 1959, all of us were looking forward to 1960. When the time came, we went on to win the Western Division title. Like all teams, we needed a little luck on our side. Baltimore lost two of its last three games, and we slipped in the side door.

As a result, when we approached the championship game with the Eagles, I am positive that we were just not sufficiently mature as a team to be a champion. Many of us couldn't really believe that we were there and had earned the right to be in a championship game. There certainly was a tremendous difference in our attitude to the 1961 championship game. The difference between our Packers of 1960 and the Philadelphia Eagles whom we were facing shaped up about as follows:

The Eagles weren't necessarily an experienced team either as they went into the championship game. However, they had a man leading them, Norm Van Brocklin, who did have championship experience. He was the prime reason for the Eagles coming as far as they had. His leadership and general savvy had made maximum use of what was really just a good team, but he had almost single-handedly moved them into a position of winning the league championship. He extended this great leadership right on into the championship game, and thanks to some great selection of plays, timely position, and adept employment of his running backs where they were needed, they beat us. We almost pulled the game out in the last few seconds, but we didn't quite make it. However, the great lesson we all learned was that we did have a right to be there. The next year we would prove it.

By 1961 we had matured fully as a team, and we honestly felt that no one could beat us.* When we went on the field against the Giants in Green Bay City Stadium in 1961, there was no way in the world the Giants could have won that day. It would have been impossible, though they had some bad breaks early in the game. Kyle Rote dropped a long pass that could possibly have changed the game's complexion a bit because it was early in the game, and there were a couple of other crucial things that happened. Still, I don't think the Giants could have beaten us, because we felt in our hearts that there was no way they could win. Here are some special plays we set up to beat the Giants.

---

* These Packers played in some or all of the championship games to be discussed:

Packer Players: #15 Starr—Qb; #31 Taylor—Fb; #5 Hornung—Hb; #22 Pitts—Hb; #88 Kramer—Tight end; #86 Dowler—Flanker; #85 McGee—Split end; #84 Dale—Split end; #81 Fleming—Tight end.

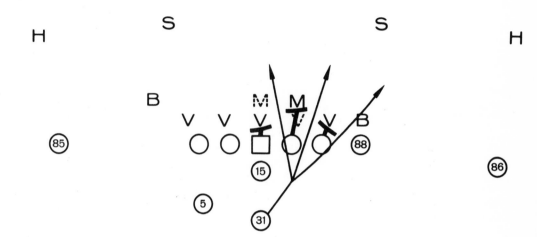

1. In 1961 in Green Bay when the Packers played the Giants for the championship, the following plays were used to take advantage of defenses the Giants employed in an effort to stop Jim Taylor.

    a. The Giants would undershift their line to try to stop Taylor's off-tackle slant whenever we got in this offensive formation, so we countered by running the ball right at the middle linebacker (M) who is normally in the middle (see dotted letters) and not being blocked quickly and straight on by a guard. With zone blocking (straight ahead blocking) you can easily see how our fullback had a lot of holes to hit. (Bold lines show blocking.)

    b. Defensive shifts and last-second stunts today would greatly reduce the effectiveness of this play.

2. In an effort to control our power sweep, the Giants defensed our split backfield formation (from which we run the sweep) with an *overshifted* line (overshifted toward our flanker). Normal positions are in dotted letters.

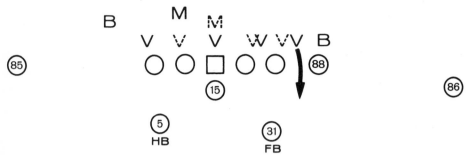

a. As you can see, their defensive left end's charge is wide and up the field, making it difficult to run wide on this side.

b. Without divulging too many counterplays for this defense, we merely did not try to run wide toward this end, but rather ran plays inside this end, ran the ball toward the *undershifted* side, plus using the following pass, which was virtually impossible to stop when in our *over* defense.

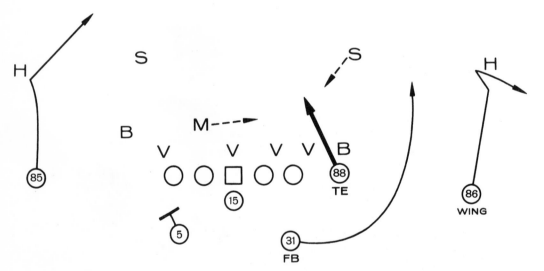

a. With the MLB (middle linebacker) removed one more position from our TE (tight end), a pass such as shown above was tough to cover.

b. The MLB cannot get to the TE quickly enough to prevent his catching the ball.

c. If the linebacker opposite the TE stays with the TE too long, then the FB is open. If the strong side safety covers the FB, then the wing is open.

Whenever we could get the Giants in a normal 4-3 defensive alignment, we liked the following flood pass in an effort to again have an option of where we wanted to throw the ball.

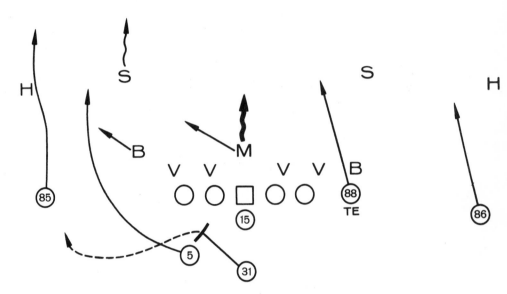

a. If the MLB left his area quickly when we flooded to our left (and he usually did since he was keying hard on the FB), we threw the ball to the TE who then had free running at the secondary. (Ron Kramer was our TE then and was big, fast, and strong.)
b. If the MLB stayed at home (bold line), we threw the screen pass out to the FB.

(Today better defensive theories and practice many times would completely nullify the preceding plays. Of course, when this happens, the offense must find new plays.)

In 1962 we encountered the Giants again. The scene had shifted to Yankee Stadium, and it was a miserable day. It was quite blustery, with the winds blowing something like 35 miles an hour or higher. They were so strong that when we got up off the benches to stand near the sidelines at kick-offs, at the half, etc., the heavy benches actually blew over.

We made a slight change. I say "slight" because we had prepared to throw the ball a great deal against the Giants in the 1962 championship game. We felt that we could throw the ball effectively on them because they were not getting great pass rush that year. We had thrown well against them in years past, and we thought we could do it again. So we had gone into the game completely prepared to pass.

When the wind factor came up, we changed slightly and decided to run the ball more than we were going to throw it.

Here are diagrams of a few pass plays that we did call again in 1962 because of some tactics the Giants were using that enabled us to control the ball a bit better by throwing just a timely pass or two on occasion.

PASSES AGAINST GIANTS 1962

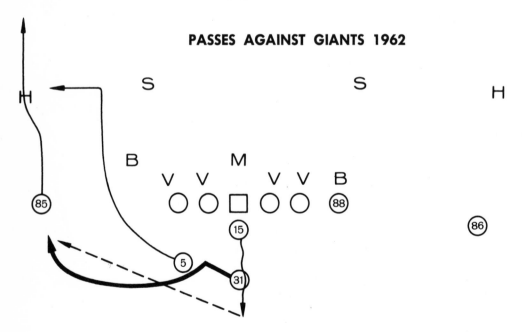

1. We threw the ball several times that day to Jim Taylor, our fullback, on flood type routes. We hit Jim because they did not cover him closely and as a result he was able to pick up sizable chunks on a trite pass pattern.

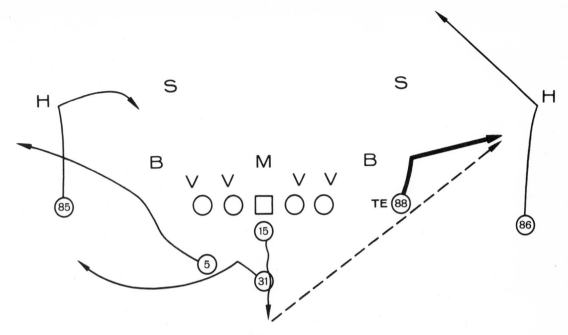

1. When we split our tight end very wide, the Giants played the strong side linebacker well inside.

2. This gave us an easy outside route to the tight end off the same flood action.

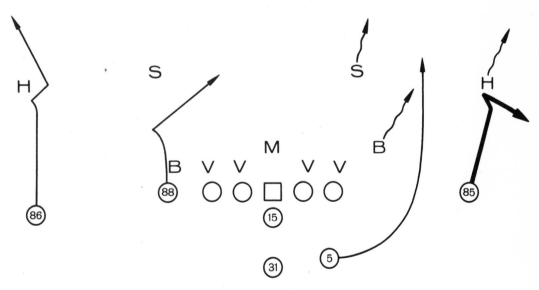

1. We also threw a few "outs" to our weak side end off the above action.

By following a disciplined game plan, we were able to run the ball, control the game, and because of a tenacious defense which also did a great job in the '61 wind-up in Green Bay, we were able to win this game. The Giants bemoan the fact that the wind hurt their passing game, and I am sure it did, because they were a passing team that year. Y. A. Tittle set many of his passing records and had an outstanding season throwing the ball, so I am sure the wind did hurt them a great deal.

However, this is how you win or lose championships. You must be able to adjust quickly and decisively under conditions that arise at the last minute. This is the mark of a championship club—to be able to win under adversity, under any sort of condition. We were able to win in 1962, and it was very gratifying to repeat as world champions.

I mentioned that we were able to call on our running game to win. The Giants did not have as strong a running game as we did that year and thus were not able to rely on it more when it was difficult to throw under windy conditions. As a result, we won. It's imperative to have a strong running game as well as an effective passing game.

When the Colts lost in 1961-62 and 1963, they did not have a complementary running game to go with Unitas' passing. He was just as effective as a passer in those years as he was in the years that they won it. However, in 1964, when they took the division title and then lost to the Browns in the playoff game, they had an outstanding ground game. Lenny Moore enjoyed a great year running, and so Baltimore had a balanced attack.

Unitas probably threw as little in 1964 as in any season in his career with the Colts because they had a balanced offense. In the previous years they did not have this balanced offensive and were defeated because teams could load up on them and concentrate strictly on Johnny's passing.

In the 1965 championship game against the Browns, we again had what we thought was a fine game plan. We felt that the Browns would give us the inside more than the outside because the Browns do an outstanding job of rushing their ends wide, even on running plays up the field, so as not to give you the end run.

The end run, if executed well, can literally chop up a defense because, if you turn the corner and get headed upfield, you've got 8, 9, 10 yards at a crack. So the Cleveland team down through the years usually has played to force you to give up the sweep. You may hurt them inside, but you're going to have to inch them to death in there. They're not going to give you anything, and they are going to cut off any big gainer you might have on the outside. You must remember also that since the sweep is our lead play, if we make that one go, a lot of other plays are opened up for us.

Since the Browns and Packers have met each other several times in the last few years, the plays shown here are certainly no big secret being divulged. We simply were able to execute some of these plays against them.

RUNNING PLAYS VS. BROWNS, CHAMPIONSHIP GAME 1965

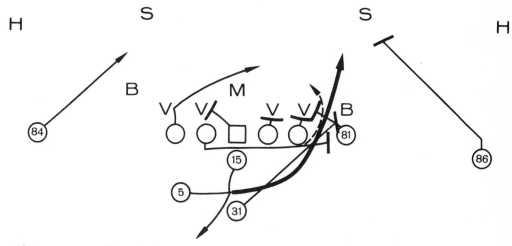

1. This was an effective off-tackle play we ran inside. (Play was also run from split backfield.)

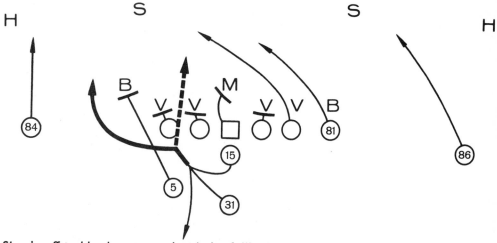

1. Simple off-tackle slant to weak side by fullback.

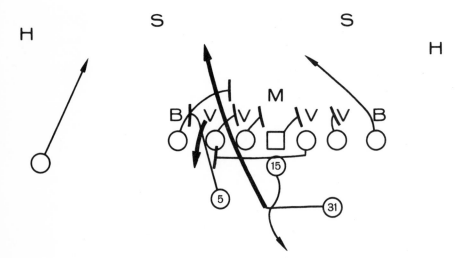

1. This simple yet effective inside play is a take-off of the sweep. Whenever a defensive end is charging wide to prevent the end run on his side, this is a good counterplay.

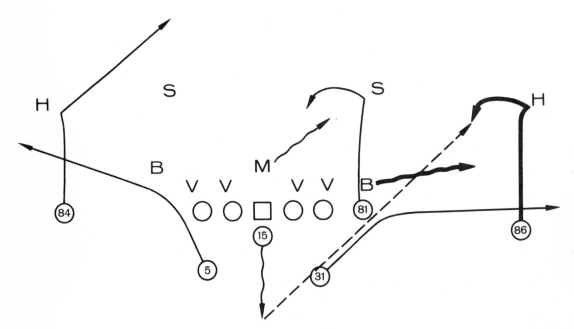

1. This is a very basic pass pattern that a lot of teams use in which the strong side receivers (flanker side) turn in.

2. As outside linebacker goes to outside with fullback, the wing curls in behind the linebacker.

3. Here's a good example of being able to throw ball at receiver while he's still on the outside of the linebacker since he and linebacker are moving in opposite directions.

4. We were able to complete this route sometimes against the Browns.

5. This is a good example of how a back is used to move a linebacker (in this case the fullback moving the outside linebacker). This action, whether you are controlling deep secondary men by halfback or linebackers by halfback or fullback is referred to as flare control (controlling the defense by the use of an offensive back).

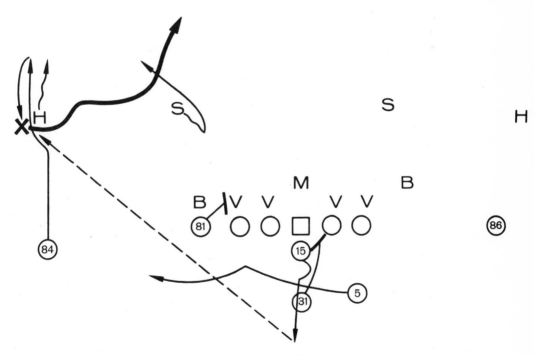

1. This pass off a play action fake got us our first score with Cleveland, though we were very lucky to score.

2. Carroll Dale (84), our wingback as flanker, ran a streak on fly route, but as the ball was underthrown, he was forced to stop and come back for it.

3. The defender slipped, and Dale eluded the safety who had come over to support and ran in for a score.

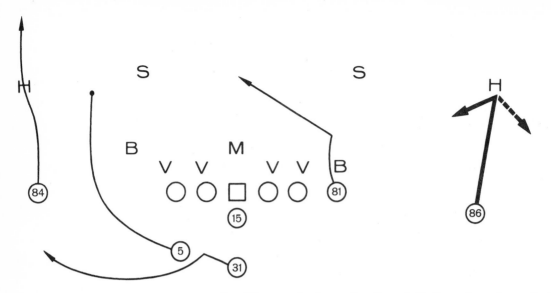

1. We ran both an "out" and "in" to the wing off the above flood action.

2. Since we were effective with the "out," this made the "in" effective also, since they come off the same look.

CHAMPIONSHIP GAME 1966— COWBOYS VS. PACKERS

For several reasons, the National Football League championship game in the Cotton Bowl in Dallas created great excitement among fans all across the country. This game pitted a young team which was born, so to speak, only a few years before against a so-called aging champion. The Dallas offense, which had run roughshod over most of its opponents, was to encounter the league's most effective defense, and the Packers' running game was to be tested by the stingiest running defense around. And, for the first time, the winner of this game would meet the AFL winner to become the world's champion.

After about a three-day layoff, following the final game of the season, we assembled to begin preparation for this all-important game. We prepared for the championship game the same way we did for any other. The only difference was we had an extra few days in which to get ready.

Since the weather was very cold in Green Bay, our physical workouts were shorter than usual. Most of the time that first week was spent in meetings, since there were more movies to be reviewed and more information to assimilate than there would be in getting ready for a game during the season.

Following Saturday's practice, Coach Lombardi wished everybody a Merry Christmas, and we scattered in all directions for a couple of days of Yuletide spirit. On Monday we flew into Tulsa, Oklahoma, and instead of warmer weather, we were greeted with snow and freezing rain. Don Chandler, who lives in Tulsa, suddenly found himself dodging everybody's blasts of humor.

Immediately after checking into the motel, we headed for the stadium and our first workout in Tulsa. Through some mixup, our equipment was an hour late in arriving, there were no lights or heat in the dressing room, and the field was covered with snow. When you are accustomed to being as well organized as we are, a situation like this becomes extremely funny.

Though the field was snow covered, the ground was not frozen, as it was in Green Bay, so we were able to get good traction with our cleats, and we held a very spirited workout there on Monday. Following dinner that night, our schedule for the week preceding the game was as follows: At 8 o'clock, breakfast; at 9 o'clock the buses left for the stadium; we had a practice session from approximately 10 to 11:30; at 12:30, lunch; at 3 o'clock, a meeting; at 6 o'clock, dinner; and at 7:30 a meeting.

The meeting Monday night at 7:30 consisted of a complete personnel scouting report and the defenses. Our game plan was presented, analyzed, and recorded.

Practice on Tuesday morning was far from pleasing to Coach Lombardi, because we spent most of the time running as though we were on eggs. We had had a hard freeze that night, and all of the slush and snow that had been on the field the previous day was frozen in hard spots, making it tough to run. In spite of the treacherous turf and the cold wind, I thought the spirit of the squad was outstanding.

We had deluxe accommodations in Tulsa, and the people who waited on us were very efficient and pleasant. The players kidded the waiters, who jested back and forth with us. There was one particularly avid Cowboy fan who kidded me because he was a Jethro Pugh fan. Every time he saw me he'd say, "Oh, Bart, before you're through, you're going to be got to by Jethro Pugh." Everyone would howl, and we had a lot of fun with him, kidding back and forth during the week we were there.

Tuesday afternoon's meeting consisted of again going over the passing game, the running game, and then settling down to studying the films. This meeting actually gets your week going because you have a chance to analyze what you are attempting to do. After the meeting was over, the quarterbacks remained to watch additional reels of film, because in this case we had even more to watch than in a normal game.

During the workout on Wednesday, it was plain to see that our game plan had a definite shape to it, and as we applied it in practice I was more and more impressed with it. I thought it was the finest game plan that I have ever seen for a particular game.

At the afternoon meeting a couple of additional passes against the Dallas defenses, which Zeke and I had seen, were suggested and accepted on the basis of our previous day's film watching.

At night, after our evening meetings, I would sit and study the game plan, the game reports, previous scouting reports, etc., in an effort to become completely familiar with what we were doing so that applying the game plan would become second nature.

By Thursday you could sense that the team was reaching a peak.

That Friday morning we flew out to Dallas, where we held a workout immediately upon arrival. We worked at a high school stadium, and there was no grass in the middle of the field.

The bags were late again, and the dressing rooms were cold, but we had an opposite reaction this time. Where we had laughed and joked about it in Tulsa the week before, by now it was Friday, the tension was beginning to build, and you could hear the grumbles.

Sunday morning I awoke with a really refreshed feeling and, after a few minutes on my feet and several thoughts of the game starting to creep in, I could feel the butterflies really dancing around in my stomach. At the pregame meal the conversation was somewhat subdued, although an occasional burst of mild laughter would indicate that another Max McGee joke was taking effect.

I don't eat much at pregame meals. In fact, I prefer a couple of eggs, over light, to the steak that most of the players eat. Our pregame meal time gives us a chance to talk about something other than the game and to get our minds off it. Immediately after the pregame meal, we always have a brief meeting in which any last-minute questions can be answered.

Our warm-up was excellent. I particularly noted that Jimmy Taylor was running like a young stallion and just itching to get the game started. You could sense that he really wanted to play that day. Back inside the dressing room we pulled on our pads and sat down to receive our last minute instructions.

After some comments by the players and the Lord's Prayer, Coach Lombardi stepped forward to talk to the squad for a minute. He was in great voice. When he was finished, I could have run through the wall. He has a tremendous way of firing you up, of getting you ready to play, and this day was no exception.

Coach had set up a special play to open the game. It was a counter play, designed to take advantage of the Cowboys' great pursuit. Elijah Pitts gained 32 yards, and we were off and rolling. We were high when the game began, and when our first special play broke for such a long gain, the feeling was electric. We knew we'd score. After six more plays, Elijah took a 17-yard pass in for the first touchdown. On the kickoff Mel Renfro fumbled, and Jim Grabowski picked it up for us and scored. With less than five minutes in the game, we led 14–0.

The Cowboys, because they were a young ball club, could literally have fallen apart at this stage of the game, being down two touchdowns this early in the ball game to a team supposedly well disciplined and well schooled in championship games. Yet this young team inexperienced at championship play came right back. Don Meredith led them beautifully for a score and later on another one that tied up the game. From this point on, the contest was a real dogfight. We scored again in the second quarter, but Dallas countered with a field goal and the score at halftime was Green Bay 21, Dallas 17.

Don Meredith hands off to Don Perkins on a counter play. Ron Kostelnick (77) of the Packers fights off his blocker. Ron is one of the best young linemen in football.

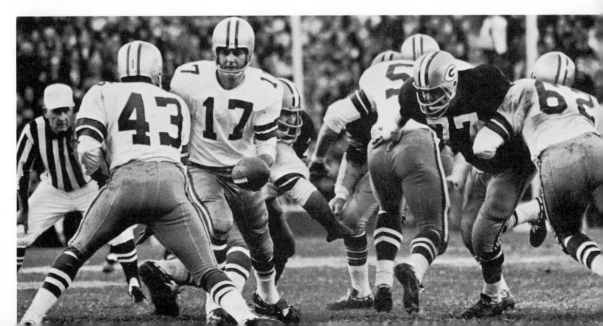

A spectacular play in the 1966 Dallas NFL Championship game: Boyd Dowler catches a touchdown pass and is then dumped by the Cowboys' Mike Gaechter.

Our defense held the Cowboys to three points in the third quarter, while we managed to score another touchdown. A fumble at a crucial point robbed us of another drive. We had a lot of momentum going, and had we been able to score, I think it would have been all over. But we fumbled, and the Cowboys turned this fumble into a field goal by Danny Villanueva.

Despite this field goal, things still looked pretty good when, in the fourth quarter, we scored again to lead 34 to 20. The extra point that was blocked following this score set the stage for a wild and furious finish.

Jerry Kramer leads Jim Taylor on a sweep against the Cowboys. Number 74 of Dallas, Bob Lilly, is being blocked by Fuzzy Thurston. Fuzzy had a great game against Lilly.

Our last touchdown came when Max McGee took a 28-yard pass. Max had called the pattern in the huddle, telling me he could beat Livingston. He did, and we had six. If the extra point had been good, the score would have been 35–20; and with only four and a half minutes to go, it would have been no sweat for us.

It's funny how the ball bounces. After Max's touchdown, we kicked off. The Cowboys got a few yards with a running play, and then Meredith hit Dan Reeves with a short pass in the left flat. Lee Roy Caffey, our linebacker, hit Reeves with a

293

jolting tackle, causing a fumble. Three Packers chased the loose ball, but a lone Cowboy, Don Meredith, touched it just before it went out of bounds. So instead of us recovering a fumble, the Cowboys kept the ball. The very next play turned the Cotton Bowl on its ear.

On third and 28 yards, Meredith found Frank Clarke with a 68-yard scoring play, and everybody in the stands suddenly realized that another score would tie up the game. Everybody on our offense team huddled hurriedly on the sideline to pledge itself to keeping the ball away from Dallas as long as possible.

I felt that the Cowboys would be blitzing, so we came right out throwing the ball, picking up two first downs. However, on the third and 7 situation that followed, I did not think they would blitz, because they knew I was going to throw. I thought they would try to keep people back and cover.

I called a flood pass, but the receivers were especially well covered and, as a result, I was forced to throw the ball to Taylor, who was immediately tackled by their middle linebacker, Lee Roy Jordan. I could have kicked myself all the way to the sideline for making that call, a typical case of outsmarting yourself. Rather than going with a proven play that we had successfully used throughout the game, I tried to cross them up with a good play but one that they hadn't seen as much of.

FLOOD PASS USED IN CHAMPIONSHIP GAME AT DALLAS

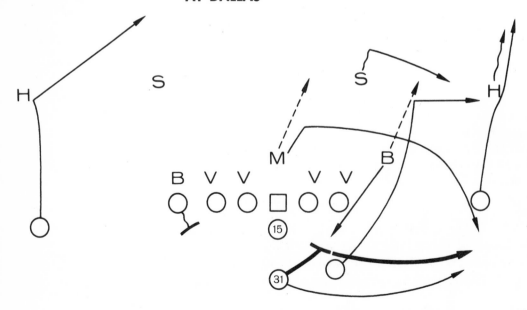

1. Since we had successfully executed this pass play earlier in the game in a critical situation—though it was from a right formation—I felt the play would work again. Linebacker coverage on the first one is shown in broken lines.

2. However, the weak side linebacker red dogged, and we had Taylor (31) running the route indicated by the thin line. Had I called Taylor on a "chuck-and-out" route (shown in bold lines), I could have had time to throw to our HB, who was covered only by the safety. Since Jimmy was out in the pattern immediately, I was forced to throw the ball to him. Lee Roy Jordan, the MLB, was right on top of him when Jimmy turned to head upfield.

Don Chandler came in to punt and was rushed, kicking the ball off the side of his foot. The Dallas fans at this point were delirious, and our bench was yelling at our defensive team to hold on.

A pass interference call moved the ball down the field to the 2-yard line, and Reeves could gain only one yard in there. At this point, a fatal penalty moved the Cowboys back to the 6, where Meredith subsequently hit Norman for four yards to the 2. On the play before, Reeves had dropped a pass out in the flat.

At this point, the whole game had come down to fourth and two yards on the 2-yard line in the fourth quarter. A situation like this can give you the shakes. It may sound a bit corny, but I honestly felt deep down inside that our defense would find some way to stifle them. I think this is the sort of faith and confidence that the players themselves have in one another on the Packers, and it is one of the reasons I am so proud to be a member of that organization.

By now everyone knows the great defensive play by our left linebacker, Dave Robinson, that forced Meredith to hurry his throw and our left safety, Tom Brown, intercepted in the end zone for the victory-saving plan. We went absolutely wild. You would have thought that we were winning our first title, rather than the fourth for some of us.

After running out the clock to preserve the win, we exchanged congratulations with our friends on the Cowboy team. I sought out Meredith and told him what a fine job I thought he had done with his team in bringing them back the way he had. As I left and walked toward the dressing room, I suddenly had a quick flashback to the year 1960, the championship game

It's all over and we won. Coach Lombardi's smile reflects the whole team's happiness at beating Dallas.

in Philadelphia, when we had come so close only to lose to the Philadelphia Eagles.

Once inside the dressing room, I went limp because of the excitement of the game. I heard many people say this was the most exciting championship game they had ever seen. I know one thing—it is the most exciting game I had ever been in.

Our dressing room was very noisy, but it was still somewhat dignified. Nobody on this ball club will ever be complacent about winning championships but, in like manner, I think we will never lose our composure and act like a bunch of idiots either. When someone asked Coach Lombardi, for example, why there was no champagne or beer around, he replied that this team was not a champagne or beer group in public and that the champagne would be forthcoming in our private confines.

Some of the pass plays which worked for us that day are diagramed as follows:

PLAYS VS. DALLAS, CHAMPIONSHIP GAME 1966

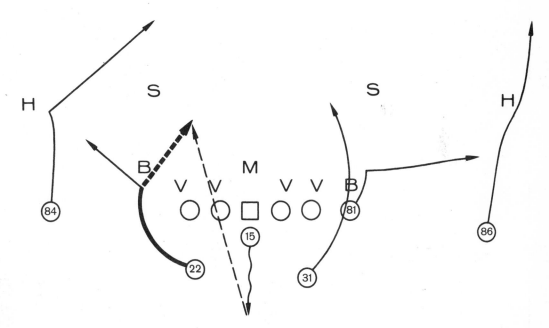

1. Our first score against the Cowboys came on a short pass to our halfback, who eluded the linebacker on his side, broke to the inside, caught the ball, and scored from about fifteen yards out.

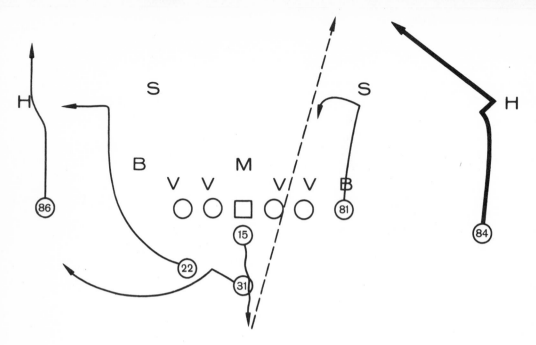

1. Our next score came on a deep pass to the middle to our flanker, who ran an excellent route.

2. The ball hung just a little too much. The defensive halfback recovered to knock it down but, in misjudging it, allowed a score.

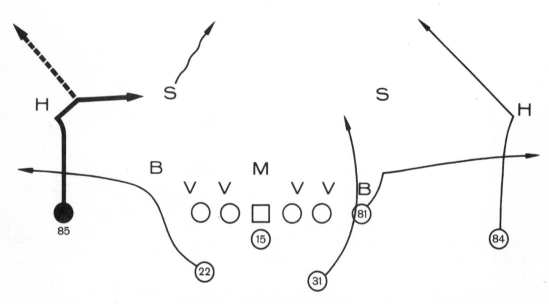

1. The above diagram shows two moves that resulted in scores. The bold-line route of the weak side end (85) shows a move to the inside.

2. The broken line shows the "Z"-out route which is a take-off of the first route. (The latter route is used when a defender starts to cover the inside move too closely.)

3. Max McGee called the "Z"-out route late in the game with Dallas after his defender had overplayed the inside route earlier. McGee's quick thinking resulted in a score for us.

SUPER BOWL

A game matching the champions of the American Football League and National Football League had been asked for by countless fans across the country for a couple of years. This game became a reality in 1966 when the Kansas City Chiefs, champions of the AFL, met the Green Bay Packers in the first Super Bowl.

The Chiefs had been in existence the same length of time as the Dallas Cowboys. They also had a high-powered offense and a stable full of fine players like Len Dawson, Mike Garrett, Otis Taylor, and others. On defense the Chiefs featured top-notch personnel in Buck Buchanan, Jerry Mays, Jerry Robinson, and Bob Bell. With imaginative coaching from Hank Stram and his assistants, the offense and defense kept opponents off balance.

The squad reassembled Wednesday morning in Green Bay to begin preparations for the game they would call the Super Bowl. Our meeting began in the normal fashion with Coach Lombardi commenting on the Dallas game. He complimented the offense on a spirited game but emphasized again how our defense had come through when we really needed them. He further added, half laughing, that he really wasn't worried, though, for he felt we would have won even in overtime. You know it's just this kind of confidence that I think is infectious. It runs throughout our ball club to the point that when we are beaten, we have the feeling that the game just wasn't long enough for us to win.

After watching the movies of the Dallas game, we ran through a brief loosening up workout prior to getting a scouting report on the Kansas City Chiefs personnel from Wally Cruice, our chief scout.

Workouts and meetings on Thursday and Friday were similar to those of comparable days prior to the Dallas game. In watching movies of the Chiefs, it was apparent that this club had done well in drafting and signing its players through the years. They had a good looking ball club. Our chief concern was just how good they were, because we knew nothing of the opposition that they were playing.

We flew to Santa Barbara, where we would spend the week in preparing for this historic game. As the chartered jet circled around Santa Barbara before landing, we were kidding Bill Anderson, one of our tight ends, that the runway didn't look long enough for us to land. Bill is not the keenest guy in the world about flying anyway, and when we came to a screeching halt about 50 yards from the end of the runway, he was the most relieved guy on the airplane.

Coach Lombardi warned us not to be overconfident and complacent about the Kansas City Chiefs, pointing up again the fact that Kansas City had excellent personnel. However, his theme for this game was to be quite clear to all of us. In fact, I don't really think he had to mention it to any of us. We had the privilege of playing in the first Super Bowl game and the responsibility to uphold the finest tradition of our own league.

The practice sessions were held in a stadium at the University of California at Santa Barbara, where they had excellent facilities. I don't really know if it was the weather, or the chance to be in this all-important game, or what it was, but our practice sessions were so full of pep and precision that by Wednesday I was ready to play the game. As I had mentioned about the Friday before the Dallas game, I wished that we could have played the Super Bowl game on Wednesday. I thought by that time I had never seen our team look sharper.

Though I have played 11 seasons in the National Football League, each Sunday morning I start to think about the game, and those old butterflies really act up. Though I have been told this is a normal reaction, you would think it would get a little bit better as you get older. Sometimes I think it gets a little bit worse.

In our last meeting, Kansas City's stack defenses were covered one last time for clarification. I think there was a lot more emphasis placed on these defenses than was necessary. Though Kansas City played them in a stack form, we had seen these defenses with the linebacker slightly out of position, as Kansas City would do on occasions, so those defenses really weren't unfamiliar to us.

Coach Lombardi's pregame talk was centered around three things: (1) the pride of performance that he felt we had displayed all year long, of not being satisfied with giving anything less than the best that we had within us; (2) the prestige that was at stake of being the first World's Champion, and (3) the

Here is a great picture. Max McGee had a fantastic day against the Chiefs. As he returns to the huddle after catching a pass, Max's grin says it all.

moral responsibility to play as well as we could in upholding the pride and prestige and tradition of our great league.

The game started somewhat slowly for us on offense although Max McGee got us uncorked after a couple of sputtering series in the first quarter by making a very difficult catch behind his back and taking it in for a score.

Kansas City came right back and scored in the second quarter to tie up the game and later added three more after we had scored to make the score, at halftime, Green Bay 14 and Kansas City 10. We were a disappointed group of players at halftime, not with the score, but with the performance we had given. We realized that we had played much too cautiously in the first half, both offensively and defensively, and one of Coach Lombardi's axioms is that you cannot play cautiously. You have to play with total abandon, or you are going to get beaten.

Forrest Gregg (75) and Jerry Kramer gave me great protection against the Kansas City pass rush.

Henry Jordan and Lee Roy Caffey stop Mike Garrett for a loss.

We were guilty of being cautious and we knew it, and we were most embarrassed with our performance. We knew that we had not played well and that every player had to rededicate himself to going out and doing a better job in the second half.

Our defense shut them out in the second half and did a tremendous job of mixing in some blitzes with their normal defenses. As a result, we were able to open the game up and win going away. I guess the play that opened the flood gates was a pass intercepted by Willie Wood that took us down to about their 3- or 4-yard line from where we scored. From here on, it seemed that we were able to keep things pretty much under control.

The blitzing tactics by our defense got to Dawson in the second half, and we were able to put a lot more pressure on him and force him to turn the ball over to us. We were able to get our running game going a little better in the second half, although we didn't at any time have it go as well as we thought we could against their defense. We ended up throwing the ball perhaps a bit more than we normally would have.

Len Dawson starts to scramble as Willie Davis (87) beats his man and starts after Dawson.

Down through the years Bob Skoronski has been one of the outstanding pass protectors. Here he comes off the field receiving congratulations from Coach Lombardi after the 1966 Super Bowl.

When the final gun went off in this game, sheer ecstasy prevailed. This had been a year when we had had a lot of hard work toward the goal of being the first World's Champion, and we were extremely pleased with the way the season had turned out for us.

The dressing rooms were ridiculously crowded, and you could hardly move inside. I have never seen so many writers in my life. They could have assigned about five to each player and had some left over.

Coach Lombardi received some undue criticism for his comments after the game, when someone pinned him in a corner and asked how he rated the two teams. He's an honest man, a straightforward man, and he gave them a straightforward answer when he said he felt there were some teams in our league that were better than Kansas City.

Now, I don't think he was downgrading the Kansas City club. I merely think that from the simple fact that our league has been in existence longer than the American Football League, there were some clubs—the Dallas Cowboys for one, though they came on the scene the same time the Chiefs did, and also the Cleveland Browns, and Colts, and the Bears—who have been very strong through the years. I think that Coach Lombardi felt they were strong enough to have beaten Kansas City, but I don't think he was knocking Kansas City at all.

As for comparing the two leagues on the basis of one game, I think that is rather difficult. I feel that in the coming preseason games, and in games to come in future years, a lot more of these questions will be answered. Many people said they didn't feel this was the difference between two leagues, but a difference between two teams. If there was a difference between two teams, we would like to think this is the difference between the two leagues, because we led our league and are representative members of it.

The following diagrams show three of the successful plays we used in the Super Bowl.

SUPER BOWL, KANSAS CITY CHIEFS

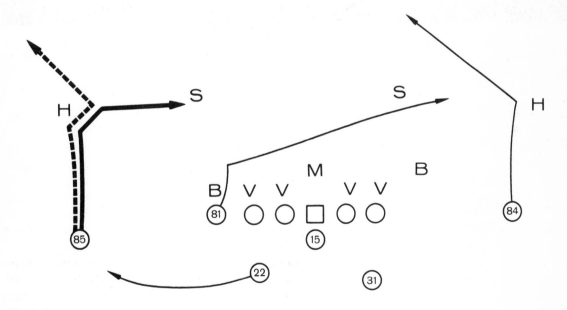

1. This complementary route was effectively used against the Chiefs. The tight end, split end, and flanker each caught passes off this route.

2. To counter the inside move by the wing, we also used a "Z"-out move (broken line).

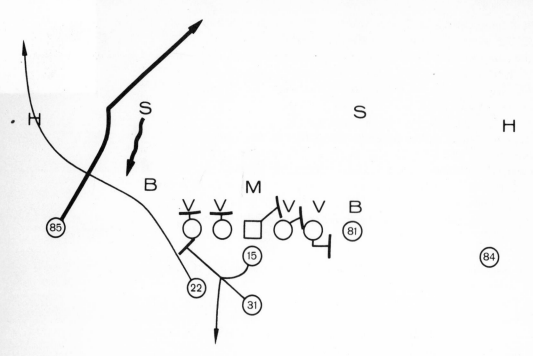

1. On a play action pass such as the one above, good faking by our fullback enabled our split end to get clear for a pass as safety came up with fake.

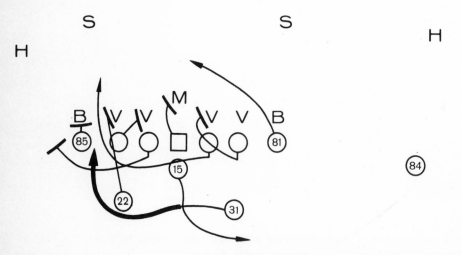

1. The above diagram illustrates the sweep to the weak side which Jim Taylor ran in for a score.